Making Organizational Change Stick

Business needs change. And it needs it in ways, at a rate and on a scale that is unprecedented. Current success rates for business change projects are dismal and are likely to remain so until organizations reinvent their approach to project delivery, and learn how to integrate Change Management and Project Management successfully. In this ground-breaking and innovative book, Gabrielle O'Donovan shows you how to design strategy, structures and processes to realize this integration and deliver sustainable and commercially powerful business change.

She opens the book by providing the context, describing both the problem with change projects and the solution; how the disconnect between Project Management and Change Management feeds the 40–70 per cent failure rate and the laying of many a dud egg; how cross-discipline integration efforts thus far have only addressed the tip of the iceberg, ignoring the subterranean cultural element that can divide or unite project teams; and how an effective joint value proposition must incorporate both above and below the surface components. From there, she profiles Project Management and Change Management in turn and, crucially, the value proposition of these respective disciplines and the different theories, models and tools they employ.

In the second half of the book she makes a 'Project and Change Partners culture' (PCP) explicit and measurable, articulating those cultural assumptions that will support an effective alliance, and that relate to universal problems all organizations face regarding the macro environment, external adaptability and survival, and internal integration. From there, she describes how Project Managers and Change Managers can cooperate on a daily basis by dividing work packages and activities throughout the end-to-end project lifecycle, offering a toolkit to enable you to bring this change partners culture to life and ensure that change is not only implemented, but embedded.

Those leaders who create a PCP culture will benefit from the unique value that these interdependent disciplines bring to project delivery. It is they who will drive up project success rates and lay golden eggs, not only implementing, but embedding change and securing business benefits.

Making Organizational Change Stick is written for Change Managers, Project/ Programme Managers, design thinkers, business architects and anyone concerned with the structure, process and people of business change.

Gabrielle O'Donovan has clocked up more than 30,000 hours over 20-plus years working on transformational change projects that have covered the full spectrum – culture transformation, process reengineering, restructuring, regulatory, infrastructure and technology, plus M&A. Edgar Schein, Professor Emeritus, Sloan School of Management, MIT, USA, has remarked on Gabrielle's work on culture as 'notable'. She is an accomplished Change Management and Organizational Culture practitioner, author, university lecturer and conference speaker.

Making Organizational Change Stick

How to Create a Culture of
Partnership between Project
and Change Management

Gabrielle O'Donovan, M. Ed.

Routledge
Taylor & Francis Group

LONDON AND NEW YORK

First published 2018
by Routledge
2 Park Square, Milton Park, Abingdon, Oxon OX14 4RN

and by Routledge
711 Third Avenue, New York, NY 10017

Routledge is an imprint of the Taylor & Francis Group, an informa business

British Library Cataloguing-in-Publication Data
A catalogue record for this book is available from the British Library

Library of Congress Cataloging-in-Publication Data
A catalog record for this book has been requested

ISBN: 978-1-138-73629-0 (hbk)
ISBN: 978-1-315-18599-6 (ebk)

Typeset in Bembo
by Florence Production Ltd, Stoodleigh, Devon, UK
Printed and bound by CPI Group (UK) Ltd, Croydon, CR0 4YY

For two special girls – Alison and Romavida

Contents

Illustrations

Figures

About the author

Gabrielle O'Donovan has clocked up more than 30,000 hours over 20-plus years working on change programmes that have covered the full spectrum – culture transformation, process reengineering, restructuring, regulatory change, major infrastructure, technology and mergers and acquisitions. Clients have included Bank of America Merrill Lynch, Unilever, the London Metropolitan Police, Lloyds Banking Group, Friends Life Insurance, the Ministry of Justice UK, Dublin Airport Authority, Cathay Pacific Airways and HSBC Hong Kong. Gabrielle has worked across the globe in Tokyo,  Jakarta, Johannesburg, Geneva, Rome, Dubai, Vancouver, Brussels, Madrid, Dublin and London – to name but a few. Projects and programmes have been primarily global in scale, but have included regional and national ones also.

Gabrielle has some significant achievements under her belt:

- Her culture transformation programme for HSBC Hong Kong plus five subsidiary companies embedded a customer-centric culture and won awards including an ASTD Excellence in Practice Award (USA, 2005).
- Her first book *The Corporate Culture Handbook* (Liffey Press, 2005)[1] was 'In the top 1% of best business books for 2005' (*Business Book Review*, USA).
- At Dublin Airport Authority, Ireland, her work as Stakeholder Management Lead for the building of Terminal 2 was deemed by executive leaders as 'instrumental to securing capital expenditure', while the Independent Verifier accorded the engagement process, which Gabrielle established, 'best practice' (2008).

- In 2010, Edgar Schein, Professor Emeritus of MIT Sloan School of Management and founding father of organizational culture, referenced Gabrielle and her HSBC culture change programme in his fourth edition of *Organizational Culture and Leadership* (Jossey-Bass, 2010). Schein also shared Gabrielle's 'Characteristics of a Healthy Culture' typology in his book, referring to her 23 new culture dimensions as 'notable in how they were designed and conceived'.[2]
- Gabrielle is a sought-after speaker on the international conference circuit.

Gabrielle also served as Associate Professor at master's degree level on culture and change programmes at Danube University Krems, Austria, and Hong Kong Polytechnic University, Hong Kong SAR, over a five-year period.

From the outset of her career, Gabrielle has been results focused and has applied Project Management models and tools to add structure and rigour to her work, anchoring Change Management activities into project plans. Gabrielle incorporates the best of both classic and new models, and keeps abreast with new Change Management and Project Management trends and developments. She is PRINCE2® qualified and has served as both Change Manager and Change Director over the course of her career.

Gabrielle's experiences over the past 20-plus years have given her strong insights into those cultural assumptions at work in the projects environment and how they can be constructive or otherwise. Exposed to a variety of approaches and methodologies in an array of global organizations, she has a clear line of sight into what works and what doesn't work. Gabrielle has revelled in all of the insights, translating them into best practices and lessons learnt. The result is her Project and Change Partnership (PCP) methodology – an informed, practical and holistic solution to the problem with change projects.

Notes

1 O'Donovan, G. (2005) *The Corporate Culture Handbook.* Dublin: The Liffey Press.
2 Schein, E. (2010) *Organizational Culture and Leadership.* (4th edn). San Francisco, CA: Jossey-Bass, pp. 168–72.

Foreword

The dismal results achieved by business change projects over the past decades drive home the need for a step change in how we deliver projects. We can no longer be satisfied to hop along with a 'one-legged approach', where only Project Management methodologies are used or, alternatively, limp with Project Management in the driving seat and Change Management playing second fiddle. Rather, a firm-footed 'two-legged approach' that employs both Project Management and Change Management methodologies and expertise, will enable projects to stride confidently to reach their goals. This requires the thoughtful integration of Project Management and Change Management methodologies throughout the end-to-end project lifecycle, and the cultivation of a culture of partnership between Project Managers and Change Managers – a twenty-first century solution to a twenty-first century problem.

Over time, a shared occupational subculture between Change Managers and Project Managers needs to evolve. To progress this process, awareness and understanding needs to be raised on the following:

- What a culture of partnership between Project Managers and Change Managers looks like and those particular cultural assumptions that either facilitate, or obstruct this.
- Why a culture of partnership is important for business benefits realization, and why it informs the next evolution of maturity in both Change Management and Project Management theory and practice.
- How to create, foster and participate in a culture of partnership between Change Management and Project Management throughout the project lifecycle.

Making Organizational Change Stick: How to Create a Culture of Partnership between Project and Change Management is the first book to identify these issues and offer a solution.

Industry needs to embrace the ongoing tending to culture across the organization, and in their programme and projects environments particularly. The latter involves fostering and reinforcing desired cultural assumptions between employees, interim managers, contractors and consultants who come together to form project teams (physically or virtually), so as to create a culture of partnership. An integrated approach needs to be adopted as the best way to get things done on change projects, with Project Management and Change Management methodologies and tools complementing each other and deriving synergies.

Undergraduate and graduate programmes that specialize in Project Management and Change Management have a very important role educating the next generations on this evolution and the role of culture on project teams, so that the lessons of the past are learnt and result in a step change in the way that change projects are delivered.

Professional associations for Change Managers and Project Managers carry a similar duty to educate trainees on how these two disciplines complement and rely on each other, for successful delivery on benefits. This involves integrating the cultural component in their respective bodies of knowledge, training and assessment programmes, and promoting cross-discipline, cooperation and partnership.

Acknowledgements

To the team at Routledge, in particular to senior editor, Amy Laurens, and editorial assistant, Alexandra Atkinson.

To Edgar Schein, Professor Emeritus, Massachusetts Institute of Technology, USA, for being an endless source of inspiration throughout my career, and to the other great thinkers such as Kurt Lewin and Peter Senge.

To all who are contributing to the next evolution of how we deliver change; we are each pioneers on this journey to build an effective Project and Change Management joint-value proposition that will ensure that organizational change sticks.

To the ongoing evolution of the Project Management and Change Management disciplines, and to the continuous professional development of both Project Managers and Change Managers.

Finally, to my mother Christine, for her fantastic encouragement and support.

About this book

As organizations evolve to meet the challenges posed by a changing environment, so too must our methods. It is not enough just to implement organizational change; we must make it stick so that benefits are realized and change can be built upon. This involves cultivating a culture of partnership between Project Managers and Change Managers, to benefit from their respective areas of expertise and maximize synergies. It also involves the ongoing tending to organizational culture, both in daily operations and on projects.

Structure

Part I describes the problem with change projects and identifies how the disconnect between Project Management and Change Management feeds the 40–70 per cent failure rate. It also gives an overview of Project and Change Partnership (PCP) methodology, which is based on a culture of partnership between Project Managers and Change Managers.

From there we take Project Management and Change Management in turn, describing their respective history and trends, together with major theories, models and tools which Change Managers and Project Managers use. This ensures grounding in a common understanding, a common language, and a common frame of reference, before considering how Project Management and Change Management can join forces on projects.

In Chapter 5 the nature and role of culture are explored. The overall framework presented for the creation of an inventory of desired cultural assumptions for Project Managers and Change Managers is based on the model put forward by Edgar Schein, Professor Emeritus at the MIT Sloan School of Management, on those archetypical problems faced by all groups as they strive to ensure the group's capacity to survive and adapt. These can be organized into three main categories: managing external adaptation and survival, managing internal integration and achieving consensus on key abstract problems relating to the macro environment.

Part II describes what a PCP culture of partnership looks like and how to implement it. In Chapters 6–8, we go down a level from the overall framework to explore three original inventories of assumptions that pertain to the projects' context specifically, and that inform the content of a culture of partnership between Project Managers and Change Managers. In Chapter 9, we reach above the surface to learn how to implement PCP methodology throughout the end-to-end project lifecycle.

Every effort has been made to acknowledge sources and copyright permissions have been secured. If any oversights come to light, these will be gladly corrected in the next edition. The author can be contacted at gabrielle.odonvan@icloud.com.

Audiences of this book

For leaders:

- Explains how to make projects and programmes more effective by creating a culture of partnership between Project Managers and Change Managers.
- Emphasizes the need for more business focus to be placed on managing culture evolution and organizational adaptability in the twenty-first century.

For change sponsors:

- Highlights the importance of utilizing Change Management expertise, particularly during the initial project phases where decisions are made on business benefits to be achieved, impacts, project success measures, resource allocation, etc.
- Enables sponsors to define the Change Management services, skills and resources requirement.
- Describes the pros and cons of different project team organisational structures and approaches that will either enhance or undermine a culture of partnership and smooth delivery.

For PMOs:

- Describes key Project Management and Change Management activities, work packages and measures that will need to be tracked and reported on.

For Project Management practitioners:

- Provides an overview of the Change Management service proposition and how Change Management can enhance each phase of a project.

- Describes what a culture of partnership between Project Managers and Change Managers looks like, and why they need to sign up to it and how.

For Change Management practitioners:

- Provides an overview of the Project Management service proposition and the projects context where Change Management specialists work.
- Provides a robust service proposition with clearly defined requirements and deliverables that will help them position their service offering on any given change project.
- Describes what a culture of partnership between Change Managers and Project Managers looks like, and why they need to sign up to it and how.

For students:

- Excellent overview on how methods for approaching change projects are evolving.
- Clarifies on how Change Management and Project Management epistemic cultures differ, and how they can be best integrated for a common purpose.
- Provides an innovative approach to Change Management and Project Management integration, which targets both above and below surface levels to include the neglected cultural component.

For professional organizations:

- Organizations and societies for Change Managers and Project Managers can use PCP methodology to educate and train members on their role in embedding a culture of partnership.

This book is relevant for all change managers who have a role in making organizational change stick.

Part I
Setting the scene

1   Introduction

The business environment is changing at an unprecedented rate, driven by the exponential growth in information and technology. Innovations such as online shopping, business models based on collaborative consumption, and declining customer loyalty are just some of the effects being felt. Adapting to disruptive change has become critical to strategic performance, dominating the business agenda like never before. Industry responses include:

- Driving adoption of cutting-edge technologies and the mass movement to the Cloud.
- Driving innovation to ensure a steady stream of cutting-edge products and services.
- Creating a customer-centric organization to give the business a competitive edge.
- Fostering a culture of ethics to retain existing customers and attract new ones.
- Restructuring and consolidating to secure a market place.

However, for any such changes to stick and meet business needs, leaders need to become as good at embedding change as they are at rolling it out. Huge fortunes are spent every year on change projects with a view to delivering on strategic visions. (Price Waterhouse Cooper forecasts global capital expenditure on infrastructure projects alone to be $78 trillion between 2014 and 2025.) Yet, despite the best brains and efforts, study after study tells us that project failure rates are unacceptably high. In fact, in a time where the only constant is said to be change, if there *is* another constant, it's those high failure rates.

1.1 The preferred vehicle for organizational change

Organizational change is increasingly being introduced via projects. However, although different disciplines feed into the management of effective organizational change, industry seems to view it as largely the domain of project/programme managers. Yet, research has shown, time and time again, that Project Management bodies of knowledge, standards and practices are ill equipped to deal with the challenges posed by the management of complex organizational change.

1.2 The problem with change projects

1.2.1 A track record for high failure rates

The shortcomings of the project, as a vehicle for introducing and implementing change, has been apparent for decades:

- In the 1980s, the microelectronics industry, which saw the rapid expansion of computers and computer-based processes into most areas of organizational life, was the subject of a great many studies (Bessant and Haywood, 1985; Morris and Hough, 1987). These found that the failure rates of new technology projects was anywhere between 40 and 70 per cent.
- In 2002, a Mckinsey & Company study of 40 organizations found that those with the lowest investment had poor Change Management capabilities, while those that gained the biggest returns had strong ones.
- In 2008, an IBM survey on the success/failure rates of change projects surveyed 1,500 change leaders and found that only 40 per cent of projects met their schedule, budget and quality goals, with the biggest barriers to success listed as people factors; changing mindsets and attitudes (58 per cent), corporate culture (49 per cent) and lack of senior management support (32 per cent) (IBM Global Making Change Work Study 2008, www.ibm.com).
- In 2012, McKinsey & Company carried out a survey in conjunction with the University of Oxford on large-scale IT projects (with initial budgets greater than US$15 million) and found that 17 per cent of large IT projects go so badly that they can threaten the very existence of the company; on average, they found that large IT projects run 45 per cent over budget and 7 per cent over time, and delivered 56 per cent less value than predicted. Factors that contributed to the problem included little heed to strategy and shareholders, with projects managed purely to budget and schedule targets; a disproportionate focus on technical issues and targets; and a lack of common vision, processes and culture on the project team.

In recent years, Project Managers have tried to address these issues and improve success rates by borrowing from the Change Management toolkit, but such arrangements are typically ill conceived and vary from project to project.

The case study overleaf illustrates why Project Management needs to partner with Change Management from the outset, to deliver successful change. A projects environment that is weak on Change Management expertise is a breeding ground for 'black swans' – those projects that prove not only to be dud eggs but which threaten the very existence of the organization.

Deploying technology as a bolt-on using Change Management

Case study

In a global financial services organization, different technologies were rolled out during the same two-year period – various employee productivity tools, function specific tools, a sign-in security application and a host of other applications. Reducing IT costs and efforts, and future proofing the organization were key objectives, with speed of implementation and cost reduction prioritized over solution quality (which was taken as a given). In this portfolio, Change Management expertise was not employed for the majority of projects and, where it was, this occured only late in the project lifecycle. The approach indicated low Organizational Change Management Maturity (see Chapter 4, section 4.3.17) and a 'Bolt-on' approach to Change Management (see Chapter 7, Figure 7.6).

For most projects, Project Managers had to cope with Communications and Training support only. The end-user experience was not analysed up-front, so user impacts and the likely level of disruption to the business were not well understood. Even the needs of senior executive end-users were not scoped, and no business intelligence was held on what technologies and tools they were currently using. Also, there was little clarity on the project teams as to how the different technologies would impact on each other. Consequently, solutions provided by the projects were neither configured nor customized to an appropriate level to ensure that they met end-user requirements and landed smoothly in the business. When a push came to aggressively close projects out at the year-end, user issues kept below the radar became visible. Senior executives, who should have been engaged early in the project lifecycle and recruited as change advocates, made the most noise as they couldn't perform key tasks as they travelled and worked 'on the go'. The noise met the ears of the CIO, and understanding business impacts and ensuring a good user experience became the hot topic – for a moment – and long after the horse had bolted.

Looking across to daily operations, there was no Organizational Development (OD) team and efforts to build adaptability in the face of change consisted of sporadic Change Management training for individuals and teams only. One has to wonder what business benefits were realized and at what cost.

1.2.2 The laments of Change Managers

According to the PROSCI® 2012 Benchmarking Study of 65 global organizations, issues that contribute to the problem with change projects are:

- Ineffective Change Management sponsorship from senior leaders;
- Insufficient Change Management resourcing;
- Resistance to change from employees;
- Middle-management resistance;
- Poor communication;
- Lack of buy-in for Change Management;
- Disconnect between Project Management and Change Management.

Study respondents noted that:

> a lack of consensus on how to integrate the two practices became a large challenge throughout the life of projects and often resulted in Change Management playing 'second fiddle' to Project Management. Specifically, study participants cited difficulty involving and getting assistance from Project Managers.

With Change Management and Change Managers playing a secondary role, they will often have little or no access to the programme sponsor and may not fulfil a key part of their duties – that is, to coach the sponsor on their role and shape the strategic conversation. They will often not be sufficiently resourced and so may not be able to engage stakeholders so as to maximize support and adoption and minimize resistance. In effect, they may not be positioned to deliver.

Having worked on change projects for more than twenty years, I have my own observations on additional issues that cloud the space:

- *Lack of a common language and concepts*: There is a mistaken notion held by many in the projects environment that Project Managers are Change Managers and that Project Management is Change Management.
- *Narrow measures of success*: Traditional project measures of success have been limited in scope, focusing on successful implementation not successful adoption and benefits realization.
- *Lack of clarity* on the Change Management service proposition, activities, deliverables and tools.
- *The macho culture* of change projects.
- *Life is messy* and change projects are invariably messy, too. Poor general management practices can undermine the value that both Project Management and Change Management bring to the table.

These issues, and others, emerge from the fact that the Project Management and Change Management disciplines and practices developed separately, leading to different ways of doing things among Project Managers and Change Managers, which has resulted in inherent conflicting assumptions about how to best implement organizational change. We need a clear line of sight to these assumptions, so we can adopt those that facilitate a culture of partnership in our projects and programmes environment, and prune those that get in the way of embedding organizational change and realizing business benefits.

1.2.3 Small caps or large caps?

Before going any further, we first need to clarify whom we are referring to when we talk about two key project roles – the Project Manager and the Change Manager.

Any one of us could claim to be a 'change manager'. For key life events, we all make plans around births, marriages and deaths in the family to ensure that things go as smoothly as possible. In the workplace, we transition in and out of employer organizations and learn to work with new colleagues who bring with them different ways of doing things. Most of us, at some point in our career, will have to manage a project, even if it is just a very small one such as building team capability over a specific time frame. Basically, without ever opening a book on Change Management, and with absolutely no formal learning on related theories, models and tools, we each can manage change in both our personal and professional lives, albeit with varying degrees of success. That makes us all 'change managers' (note the small 'c' and 'm'). It does not make us Change Managers (capital 'C' and 'M') who are well versed in models, theories and tools of the Change Management discipline and who practise Change Management as a profession and primary skill set. On workplace change initiatives, there is a role for both Change Managers and change managers – the former can lead and drive Change Management processes to partner with Project Management processes and ensure adoption of a new product, service or approach, while change managers can help support the embedding of new ways of working in the business.

Likewise, any one of us could claim to be a project manager (note the small 'p' and 'm') in both our personal and professional lives. At home, f we have applied our knowledge, skills and tools to plan and manage a family event such as a summer holiday or a religious rite of passage for a family member, we can claim to be project managers. At work, if we have applied such knowledge, skills and tools to plan and manage an initiative such as a leadership event or the car pool for getting colleagues to and from the office, we can make a similar claim. Again, without ever opening a book to learn the theories, models and tools of Project

Management, we can demonstrate related skills in both our personal and professional lives. It does not make us Project Managers who are well versed in the models, theories and tools of the Project Management discipline and who practise Project Management as our primary skillset.

So, what's the big deal? What does it matter whether a person is a change manager or Change Manager, a project manager or a Project Manager? It matters greatly because:

- Most people working on projects like to position him- or herself as a 'Change Manager', as managing change is a very important capability to be seen to have in the modern workplace. However, only a very small percentage of people can actually live up to the title and bring Change Management expertise to the table.
- Senior executives whose primary skill set will be something else, typically think their projects are awash with Change Managers, when in fact they might be lucky to count just one genuine Change Manager in their ranks.
- Project Managers most often are not even aware of the full Change Management service offering and, subsequently, don't know how to work with Change Managers.
- While Project Managers are recruited for their Project Management skills, Change Managers can often be recruited primarily for Project Management skills, or their communications and/or training skills!
- Much of the recent literature, which can claim to advance the Change Management profession is, in fact, written for 'change managers' and does little to clarify how the role of the 'Change Manager' differs to the role of the change manager. Content covered can include lots of general and strategic management activities and tools, leading to fuzzy boundaries around the Change Manager role scope. This is very confusing, no doubt, for new recruits into the Change Management profession.

1.2.4 Project Management methodologies and Change Management

The role of effectively managed projects and programmes in building organizational capability is a given for successful organizations. With the Project Management profession now in stages of early maturity (with a key criteria for full maturation being defined here as successful partnership with Change Management) and the Change Management profession in its formative stages,[1] we are all pioneers on the journey to figure out how to work together so ensure higher success rates. In recent years, a great deal of thought and effort has gone into understanding how the two can come together, with 'integration' being the current hot topic in articles and books. However, often this work is conducted either by academics (who, with all due respect, would not survive a week working on a global change project), by consultants who are too expensive to stick around and see how their vanilla strategies and recommendations work in practice, or by Project Managers who have a superficial understanding of Change Management theories, models and tools, and whose inherent bias, interest and talent is Project Management and managing tasks, not people. Over time, some of this input has filtered through to those major Project Management methodologies and amounted to an evolution of sorts.

In the PRINCE2® context, the term 'Change Management' relates to what is also known as 'configuration management' or 'change control', and not the business of managing people through change. With PRINCE2®, the focus is on management products that are required to manage the project, with specialist products such as those emerging from (Organizational) Change Management considered additional and outside the scope of this approach. While PRINCE2® does recognise that specialist products needs to be identified and included within project scope and plans, it leaves it to the Project Manager and specialist to determine what this might look like. Here, the Change Manager is positioned in a support role, and not as an equal partner to the Project Manager.

With MSP® methodology, a programme board oversees projects and portfolios. The board includes 'Business Change Managers' who have roles in the business. In addition to their work in daily operations, Business Change Managers are tasked with ensuring that capabilities delivered by the programme are adopted by the organization and benefits realized. However, as Change Management is not their primary skillset and as they will already have full-time jobs in the business, this group will be at a disadvantage on how best to deliver on their programme responsibilities. To bridge this gap, and allow also for Change Management expertise to shape the conversation at programme board level, provision needs to be made for the role of a Change Director whose primary skillset is Change Management. The Change Director will provide overall leadership and coordination of Change Management activities across projects and portfolios, and serve as subject-matter-expert and trusted advisor for Business Change Managers and the board.

In the 'PMI's 2012 Pulse of the Profession™ In-Depth Report: Organizational Agility', it was highlighted that 'organizations achieving higher-than-average success rates from their portfolio of programs and projects have not only increased their use of standardized portfolio, program and project practices, but have adopted, among other things, rigorous Change Management to better adapt to shift market conditions.' Fewer than 20% of organizations surveyed were found to have Change Management capabilities. In the following year, the PMI® produced a discussion document 'Managing Change in Organizations: A Practice

Guide' (2013), recognising that there may not yet be consensus on what constitutes good practice. Interestingly, in the PMI® standards, some elements of Change Management such as communications appear throughout but are not identified as 'Change Management' (or OCM) activities, while the term OPM is called out to position Project Management as a discrete discipline and profession. The PMI® approach does make provision for a dedicated Change Management workstream, but not for a dedicated Change Manager/Director at either project or portfolio level. Instead, the PMI® recommends a designated lead for Change Management activities 'who may be the Project Manager, the programme manager, integrator, sponsor or a dedicated employee who reports into the Project Manager'. The PMI® methodology does not require a comprehensive Change Management strategy or plan, with elements picked up elsewhere. With this set-up, it's easy to see how Change Management priorities would be pushed aside when the Project Manager is under pressure.

It is easy to see why many global organizations blend methodologies in an attempt to design their own internal approach to meet their needs. The analysis above also sheds light on the fact that while a Project Manager can reasonably assume to have the responsibility, accountability and authority (see Figure 1.1) they require to deliver on their remit, how a Change Manager fares on these three counts will vary greatly. Often, roles will communicate a lot of responsibility and accountability but insufficient authority, meaning that the Change Manager and their team have an inadequate platform to enable successful delivery. If not challenged, this can marginalize Change Management practitioners and lead to a myriad of issues during implementation.

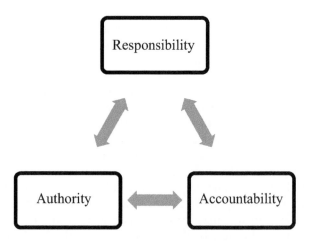

Figure 1.1 Being positioned for success: three basic criteria

1.2.5 What do we need to do differently?

Change Managers can have a good line of sight into those issues that emerge as Project Managers and Change Managers deliver together on projects and how these should be addressed. In the PROSCI® survey mentioned earlier, respondents shared their views on future improvements:

- *Utilize a holistic approach*: Apply a proven model that ensures rigour; establish Change Management milestones and scope; use concrete deliverables.
- *Structure the Change Management team*: Assign a Change Management Lead with necessary experience and expertise.
- Start Change Management activities earlier, preferably at initiation.
- Engage the project team:
  - create a cooperative and collaborative relationship with the project team;
  - integrate Change Management and Project Management activities;
  - build project team support for Change Management, educating them on methodology.
- *Enhance planning activities*: Dedicate more time to planning the Change Management effort, including readiness assessments, scaling exercises, and impact identification and analysis.[2]

1.3 The solution

A holistic methodology that utilizes and aligns both Project Management and Change Management expertise, and that is anchored in a common culture, can neutralize those issues shared above and other related issues.

Project and Change Partnership (PCP) methodology is designed to do just that and is the first of its kind. Not only does PCP methodology enable operating assumptions alignment to create a common set of steps, activities and deliverables that can be applied by any project to ensure that it addresses both the technical side and people side of change, it is underpinned by a culture of partnership between Project Managers and Change Managers, and explains in detail to leaders how to establish such a culture. PCP methodology provides more visibility and structure of Change Management activities and work packages than any of the major Project Management methodologies.

1.4 Chapter summary

The issues of change and keeping ahead of the curve dominate the business agenda like never before. Yet, despite the vast resources put into successful project delivery, industry studies continue to report high failure rates, indicating a serious problem that exist across a broad cross-section of industries. To get a different result, we simply have to start doing things differently, and this requires a step change in how we deliver change projects.

The widespread disconnect between Project Management and Change Management is a key contributor to the problem with change projects, leading to a myriad of issues that undermine benefits realization. These can be resolved with a unified and integrated approach to delivering change projects that adopts a firm-footed approach. PCP methodology delivers on this, adopting a parternship approach to project delivery.

Notes

1   While the Project Management profession is more mature than the Change Management profession, the Change Management discipline is the more mature of the two. To learn more, see Figures 3.18 and 4.27.
2   PROSCI Benchmarking Report (2012).

Bibliography

Book

Morris, P. W. and Hough, G. H. (1987) *The Anatomy of Major Projects*. New York: John Wiley & Sons.

Online

PWC. *CPI Outlook to 2025*. Retrieved from www.pwc.com/gx/capital-projects-infrastructure/publications/cpi-outlook/assets/cpt-outlook-to-2025.pdf (accessed August 2017).

Reports

Bloch, M., Blumberg, S. and Laartz, J. (August 2012) *Delivering Large-scale IT Projects on Time, on Budget and on Value*. Retrieved from: www.mckinsey.com/business-functions/digital-mckinsey/our-insights/delivering-large-scale-it-projects-on-time-on-budget-and-on-value (accessed14 January 2017).

Creasy, T. and Hiatt, J. (eds) (2012) *Best Practices in Change Management – 2012 Edition*. Prosci Benchmarking Report, USA.

LaClair, J. and Raa, P. (2002) *Helping Employees Embrace Change*. Retrieved from www.mckinsey.com/business-functions/digital/mckinsey/our-insights/helping employees embrace change (accessed 14 January 2017).

2   Project and change partnership

Methodology overview

While reviewing methodologies that propose to integrate Change Management and Project Management, it struck me that any attempts thus far have only addressed the tip of the iceberg. Their focus has been on those things above the surface – targeting strategies, structures, frameworks and tools used by Project Managers and Change Managers alike. However, there is a far bigger force at play that can turn such interventions on its head. That force is culture and it exists below the surface, while influencing that which is above it. Therefore, the next evolution in Project and Change Management integration must incorporate the cultural perspective. Project and Change Partnership (PCP) methodology is the first to take this step.

With PCP methodology, any recommended 'above the surface' interventions are based on, and will reinforce, a clearly defined culture of partnership between Change Managers and Project Managers.

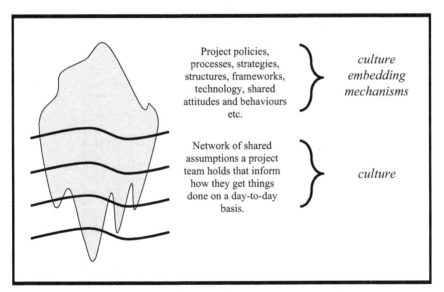

Figure 2.1 PCP methodology: above and below surface integration

Integration is a central tenet of PCP methodology. The integrated approach involves Project Management and Change Management joining forces and aligning on a number of key dimensions. How much value is created is dependent on the level of integration employed. Insufficient integration can leave Change Managers and Project Managers working in parallel with little communication, while too much integration can be value destroying, as the unique strengths of Change Management and Project Management are diluted. The trick is to get the right balance and PCP methodology is designed to deliver on this.

2.1 A joint value proposition

PCP methodology (Figure 2.2) offers a unique Project Management–Change Management joint value proposition by underpinning all activities and deliverables with specific cultural assumptions that promote a culture of partnership, while promoting *integration, but not assimilation* so as to safeguard the unique strengths of Project Management and Change Management.

2.2 Project lifecycle phases and aims

Lifecycle and evolutionary theories present change as a predetermined process that unfolds over time in a pre-specified direction.[1] Common project and programme management methodologies such as PMI®,

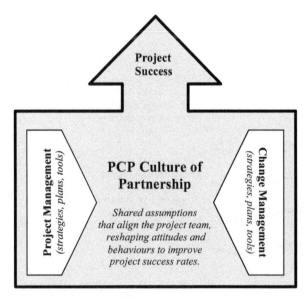

Figure 2.2 PCP methodology: joint value proposition based on a culture of partnership

PRINCE2®, APM™ and MSP® follow a process that typically has four to six phases that cover set-up through to closing. PCP methodology has six such phases, the aims of which are as follows:

1   *Discover*

- Determine whether there is a viable business challenge or opportunity that needs to be addressed.
- Determine whether there is a credible plan in place to move to Phase 2 and formally kick off a project.

2   *Plan and analyse*

- Establish the project organization.
- Assess all viable solution options and recommend a preferred solution that is based on agreed evaluation criteria.

3   *Build and engage*

- Develop and refine design plans for preferred solution.
- Build the preferred solution.
- Further collation of stakeholder requirements and end-user impacts.

4   *Get ready*

- Test and pilot the final solution.
- Conduct final preparation of all deployment-related materials.
- Engage change advocates and mobilise the business.
- Prepare end-users for the impending change.

5   *Go live*

- Ensure the smooth rollout of the solution to end-users.
- Monitor developments so that remedial action can be taken as necessary.

6   *Embed and close*

- Maintain strong, visible change advocacy.
- Support end-users, creating a change-friendly work environment.
- Ensure that the organizational change implemented now sticks.

2.3 Integration across six dimensions

PCP methodology integrates Project Management and Change Management throughout the project lifecycle and across the following six dimensions:

1   *Structure alignment*: The project team is organized so that the Project Manager and Change Manager are positioned as peers and on an equal footing.

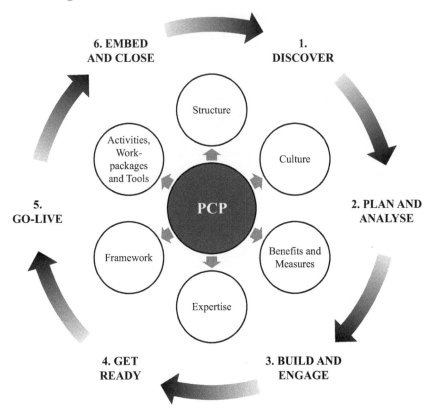

Figure 2.3 PCP methodology: across six phases and six dimensions

2   *Culture alignment*: The project team operates from a common set of cultural assumptions that define how the team works in partnership to deliver on both solution development and adoption.

3   *Benefits and measures alignment*: Business benefits, end-user benefits, and measures of success are unified and agreed by the Project Manager and Change Manager to create one shared set of benefits, measures and tracking activities.

4   *Expertise alignment*: The project team is educated on the role of Project Management and Change Management in successful delivery, and how the success of one depends on the other.

5   *Framework/project lifecycles alignment*: The PCP methodology framework is made up of six lifecycle phases that align both Project Management and Change Management end-to-end and not only 'above the surface', as is typical with other methodologies, but 'below the surface' also. Change Management activities and deliverables are just as dependent on the overall project timeline, key

milestones and dependencies as Project Management activities and deliverables are.

6   *Activities, work packages and tools alignment*: PCP activities and work packages have clear descriptions and owners to facilitate the use, and benefit, of Project Management and Change Management expertise and areas for joint enterprise.

PCP methodology is not just a series of activities and work packages. Rather, it is a philosophy that guides project team attitudes and behaviours to create a culture of partnership. Therefore, PCP is most effective when used as a stand-alone methodology, but it can also be used to augment in-house and mainstream Project Management methodologies that support, on a practical level, Project Management and Change Management integration and the creation of a culture of partnership between Project Managers and Change Managers.

2.4 Key cultural assumptions

A collection of cultural assumptions is at the heart of PCP methodology. For any 'above the surface' interventions to stick (those policies, processes, rites and rituals that are designed to embed change), they must be aligned with those shared cultural assumptions that are held by the project team and that exist 'below the surface', otherwise these interventions will falter and be rejected. Articulated key assumptions make transparent thinking on key issues and minimize opportunitiesfor miscommunication or misunderstanding. They inform ways-of-working and decision-making. Below, PCP cultural assumptions are organized into three categories – assumptions about 'macro concepts', assumptions about 'external survival' and assumptions about 'internal integration'.

2.4.1 Summary of cultural assumptions: macro concepts

Macro concepts are general issues that project teams need to agree about – for example, the nature of projects, the nature of the project and organization relationship, etc. Related cultural assumptions that support a culture of partnership between Project Managers and Change Managers are outlined overleaf in Figure 2.4.

2.4.2 Summary of cultural assumptions: external adaptation

Shared assumptions about external survival determine how the project team will align with, and support delivery of, corporate strategies so the organization can adapt with the ever-changing business environment (see Figure 2.5 overleaf).

- *Life is messy and projects are messy too.*
- *The project is a series of linear and non-linear tasks and activities arising from the needs of people and the business.*
- *Projects don't exist in a vacuum; they emerge, grow, decline and die in their host organizations.*
- *The Project Manager and Change Manager develop the plan, lead the team to deliver the plan and work with stakeholders to integrate diverse perspectives.*
- *Project Management and Change Management are separate, but interdependent partners that, together, can both implement – and embed – change.*
- *Project Management and Change Management epistemic cultures fundamentally differ, attracting students and practitioners with different, but complimentary, interests and talents.*
- *Neither masculine nor feminine ways of reasoning are inherently superior to the other.*
- *Male and female roles are not bound by stereotypes that are harmful to both, but to women in particular.*
- *The male and female contributions to the project are equally appreciated and respected.*

Figure 2.4 PCP methodology: cultural assumptions about macro concepts

- *Project success is defined as successful implementation and embedding of the change, enabling the realisation of business benefits*
- *Project goals and objectives must embrace both Project Management and Change Management perspectives*
- *Project resources need to be allocated equitably so that both Project Management and Change Management expertise and methods are utilised to deliver on the joint value proposition*
- *Project Managers and Change Managers are interdependent partners whose combined expertise can effectively implement and embed change*
- *Project Management and Change Management methodologies are semi-integrated to support overall alignment, while operating interdependently so as not to dilute the unique value propositions each brings to the project*
- *Change Management and Project Management have their own toolkits that, for the most part, differ*
- *Expert leadership, coupled with a culture of problem solving via a trial-and-error approach, maximises adaptability to change*
- *Transparent processes and practices for risks and issues management will ensure that information gets to the right people and that the right corrective action is taken*
- *Successful change programmes begin with a focus on results*
- *Both Project Management and Change Management deliverables are tracked by one Project Management Office (PMO), using key performance indicators (KPIs) that unify Project Management and Change Management priorities as one set*
- *Effective remedial action depends on a good information flow and processes that ensure that any information is acted upon appropriately.*

Figure 2.5 PCP methodology: cultural assumptions about external adaptation

- *We are all equally creative and each of us has an important role to play if overall team problem solving capability is to be maximized.*
- *Feedback ensures a good line of sight to project risks and issues, allows for moderation of ways to support project goals, and motivates goal attainment.*
- *One official project language permits the setting of goals, and interpreting and managing what is going on.*
- *One official definition for conceptual categories supports the setting of goals, and the interpretation and management of what is going on.*
- *Team boundaries and identity are clearly defined so the team can direct their energies towards delivering.*
- *Power, authority and status on our project team are determined by formal and informal processes, and not by social processes.*
- *Getting along with team members is important and it is reliant on a shared sense of how to behave with one another.*
- *Sanctions for obeying and disobeying our cultural norms and rules need to ring true and be evident to the project team, with rewards and punishments appropriate to local culture.*
- *Stories and myths help explain the unexplainable.*

Figure 2.6 PCP methodology: cultural assumptions about internal integration

2.4.3 Summary of cultural assumptions: internal integration

Finally, shared assumptions about internal integration define how the project team will work together and get things done within the project organization and when working across the broader organization (Figure 2.6).

In Part II of this book, Section A explores each of these assumptions in turn and how they, and alternative cultural assumptions, can manifest in attitudes and behaviours during project operations – for better or for worse. Section B explains how to embed these desired cultural assumptions on a practical level during the project lifecycle and project operations.

2.5 PCP methodology: project lifecycle phases

2.5.1 Features

PCP methodology has the following features:

- *Unique*: The first solution to the problem with change projects that targets both 'above the surface' and 'below the surface' integration.
- Two-pronged approach:
  - *Below the surface*: Lays the foundations for a culture of partnership between Change Managers and Project Managers as they deliver on projects.

- *Above the surface*: Uses 'culture embedding mechanisms' to ingrain this culture in the DNA of the project team, aligning methodologies and processes across the project lifecycle and across six dimensions.

- *Adaptable*: Can be used as a stand-alone or to supplement and enhance existing methodologies that embrace the principle of culture of partnership between Project Managers and Change Managers.
- *Flexible*: Is not overly prescriptive; the sponsor, Change Manager and Project Manager can agree among themselves about which work packages and activities are required, and how to allocate responsibilities to Project Management specialists, Change Management specialists and other team members. PCP methodology can be customized to suit big and small organizational change projects.
- *Academically grounded*: Informed by the work of the founding fathers and great thinkers on Change Management, Project Management and Organizational Culture.

2.5.2 Benefits

PCP methodology creates value on any given project.

- *Creates a common culture* – defines 'how we do things around here' so that project teams can utilize both Project Management and Change Management expertise for improved project delivery:
  - Alignment on what change project success looks like, vision and objectives and rounded set of measures to track against;
  - Alignment on means to achieve goals;
  - Clarity and alignment on roles, responsibilities and touch-points/boundaries;
  - Balanced and constructive power distribution that supports getting the job done;
  - Common language and concepts;
  - Appreciation of abstract themes that impact operations – e.g. the messy nature of projects, the nature of the Change Management/Project Management relationship.

- *Enables a firm-footed approach* – when Change Management and Project Management are integrated to an appropriate degree that facilitates *interdependence*, both can contribute their respective expertise towards a common objective.
- *Supports project goals and maximizes business benefits realization* – timely identification and management of risks and dependencies, and early resolution of issues minimizes resistance to change and impact to the project.

- *Enables project team cooperation and alignment* – when Project Management and Change Management activities are sequenced clearly, both Project Management and Change Management specialists understand how they all fit together and how they individually contribute to team activities and deliverables.
- *Maximizes stakeholder buy-in and end-user adoption* – when Change Management expertise is involved from the outset, and at a strategic level, early plans can reflect Change Management expertise and ensure business and end-users get timely and effective support.
- *Enables communication* – within the project, clear articulation of aims, activities and deliverables enhances the flow of information while, across the organization, the business and end-users are receiving the right messages, at the right time from an aligned project team.
- *Provides one voice and one vision to the business and stakeholders* – protects operations from any disconnect between the Project Manager and Change Manager, which can happen when the project team is more focused on technical solution and neglecting broader stakeholder management and change adoption.
- *Ensures solution meets the needs of the organization and end-users* – a robust 'Impacts Disposition' process ensures communications, training and other such plans are based on end-user impacts which have been identified at a granular level.
- *Builds organizational capability to embrace change* – the culture of cooperation that develops between Project Managers and Change Managers will be mutually beneficial and help change stick.

2.6 Critical success factors

Certain things need to happen on any change project or programme to ensure successful delivery. The critical success factors (CSFs) of PCP methodology are to:

1 Establish the Change Triad and strong sponsorship;
2 Kick off a Project and Change Partnership culture;
3 Establish a powerful governance committee;
4 Instil a sense of urgency;
5 Engage stakeholders to maximize understanding and buy-in;
6 Ensure solution meets business requirements;
7 Align all with a common vision and objectives;
8 Overcome resistance;
9 Maintain momentum, share successes and celebrate wins;
10 Reinforce change via culture-embedding mechanisms;
11 Ensure organizational alignment with the change;
12 Give the business ownership for success or failure;
13 Capture business benefits and build on the change.

These CSFs are based on the extensive research of Jick's, Kotter, and the team at General Electric, and on my own insights gained over the past 25 years in the projects environment. They can be incorporated into the Risk Register to balance technical risks with people-related risks.

2.7 Other considerations

For all its benefits, PCP methodology is not a magic potion to the problem with change projects:

- Where PCP methodology is being used to augment other methodologies, the degree of success integrating the two methodologies will depend on how receptive the other methodology is to a culture of partnership between Project Managers and Change Managers. The greater the gap in underlying philosophy, the more difficult it will be to align Project Management and Change Management expertise to ensure a firm-footed approach to secure project success. This has implications not just for disciplines and professions, but also for industry.
- While the project has become the preferred vehicle for introducing organizational change, the people side of change can be unpredictable and needs to be responsive and dynamic. Therefore, flexibility will be required for activities and deliverables.

2.8 Chapter summary

PCP methodology offers a unique Project Management–Change Management joint value proposition that underpins all activities and deliverables with specific cultural assumptions that foster a culture of partnership. It consists of six lifecycle phases – Discover, Plan and Analyse, Build and Engage, Get Ready, Go Live and Embed and Close – and identifies thirteen critical success factors. PCP methodology works best as a stand-alone, but can be used to augment methodologies that are receptive to building a culture of partnership between Project Managers and Change Managers.

Bibliography

Book

Hayes, J. (2014) *The Theory and Practice of Change Management*. Basingstoke, UK: Palgrave Macmillan.

3 An overview of Project Management

As established earlier, the project is a vehicle for introducing organizational change. It will be temporary in nature, have discrete start and end points, and be designed to meet specific goals and objectives.

The value proposition of Project Management is the design, development and delivery of a solution that meets business requirement. Traditionally, this has been achieved thorough the application of Project Management theories, models and tools as sold by service providers. But, in the organizational content, where the product of the project must be adopted by end-users, projects are increasingly being managed using a blend of Project Management and Change Management.

The most widely accepted standards for the Project Management profession include those of the International Project Management Association (IPMA®) which was founded in the 1950s, the UK-based Association of Project Management (APM™), and the USA-based Project Management Institute (PMI®) publisher of *A Guide to the Project Management Body of Knowledge* (PMBOK® Guide). How these and other professional associations and service providers perceive Project Management influences their varying definitions and methodologies. Some see Project Management as traditional project execution (delivering on time, on scope and to schedule), while others define Project Management to encompass project, programme and portfolio definition, development and execution so as to deliver on business strategies and realize business benefits. This more holistic and commercially attuned view has to be preferable. It requires more of the Project Manager and cross-discipline coordination.

Although projects are concerned with change, professional Project Management guidance regarding Change Management on projects has, until recently, related to controlling scope change (aka 'Change Control') and not the business of bringing people on the journey and securing buy-in and adoption of change by the organization. In a study, Griffith-Cooper and King (2007) outline the very great difference between directly controlling change relative to the non-human aspects of a project (Change Control) and effecting change in the human dimensions of a project (Change Management). Efforts to unite Change

Management and Project Management has amounted to the piecemeal inclusion of a few Change Management theories, models and tools, with such efforts largely led by 'change managers' (note the small 'c' and 'm'). They do not make use of the full Change Management service proposition (see Figure 4.3) or demonstrate how the Project Manager can partner with the Change Manager during the project lifecycle and drive up value for the business.

In an alternative universe where Change Managers dominate project activities, it would be considered naive to suppose that – across the board – Change Managers could also bring Project Management expertise to the table to the same standard as Project Managers . The opposite is true in our current universe. Project Managers cannot be expected to bring the same level of Change Management expertise to a project as a Change Manager can. Indeed, the respective Project Management bodies of knowledge do not even make this a requirement, although there is some heaving hinting in that direction. Project Managers who are given Change Management responsibilities in their daily operations typically flounder as they are operating outside their comfort zone. 'This is not what I was hired for', they will complain. Project Managers and Change Managers have different biases, interests and talents that complement each other. Forcing one to become the other can only end badly.

Gorksky *et al.* (2010) describe a discipline as a branch of learning or scholarly instruction. According to Kwak and Anbari (2009), there has been a long-standing debate in the management education community as to whether 'Project Management' is a practice or an academic discipline. Carden and Egan (2008) maintain that 'Project Management is an evolving field of study and as such does not have a fully established theoretical background', a view which is reasserted by Turyahikayo (2016) who asserts that 'the discipline is still young but growing'. J. A. Hanford (2017), Dean of Metropolitan College and Extended Education at Boston University, USA, sees Project Management as but 'on the cusp of becoming a bona-fide discipline', with a robust Project Management academic credential requiring

> a faculty with gravitas who serve on editorial boards, connect academic research and industry needs, and generate and disseminate knowledge. Their success distinguishes a world-class program from a merely competent one, a passing training fad from an enduring academic field of study.

3.1 A brief history

Project Management developed from several fields of application including civil construction, engineering, and heavy defence activity (Cleland and Garis, 2006). In the mid-1950s, Project Management

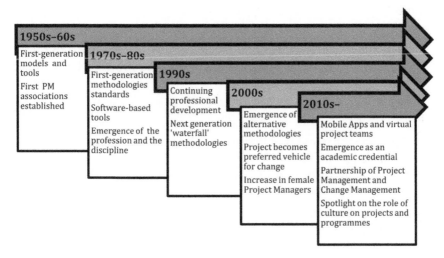

Figure 3.1 The Project Management timeline

emerged in the organizational context and, since then, each decade has marked a particular era in the evolution and growth of Project Management – as an academic discipline, as a profession, as a skill set and as a service offering.

1950s–60s

- In the 1950s, organizations started to systematically apply project management tools and techniques to complex engineering projects.
- First-generation tools invented included the 'job-specification' (which later became the basis of developing the Work Breakdown Structure (or WBS)), the Critical Path Method (CPM) and the Project Evaluation and Review Technique (PERT).
- In 1965, the IPMA® was founded in Europe, while in 1969 the USA-based PMI® was established, marking the emergence of the profession (Kwak, 2005).

1970s–80s

- This period saw the publication of first-generation 'Waterfall' methodologies (PMBOK® Guide, PRINCE Guide and ITIL® Guide), which depicted Project Management as a set of linear activities.
- More sophisticated tools were made available by newly set up software companies such as Artemis (1977), Oracle® (1977) and the Scitor Corporation (1979).
- Project Management specific academic publications and conferences went from strength to strength.

1990s

- During this decade, maturation of the profession marched on. PMBOK® becomes an ANSI standard, the evolved PRINCE2® standard was published and the PMI® initiated Project Management certification.

2000s

- This era is characterized by the introduction of some methodologies to challenge the Waterfall method – namely, 'Agile', 'Lean', 'Scrum'.
- Technological innovations and the growth of SaaS-based Project Management also defines this era.
  - The introduction of low-cost multi-tasking PCs led to higher efficiency in managing and controlling complex project schedules, while low-cost Project Management software became widely available, making Project Management techniques more easily accessible.
  - The rise of the internet and software with internet connectivity features allowed for anyone based anywhere in the world to access their project progress, activities and developments, which is excellent for those wishing to stay 'in the loop' for their project role, while working independently at a remote site.
- Nehauser (2007) observed an increase in the number of women taking on more roles in Project Management. By 2008, females accounted for 30 per cent of the Project Manager population.

2010s–present

This current era has seen developments in four different areas:

- *Mobile Apps* – The IT explosion and the growth in mobile applications has led to a growth in virtual project teams where members are located in different geographies to one another.
- *Emergence as an Academic Credential* – According to J. A. Hanford (2017), at present, postgraduate courses in Project Management tend to be delivered online and not by a full-time faculty with research-based doctorates who are actively engaged in scholarship.
- *The role of Change Management on projects and programmes* – Increasingly, it is understood that Change Management has a critical role to play on projects and that the 'integration' of Project Management and Change Management expertise is inevitable to derive business benefits.
- *Spotlight on the role of culture on projects and programmes* – This book raises visibility on a previously undetected issue relating to the role

of culture on effective project teams that include both Project Management and Change Management professionals.

3.2 Theories, models and tools

The founding fathers of Project Management include Frederick Winslow Taylor, Henry Gantt and Henry Fayol. The scientific management theories of Taylor informed modern Project Management tools such as the Work Breakdown Structure (WBS) and resource allocation, while Gantt is famous for his 'Gantt Chart' project scheduling tool. Fayol's contribution is those five management functions that he identified (planning, organizing, commanding, coordinating and controlling) and that form the foundation of the Project Management body of knowledge.

Below, we take a look at the most common Project Management tools and techniques. Increasingly, many of these can be applied digitally using software packages.

3.2.1 The project lifecycle

This lifecycle marks the start and end dates of a project and the period that exists in between. To facilitate the orderly sequencing of activities and deliverables and support effective resources management, Project Management organizes the project lifecycle into a framework of phases that underpin the Project Management service proposition. Each service provider and professional body has their own view on what this cycle looks like. Below, we see the approach of the Association of Project Management (APM™).

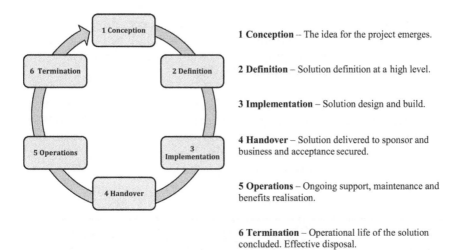

1 **Conception** – The idea for the project emerges.

2 **Definition** – Solution definition at a high level.

3 **Implementation** – Solution design and build.

4 **Handover** – Solution delivered to sponsor and business and acceptance secured.

5 **Operations** – Ongoing support, maintenance and benefits realisation.

6 **Termination** – Operational life of the solution concluded. Effective disposal.

Figure 3.2 APM™ Project Management lifecycle

APM methodology is similar to that of the IPMA® and covers programme and portfolio management, strategy, technical and commercial matters as well the more traditional areas of project execution that can be the main focus of some methodologies.

While different professional associations and service providers have their own lifecycles, the nature of the project lifecycle and phases therein is the same:

- Each phase must be officially sanctioned before work can commence on that particular phase.
- A project review point typically known as a 'Phase Gateway' or 'Stage Gate' occurs at the end of each phase to review the quality of phase execution and the plan for the next phase.
- Each phase has its own unique focus but, in recent times, will be managed by the same Project Manager where possible.
- Achieving the aims of the phase under execution should be priority focus.
- Each phase must be completed to the satisfaction of project governance.
- Success in one phase will lay the foundations for success in any further phases and the realization of business benefits (and vice versa), with success criteria including a good balance of both Project Management and Change Management input to deliver and secure objectives.
- Stakeholder management must be conducted to achieve current phase objectives, but with an eye to the overall stakeholder engagement picture and how stakeholder issues and concerns will evolve across phases.
- The knowledge and skills required for the successful execution of each phase will be determined by the aims and objectives of a given phase. Therefore, the project team will expand and contract as the need shifts across the project lifecycle.

To illustrate the shortcomings of Project Management for effecting successful organizational change, an alternative project lifecycle has been put forward – 'The six phases of a big project' (Poplick, 2011). This cynical take will resonate with many and brings home to us the need for a step change in how we deliver projects.

Figure 3.3 The six phases of a big project

The programme lifecycle is similar in form to the project lifecycle, with the key difference being that, in programme management, the 'implementation' phase is concerned with managing 'tranches' or multiple projects, each with their own goals and objectives. An analysis by Praxis consulting (www.praxisframework.org) to compare the underlying lifecycle of project and programme guides such as PMI®, PRINCE2® and MSP®, found that 'despite the fact that we are talking about tranches instead of stages and now including a process for benefits realisation, the principle phases of the life cycle are the same'.

3.2.2 The Triple Constraints model

The Triple Constraints model (also known as 'Project Management Triangle' or the 'Iron Triangle') illustrates those traditionally recognized constraints that Project Managers must work with – 'time', 'cost' and 'scope'. As demonstrated below, the triple constraints are shown on the corners of a right-angled triangle to show opposition to one another. What happens in one corner affects the others, so, should a project decision-maker seek to optimize all three variables, one will be found to suffer.

This leaves decision-makers with a choice when deliberating on their preferred solution:

- A solution that is designed quickly and to scope (features and quality), but it won't be as cost-effective as it could be.
- A quality and cost-effective solution, but it will take a relatively longer time to deliver.
- A solution that is designed quickly and cheaply, but which does not have the features and is of a lesser quality than some might prefer.

The 'Triple Constraints Model' is useful when intentionally choosing project biases or analysing the goals of a project. A refinement of this model has 'quality' called out as a fourth constraint.

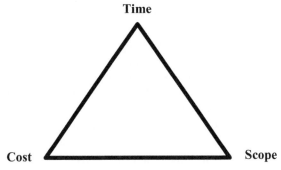

Figure 3.4 The Triple Constraints model

3.2.3 Measures of success

The 'Triple Constraints' of scope, time and cost have been the traditional measures of success for project success. But a question that has been explored in recent years is whether project delivery success is synonymous with the successful delivery of business change. The dismal failure rates suggest not, and this is the conclusion that most have come to. Now, it is understood by those who keep up-to-date with best practices and lessons learnt in both industry and academia, that Change Management expertise needs to have a greater bearing on project definition, development and execution, and additional measures of success need to capture the benefit that Change Management brings to the equation. For project delivery success to be synonymous with successful delivery of change, additional measures must include 'business adoption of the change', 'end-user proficiency' and 'benefits realization'.

3.2.4 Brainstorming analysis

Brainstorming is a group creativity process. The term was popularized by Alex Faicknewy Osborn in the 1953 book *Applied Imagination*. The idea is to encourage spontaneous ideas about how to solve a problem. The technique is particularly useful in the early phases of the project lifecycle.

Osborn (1953) identified two principles that contribute to *ideative efficacy* (the ability to brainstorm ideas) – 'defer judgment' and 'reach for quantity'. He established four general rules of brainstorming (below) to reduce any social inhibitions among group members, stimulate idea generation and increase the overall creativity of the group:

1   *Go for quantity*: This rule is a means of enhancing divergent production, aiming to facilitate problem solving through the maxim *quantity breeds quality*. The assumption is that the greater the number of ideas generated, the bigger the chance of producing a radical and effective solution.
2   *Withhold criticism*: In brainstorming, criticism of ideas generated should be put 'on hold'. Instead, participants should focus on extending or adding to ideas, reserving criticism for a later 'critical stage' of the process. By suspending judgement, participants will feel free to generate unusual ideas.
3   *Welcome wild ideas*: To get a good long list of suggestions, wild ideas are encouraged. They can be generated by looking from new perspectives and suspending assumptions. These new ways of thinking might give you better solutions.

4 *Combine and improve ideas*: As suggested by the slogan '1+1=3'. It is believed to stimulate the building of ideas by a process of association.

A well-facilitated brainstorming session can encourage Project Managers, whose strengths are most often processes and systems related, to think creatively.

3.2.5 The Business Case

The Business Case aims to establish whether, at face value, a sufficient case exists for considering a proposal in more depth. It establishes the Terms of Reference for a project, and leads to a recommendation on whether or not to proceed. A comprehensive Business Case will cover the following:

1	Business challenge or opportunity	The business problem or opportunity that the proposed project will address.
2	Outcomes and benefits	How the project will benefit the business.
3	Recommendations	Key findings and proposals for addressing them.
4	Justification and feasibility	Project rationale. Outline of project constraints and any previous lessons learnt.
5	Business case team	The roles of the team members.
6	Problem statement	What problem this project is to address.
7	Change impact	Impact on the business and end users.
8	Technology migration	How new solution will be implemented and how data from the legacy tools will be migrated.
9	Project overview	Goals and objectives, measures and milestones.
10	Project description	The approach the project will use to address the business challenge or opportunity.
11	Goals and objectives	Business goals and objectives.
12	Project performance	Measures to gauge performance and outcomes.
13	Risks, assumptions, issues and dependencies	Preliminary risks, assumptions, issues and dependencies.
14	Major milestones	The milestones and their target completion date.
15	Strategic alignment	How the project supports the strategic plan.
16	Cost benefit analysis	The financial benefits of the project.
17	Alternative analysis	Alternatives plus the reasons for rejecting them.
18	Approvals	Executive review board.
19	The scope	Departments and functions affected; stakeholders; duration of spending proposal.
20	Appendices	Support documentation

Figure 3.5 Business Case content areas

While the level of detail required will be dependent on the level of expenditure expected, the Business Case must help decision-makers answer the following:

- What will the project create (new product, service, approach)?
- What business challenge or opportunity will the project address?
- What benefits will the project afford the organization?
- What are the expected disbenefits and risks?
- How much is the project expected to cost and is funding available?
- What other resources are required and can they be supplied?
- How long will the project take?

3.2.6 Work Breakdown Structure

When getting into the actual planning of a project, it is not unusual to feel somewhat daunted by the scale of the challenge and the level of detail involved. To overcome this, the Work Breakdown Structure (WBS) method is used to 'eat the elephant in small chunks' – breaking the project into manageable parts and organizing those parts in a logical fashion so the project team can add the detail over time (see Figure 3.6 overleaf).

The WBS is a chart in which the critical tasks of a project are organized to illustrate their relationships to each other and to the project as a whole. The key objectives are defined first and then those tasks that are required to achieve the objective. In the example below, the WBS for a project team-building event is shown. For large projects, the WBS would be a great deal more complex.

The WBS is used at the beginning of a project to help build the Business Case and define project scope therein. A well-designed WBS can help with all aspects of Project Management (e.g. effective resource allocation, budgeting, procurement, product delivery, quality control, risks management and scheduling).

3.2.7 Statement of Work

A Statement of Work (SOW) defines project-specific activities, deliverables and timelines for a vendor providing services to the client. It is often a binding contract, the terms of which will be governed by the Master Services Agreement which serves as the master contract. Figure 3.7 on p. 34 shows what a SOW typically includes.

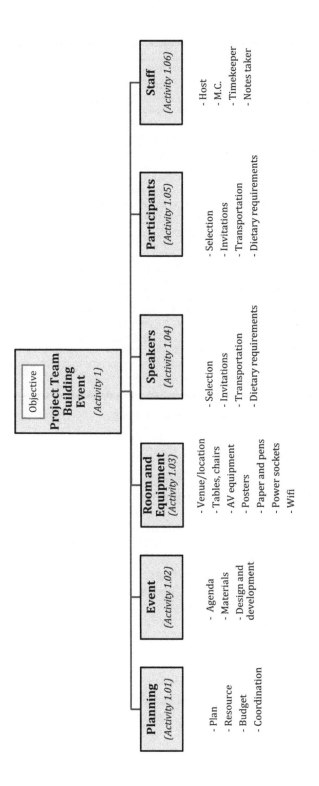

Figure 3.6 Work Breakdown Structure for project team-building event

1	**Purpose statement**	• Explains the reason for the project.
2	**Scope of work**	• Describes the work to be carried out and any hardware and software involved.
3	**Location of work**	• Describes where the work is to be performed.
4	**Performance time frame**	• Specifies the start and finish time, number of hours that can be billed per week or month, where work is to be performed and anything else that relates to scheduling.
5	**Deliverables schedule**	• Lists and describes what is due and when.
6	**Applicable standards**	• Describes any industry specific standards that need to be adhered to in fulfilling the contract.
7	**Acceptance criteria**	• Specifies how the buyer or receiver of goods will determine if the product or service is acceptable, usually with objective criteria.
8	**Special requirements**	• Specifies any special hardware or software, specialized workforce requirements, such as degrees or certifications for personnel, travel requirements and anything else not covered in the contract specifics.
9	**Type of contract/ payment schedule**	• Project acceptance will depend on if there is a budget to cover the work required. A breakdown of payments and whether they are up-front or phased will usually be negotiated in an early stage.
10	**Miscellaneous**	• Many items that are not part of the main negotiations may be listed because they are important to the project, and overlooking or forgetting them could pose problems for the project.

Figure 3.7 Statement of Work: outline of contents

3.2.8 The Project Charter

A Project Charter document has three main purposes: project authorization, project promotion and project point of reference.

1   *Project authorization* – Using a standard charter template, projects in the pipeline can be ranked and authorized based on standard criteria and expected business benefits.
2   *Project promotion* – Senior stakeholders have an executive summary they can use as they see fit to promote the project and defend it from any challenges to the project or project resources.
3   *Project point of reference* – Useful for existing project team members and for new team members who need to understand matters such as the project rationale, project stakeholders and what is in and out of scope.

A review of project charter templates used across industries has found that although templates vary by organization and according to the Project Management methodology used, the core contents tend to include the following:

- *Purpose or justification/benefits* – May refer to the business case, strategic objectives or external factors that justify the use of resources;
- *Scope* – What is in scope and what is out of scope; as the programme gets underway the scope may be revisited;
- *High-level requirements* – Initial high-level business and compliance requirements that meet customer expectations;
- *Objectives and success criteria* – Measurable objectives for the scope, schedule, cost, quality, customer satisfaction, etc., and measurable criteria to indicate successful completion of each objective;
- *Deliverables* – List of key products/work packages;
- *Methodology* – e.g. PCP methodology;
- *Risks and issues* – Initial global risks (to be progressively elaborated upon);
- *Assumptions* – Initial high-level assumptions about scope, resources, funding, limitation, budget or fixed due date;
- *Dependencies* – High-level dependencies and constraints;
- *Milestones* – Timeline of significant high-level events and/or deliverables;
- *Financial* – High-level range of expenditures estimate;
- *Stakeholder list* – Initial list of people who can influence or be influenced by the project;
- *Key manpower* – sponsor, Change Manager, Project Manager and any other relevant resources;

Change Project Charter		
Project name	**Project date**	**Purpose**
High-level requirements	**Scope**	**Business case**
Benefits	**Objectives**	**Success criteria**
Methodology	**Financial**	
	Budget	*Costs*
Assumptions	**Risks and issues**	
	Risks	*Mitigation*
Dependencies	*Issues*	*Mitigation*
Stakeholder list	**Key manpower**	**Project and Change Manager authorities**

Figure 3.8 Change Project Charter template

- *Authorities* – Authority regarding hiring, firing, discipline, accept or reject; authority regarding technical decisions; authority to resolve conflict within teams or with external stakeholders; authority to manage funds variance.

This content can be organized as shown in the sample Change Project Charter (Figure 3.8).

3.2.9 Stakeholder analysis and engagement

For large and complex projects, stakeholders can run into large numbers that can prove difficult to manage and, as having a clear line of sight across stakeholder-related risks, issues and concerns is imperative, good planning needs to go into stakeholder management. The stakeholder management toolkit used needs to place the emphasis of effort on actual stakeholder management (together with related risks and issues management) and not on the upkeep of complex and convoluted tracking and reporting spreadsheets and databases. The toolkit below was designed with this in mind to support PCP methodology.

Stakeholders fall into four broad roles:

1   *Senior executives and decision makers*, most active during project phases 1–4 when the business case and solution are being defined;
2   *Project support* groups such as super users, local leaders and other projects, who will be active and influential during project phases 3–6 as the solution is developed, tested and deployed;
3   *Change advocates* who will contribute and be active and influential during project phases 2–4;
4   *End-users*, who will be active and influential during project phases 5–6 and may either embrace the change being implemented or reject it.

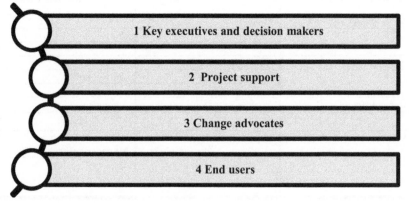

Figure 3.9 The four tiers of stakeholders

These categories can overlap, for example, and an individual may contribute to the project in the early stages of solution design and become an end-user once the final solution is deployed.

Step 1: The Stakeholder Map

The term 'Stakeholder Map' can mean different things to different people. Here, it is presented as a handy visual image of stakeholders that may be grouped in a number of different ways – for example, by industry, by geography, or by relative power and influence. In the example below, which is based on work I did as Stakeholder Management Lead for the building of the new terminal airport at Dublin Airport, Ireland, the project is the construction of an airport terminal and the stakeholders are categorized according to their role and relationship with the airport authority. Each of the categories can be further subdivided – for example, 'airport workers' will include airport police, airport security, retail outlet staff and cleaners, and taxi drivers, while 'near neighbours' will include local churches, residents, schools, businesses, etc.

Using this method, which will appeal to visual learners in particular, it is very easy to spot which stakeholders are missing from the picture and add them. It is a good idea to post this chart up so the team can add to it as they work.

Figure 3.10 Airport construction: project stakeholder map

Step 2: Stakeholder profiling

Once a stakeholder has been identified, they can be profiled according to agreed criteria. Different tools are available to assist this process. A favourite is the 2 x 2 'Power/Interest' stakeholder matrix. As the description suggests, stakeholders are profiled according to the power they wield to impact the project and nature of their interest in the project. So a stakeholder may be profiled as 'high power, high interest' (HP/HI), 'high power, low interest' (HP/LI), 'low power, high interest' (LP/HI), or 'low power, low interest' (LP/LI), and be positioned on the stakeholder matrix accordingly. This profile will determine the strategy the project adopts to manage the stakeholder:

- High power/high interest – manage closely;
- High power/low interest – keep satisfied;
- Low power/high interest – keep informed;
- Low power/low interest – monitor.

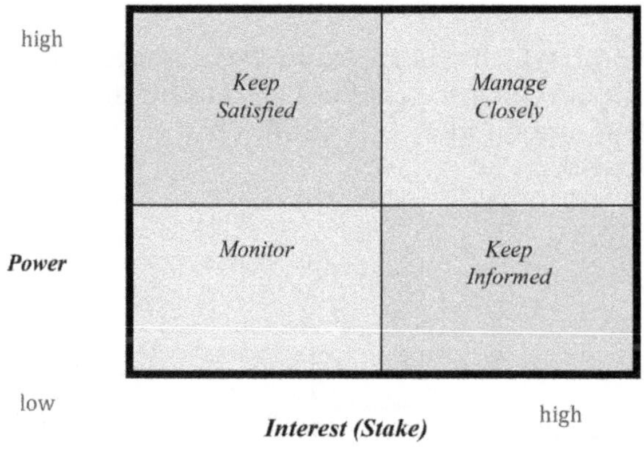

Figure 3.11 Stakeholder Power/Interest matrix

Step 3: The Stakeholder Governance Plan

Once stakeholders are profiled, thought needs to go into which project representative will manage which stakeholder, and agreement will need to be reached on this. The Stakeholder Governance Plan names the confirmed Relationship Owner for each stakeholder. It can also name an Interface Manager where the Relationship Owner has appointed someone else to manage the relationship on his or her behalf. Where such an arrangement exists, the Relationship Owner will continue to own the relationship, and the Interface Manager should either be a direct report or someone who has the required gravitas and with whom the Relationship Owner works closely.

Airport workers	Profile	Contact	Relationship owner	Interface Manager
Airport Police	LP/HI	Jay Chan, Head of Airport Police	Alex Rudd, Airport Authority Security Director	Sam Kapur, Airport Authority Senior Manager Security
Retail outlet employers	HP/HI	Val Higgins, retailers' representative	Jake Walsh, Airport Authority Head of Operations	Kathy Connolly, Airport Authority Senior Manager Operations
Maintenance contractors	LP/HI	Maintenance contractors' representative	Jake Walsh, Airport Authority Head of Operations	Kathy Connolly, Airport Authority Senior Manager Operations
Unions	HP/HI	Union representative	Sally Delaney, Airport Authority Head of Human Resources	Victor Low, Airport Authority Senior HR Manager

Figure 3.12 Template: Stakeholder Governance Plan

The Stakeholder Governance Plan should show, at a glance, the stakeholder profile of a stakeholder and 'who' is responsible for owning and managing the relationship.

Step 4: The Stakeholder Engagement Plan

The Stakeholder Engagement Plan focuses on the 'what and how', outlining engagement objectives, channels, frequency of engagement, key issues this particular stakeholder has, and a status update on issues resolution. It will dovetail with the Project Communications Plan.

While stakeholder-related tools and templates do feature in both Project Managment and Change Management methodologies, it makes sense for the Change Manager to own stakeholder mapping, analysis and engagement activities. The Change Manager will look at the broader picture across all stakeholders, and all project phases, and will need to develop strong insight into stakeholder interests, issues and concerns.

Stakeholder group	Profile	Relationship owner	Objectives	Engagement channels and frequency	Issues	Status update

Figure 3.13 Stakeholder Engagement Plan template

3.2.10 RAID log

The acronym RAID stands for Risks, Assumptions, Issues and Dependencies. The RAID log enables the tracking of anything that has an immediate or future impact. It should be kept up-to-date through weekly reviews and team meetings. The project team should act swiftly as risks and issues are identified, check assumptions to ensure they continue to remain valid, and review dependencies to ensure they are understood and factored into plans as appropriate.

Risks	Risks are events that are likely to happen and will impact a project if they do occur. The higher the likelihood and the higher the expected impact, the greater the risk rating. The RAID log gives an account of each risk, together with an analysis and risk mitigation plan.
Assumptions	Assumptions are based on beliefs we hold to be true and which will inform our future action. Sometimes they prove to be true and sometimes they don't. Project assumptions need to be articulated and validated. The RAID log details each assumption, the reason it is assumed and the action needed to confirm whether the assumption is valid.
Issues	When risks are not mitigated, they become real issues that impact the project and need to be managed. The log details each issue, its impact, its gravity and what action needed to be taken to contain and eliminate it.
Dependencies	Dependencies are those relationships between preceding and succeeding tasks. The log details where the dependencies are in the project tasks and deliverables.

Figure 3.14 RAID log

3.2.11 Project Roadmap

The Project Roadmap (Figure 3.15) is used to communicate plans with stakeholders and project team members and ensure a shared under-standing. This example (www.business-docs.co.uk) illustrates project goals, high-level activities and milestones along a timeline, with workstreams represented by separate 'swim lanes'. The initial Project Roadmap developed might give a very high-level view across the project, with additional Project Roadmaps developed to show more detail across each workstream swim lane for each quarter or three-month period.

If space allows, the Project Roadmap can additionally show key risks and dependencies.

3.2.12 The Project Management Plan

A Project Management Plan (PMP) shows how a project's objectives are to be achieved, detailing key activities, deliverables, resources required and how the project will be executed, managed and controlled for its

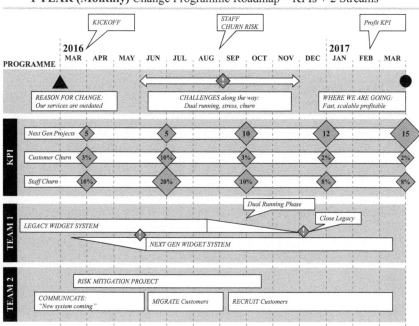

Figure 3.15 Project Roadmap

duration. It is a formal document that is approved by programme governance and used to guide project implementation. The Project Management Plan typically covers the following:

- Communications management;
- Change control;
- Financial management;
- Quality management;
- Resource management;
- Risk management;
- Stakeholder requirements management;
- Stakeholder management;
- Schedule management;
- Scope management.

An obvious oversight is the exclusion of Change Management, which would also incorporate not only front-end activities such as communications and training, but also back-end activities that feed and inform these, such as impacts analysis, and culture and readiness assessments.

The Project Plan is approved in the initial project phases and applied throughout the project lifecycle.

3.2.13 Project Schedule and the Gantt Chart

A Project Schedule is a listing of deliverables, tasks and activities, and task owners, with start and finish dates. It also includes task duration, milestones and the linkage of dependencies. The Project Schedule can be informed by the Work Breakdown Structure and the Statement of Work. It will be developed using a Gantt Chart.

As mentioned earlier, the Gantt Chart is named after US engineer and consultant Henry Gantt who devised the technique in the 1910s. The Gantt Chart illustrates a project schedule, with start and finish dates of the work breakdown structure of the project. In modern times, the Gantt Chart has evolved to show activity owners and the dependency relationships between activities. It can be very handy for showing current schedule status, using per cent-complete shadings and a vertical line to mark today. A Gantt Chart can be constructed using a spreadsheet or a software package design as seen overleaf (Figure 3.16).

The Gantt Chart is very flexible and is an excellent tool for creating the Project Schedule and checking project progress. However, it does not easily or obviously show the importance and interdependence of related parallel activities, as does the Critical Path Analysis (see overleaf). For project planning purposes, it is best to use both tools.

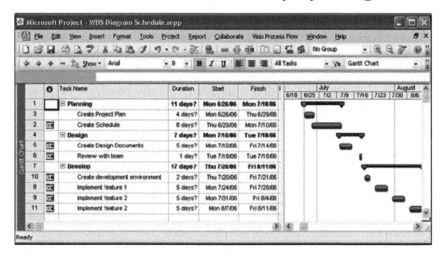

Figure 3.16 Project Schedule based on Gantt Chart

3.2.14 Critical Path Analysis

Critical Path Analysis was developed in the 1950s as a planning method for large USA defence projects. Critical Path Analysis formally identifies which project's tasks must be completed on time so that the whole project can be completed on time. It also identifies which tasks can be delayed and if manpower needs to be reallocated to tasks that were missed off or are running late against schedule.

Advantages

* Allows for the monitoring of achievement of project goals;
* Shows the importance and interdependence of related parallel activities;
* Helps to see where remedial action needs to be taken to get a project back on track;
* Helps develop and test the Project Plan to ensure that it is robust;
* Helps to identify the minimum length of time needed to complete a project;
* On an accelerated project, it helps identify which project steps need to be accelerated to complete the project within the available time.

Disadvantages

* The relation of tasks to time is not as immediately obvious as with Gantt Charts.

3.2.15 PERT analysis

The Programme/Project Evaluation and Review Technique (PERT) is a specialized tool that is an offshoot of Critical Path Analysis. Both are used to illustrate the timeline and the work that must be done for a project but, with PERT, three different time estimates for the project are calculated, working back from a fixed end date: the shortest possible amount time each task will take, the most probable amount of time and the longest amount of time if things don't go as planned. PERT allows for a very detailed analysis of numerous related activities, and of the timings, implications and opportunities arising from interconnected events. Various software systems and applications are based on its principles. Some sources suggest that PERT techniques were devised in the 1950s by the DuPont® Corporation, while other sources suggest that the method was devised in the General Dynamics Corporation. Whatever its beginnings, PERT was subsequently adopted by the US Navy and refined in the late 1950s.

3.2.16: Risk/Impact Probability Matrix

The Risk/Impact Probability Matrix is a very effective tool for raising senior management awareness of risks so that sound decisions can be made. It is based on the principle that a risk has two dimensions:

- *Probability* – A risk is an event that 'may' occur. The probability of it occurring can range anywhere from just above 0 per cent to just below 100 per cent. (Note: It can't be exactly 100 per cent, because

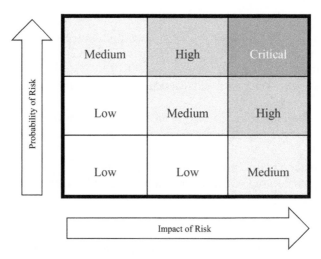

Figure 3.17 Risk/Probability Matrix

then it would be a certainty, not a risk. And it can't be exactly 0 per cent, or it wouldn't be a risk.)
- *Impact* – A risk, by its very nature, always has a negative impact. However, the size of the impact varies in terms of cost and impact on health, human life or some other critical factor.

The matrix allows you to rate potential risks on these two dimensions. The probability that a risk will occur is represented on one axis of the chart, and the impact of the risk, if it occurs, on the other. You use these two measures to plot the risk on the chart. This gives you a quick, clear view of the priority that you need to give to each. You can then decide what resources you will allocate to manage that particular risk.

The corners of the chart have the following characteristics:

- *Low impact/low probability* – Risks in the bottom left corner are low level and you can often ignore them.
- *Low impact/high probability* – Risks in the top left corner are of moderate importance: if these things happen, you can cope with them and move on. However, you should try to reduce the likelihood that they will occur.
- *High impact/low probability* – Risks in the bottom right corner are of high importance if they do occur, but they are very unlikely to happen. For these, however, you should do what you can to reduce the impact they will have if they do occur and you should have contingency plans in place just in case they do.
- *High impact/high probability* – Risks towards the top right corner are of critical importance. These are your top priorities and are risks that you must pay close attention to.

Those risks that fall into the middle and high-priority risk rankings are the ones to focus on.

3.2.17 Project Management Maturity model

A Project Management Maturity model (PMM) assesses the organization's Project Management maturity level in terms of three core areas – people, processes and tools. It helps identify gaps in capability and areas for improvement, providing comparisons against competitors. Increasing maturity requires the progressive development of competence in areas for improvement.

There are over thirty tools in the marketplace claiming to measure PMM, each using its own criteria. The standard measure for maturity in the 'people' arena is whether or not Project Managers have formal Project Management qualifications and how they rate in terms of particular subject areas. A useful refinement to such tools would be to measure Project Managers for their knowledge of Change Management (as a secondary skill set) and competence in *partnering* with Change Managers.

3.3 Trends and areas for development

The PMI® estimates that growth for Project Management will increase through the decade ending in 2020 and 15.7 million new Project Management roles will be created. The profession is expected to grow by US$6.61 trillion (www.pmi.org). This growth will drive maturation on all four fronts – as an academic discipline, as a practitioner skill set, as a profession and as a consumer product (Figure 3.18).

While certain trends are emerging, other areas in need of development I have identified and incorporate below.

3.3.1 Maturation of the academic discipline

As an area of study and research, Project Management remains in its formative years. Trends and areas for development include:

*   New theories, models and tools will deepen our understanding of Project Management.
*   The common availability of third-level courses that are backed by a faculty of staff with academic gravitas will confirm Project Management as an academic credential.
*   An ongoing refinement in thinking is required on how best to integrate Project Management and Change Management, without diluting the value and service proposition of each discipline.
*   Increased appreciation of the role culture plays for project teams delivering organizational change.

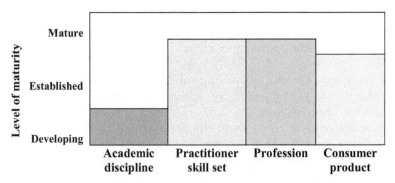

Figure 3.18 The faces of Project Management maturity

3.3.2 Maturation of the profession

Project Management as a profession is in early advanced maturity, with first generation methodologies and standards emerging decades ago, and subject to continuous improvement. Trends and areas for development include:

- Increasing professional development among Project Managers;
- New body of knowledge for Project Managers on the scope of Change Management and how Project Managers can partner with Change Managers to implement – and embed – change;
- Evolving certification programmes that require senior candidates to have a considerable number of hours experience working alongside a Change Manager and their team at project level (or a Change Director at programme level);
- Project Management will continue to incorporate the latest technology.

3.3.3 Maturation of the practitioner skill set

While capabilities can vary greatly across individuals, the practitioner skill set clarifies what skills junior, intermediate and senior Project Managers should have. Collectively, it is in its early advanced maturity stage. Trends and areas for development include:

- Greater mutual appreciation among Project Management and Change Management professionals on their complementary toolkits and skillsets; it is becoming increasingly common for Project Managers to learn about Change Management as part of their secondary skillset, and for Change Managers to learn Project Management skills as a secondary skillset.
- The ability to demonstrate attitudes and behaviours that express those cultural assumptions that will support a culture of partnership between Project Managers and Change Managers; it is time to let go of out-dated assumptions that get in the way of effective teamwork and successful delivery (see Chapters 5–8).

3.3.4 Maturation of the consumer product and consumer understanding

The Project Management consumer product is quite standardized, but it is not delivering to industry's expectations. Trends and areas for development include:

- Revised client procurement models based on an increased understanding of Change Management and which lead to an increase in the use of a Project Management/Change Management joint proposition for delivering change;

- Cultivating an in-house culture of partnership between Project Management and Change Management to secure successful delivery of change.

3.4 Chapter summary

Various practice standards are in place for Project Management professionals, including the International Project Management Association competence baseline (ICB, 2006), the APMBoK® (APM™, 2006) and the PMBOK®, 6th edition (PMI®, 2017). Existing Project Management practices, standards and theory indicate that Project Management does not adequately address the role of Change Management on projects or provide guidance on how Project Management practitioners can partner with Change Management practitioners to embed change and secure higher project success rates. The toolkit of Project Management has varied very little from its early days with innovations relating more to the use of software to digitize tools, rather than the creation of innovative theories and models that redefine our understanding of Project Management and reshape our practices.

Project Management is at varying levels of maturity as an academic discipline, a skill set, a profession and a consumer project, with a key trend being the assimilation of Change Management by Project Management. We need to stop using twentieth-century solutions to address twenty-first century problems. The world has changed and our methods need to change. Cultivating a culture of partnership between Project Management and Change Management will go a long way to securing successful delivery of change.

Bibliography

Books

Cleland, D. I. and Gareis, R. (2006) Chapter 1: The Evolution of Project Management. In: *Global Project Management Handbook*. New York: McGraw-Hill.

Kwak, Y. H. (2005) A Brief History of Project Management. In: *The Story of Managing Projects*. Elias G. Carayannis *et al.* (9th edn). Westport, CT: Greenwood.

Nokes, S. (2007) *The Definitive Guide to Project Management* (2nd edn). London: Prentice Hall, Financial Times.

Osborn, A. F. (1963) *Applied Imagination: Principles and Procedures of Creative Problem Solving* (3rd edn). New York: Charles Scribner's Sons.

Journals

Carden, L. and Egan, T. (2008) Does our literature support sectors newer to project management? The search for quality publications relevant to non-traditional industries. *Project Management Journal*, 39 (3).

Gorsky, C. A., Antonovsky, A., Blau, I. and Mansur, A. (2010) The relationship between academic discipline and dialogic behavior in Open University course forums. *International Review of Research in Open and Distance Learning*, 11(2).

Griffith-Cooper, B. and King, K. (2007) The partnership between project management and organizational change: Integrating change management with change leadership. *Performance Improvement*, 46(1): 14–20.

Hanford, J. A. (2017) Projecting project management's future within the academic landscape. *The New England Journal of Project Management*. Retrieved from: www.nebhe.org/thejournal/projecting-project-management's-future-within-the-academic-landscape/ (accessed 14 January 2017).

Kwak, Y. H. and Anbari, F. T. (2009) Analyzing project management research: Perspectives from top management journals. *International Journal of Project Management*, 27: 435–46.

Neuhauser, C. (2007) Project manager leadership behaviors and frequency of use by female project managers. *Project Management Journal*, 38 (1): 21–31.

Turyahikayo, E. (2016) Theoretical paucity of project management as an academic discipline: Implications for project management practitioners and researchers. *Journal of Good Governance and Sustainable Development in Africa*, 3(2): 28–35.

Online

www.barrypoplick.com
www.business-docs.co.uk
www.mindtools.com
www.pmi.org
www.praxisframework.org

4   An overview of Organizational Change Management

While project management techniques date back to the pyramids, the very earliest human civilizations developed cultures and managed change to ensure the survival of their communities.

Organizational Change Management (OCM), aka Change Management, emerged in the 1980s to plug a gap left by Project Management. As the project vehicle and Project Management gained popularity as the preferred method for introducing change to organizations, stakeholders were often left behind because Project Managers focused more on technical delivery and less on ensuring that the product of the project met the needs of the business and was adopted.

Change Management is the planned transitioning of the organization, teams and individuals from current state to desired state by embedding new ways of working that meet business and end-user requirements.

Where change is introduced to the organization outside of the project context, it can more usefully be referred to as Organizational Development (OD) – a field of applied behavioural science, which emerged in the 1930s. French and Bell (1999) describe OD as 'a long term effort, led and supported by top management to improve an organisation's visioning, empowerment, learning and problem solving processes, through an ongoing, collaborative management of organisation culture'. OD emerged after a series of studies on autocratic and democratic leadership found that employee participation led to improved outcomes. Initially, OD was characterized by small-scale incremental change, but in time it came to embrace larger scale change initiatives such as total quality management (TQM). As the rate of change accelerated, the need for the organization to adapt quicker became a strategic imperative and leadership focus shifted away from introducing incremental change to getting quick results. With this trend came the rise of the project as the preferred vehicle for introducing change and OD started to take a back seat as Project Management gained favour. Although OD has a critical role to play in ensuring ongoing organization readiness for change by building capability for learning and innovation, it was seen to fall short on this, placing too much emphasis on facilitating individual and team change, to the neglect of organization level change and securing business benefits. This may be due in no small part to the dominance of *action learning* as an OD intervention. Action learning involves participants working in teams on real problems and under the guidance of a process facilitator, but focuses primarily on individual and team problems, and rarely on organizational problems.

Both Change Management and OD interventions facilitate organizational change on three levels, as illustrated below:

1   The organization/enterprise – strategies, policies, processes, structures, systems, roles and competencies;
2   Teams – knowledge, skills, attitude, climate and culture;
3   Individuals – knowledge, skills and attitude.

Both disciplines take a holistic approach across the entire organizational eco-system, conscious that change in one part affects other parts. However, while Change Management has its roots in OD and the behavioural sciences, Change Management theory and frameworks have been shaped by other traditions, too, including strategic management and engineer°ing. Also, while the OD practitioner stands aloof from the substantive content of change and making any recommendations, the Change Management practitioner is a key member of the project organization and acts as subject-matter-expert (SME) and trusted adviser. OD focuses on micro-level interventions such as process consultation, while Change Management integrates micro- and macro-level interventions. Change Management in the projects environment can support the long-term work of Organizational Development by embracing culture building as part of the work of the project, and by planning for sustainable change rather than quick fixes.

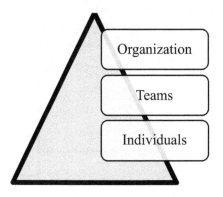

Figure 4.1 Change Management and OD: levels of intervention

4.1 A brief history of Change Management

From the early twentieth century, academics have been exploring the nature of change and how individuals, teams and organizations experience and respond to it, for example:

- Cultural anthropologist Van Gennep (1909) found that, across cultures, certain kinds of life-changing rituals such as births, weddings and funerals have similar structures made up of three distinct phases: 'separation' from the old position, 'transition' during which the individual is no longer in the old stage but not yet in the new, and finally 'reintegration', where the individual is reintroduced into society in his or her new role.
- Social psychologist Kurt Lewin (1947) postulated that although change in organizations is constant, the nature of the change is not always the same, as change comes in a variety of shapes and sizes, and can be proactive or reactive depending on contextual factors. Lewin introduced two of the most influential models on change – the Ice Cube Model (see section 4.2.2) and Force Field Analysis (see section 4.2.7).
- Aguilar (1967) presented 'ETPS' as a mnemonic to represent four environmental forces at play: economic, technology, political and social. Over time, other forces had been identified and added to the mix.

Since the 1980s, each decade has marked a particular era in the evolution and growth of Change Management on four fronts – as a discipline, as a profession, as a skill set and as a consumer product.

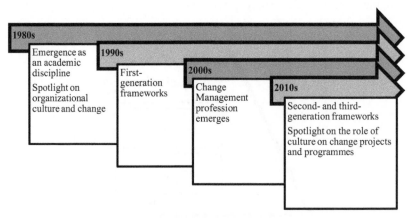

Figure 4.2 The Change Management timeline

1980s

While the term Organizational Change Management can be found in academic literature from the 1960s, it was in the 1980s that Change Management separated from Organizational Development and emerged as a discrete area of research and practice that put people at the centre of change. Early pioneers include the University of Sheffield and the University of Warwick, which count among the Russell Group of prestigious educational establishments. Also, and as a result of a significant increase in demand from industry for Change Management services, the major management consultancies rebranded their 'reengineering' practices as 'Change Management' practices (see section 4.3.7).

The second big development that came in the 1980s was the rise in interest in 'organizational culture'. One cannot sensibly discuss Change Management without discussing culture, as culture is that subterranean force that can absorb and incorporate change – or spit it out. The essence of culture is that shared mind-set of assumptions that a group holds about how to get things done. It is expressed in the shared attitudes and behaviours of the group, and reflected in outcomes and results they achieve. Organizational culture is hugely relevant in the projects space for the following reasons:

- Those different cultural assumptions that Project Managers and Change Managers hold impact their effectiveness when they work together.
- Projects introduce new ways of doing things and, at some level, drive for a shift in those assumptions held by the organization about how to get things done. That, by default, places demands for some degree of culture shift.

Understanding culture, and how to facilitate culture evolution and transformation, are essential components of the Change Manager's skill set.

1990s

As the pressure to embrace change was felt more acutely by organizations, leaders wanted some practical, proven roadmaps on how to implement change. Academics and practitioners obliged with prescriptive models based on a series of liners – for example:

- Jick (1991) put forward his ten steps for implementing successful change.
- General Electric (1992) developed their Change Acceleration Process (CAP).

- Kotter (1995) described typical failures of organizations managing change and recommended eight steps to address them.

These models are described and compared in section 4.2.13.

2000s

According to Nickols (2000), Change Management is 'an area of professional practice' as much as it is 'the task of managing change' and 'a body of knowledge'.

With the Change Management discipline established and demand for Change Management services growing exponentially, the Change Management profession started to take shape:

- Since the turn of the millennium, USA Change Management corporation PROSCI® (www.prosci.com) has played a leading role in providing insights that have helped shape the profession, conducting global research on Change Management practices across industries, and sharing best practices and lessons learnt.
- In 2005, the Change Management Institute (CMI) (www.change-management-institute.com) was established in Australia as a global, independent, not-for-profit organization to promote and develop the profession of Change Management internationally. Recognizing the need for standards, the CMI developed the first ever Change Practitioner Competency Model in 2008, followed by an accreditation scheme and a variety of professional qualifications.
- In 2006, the UK-based APMG, which specializes in Project Management examinations, started providing foundation examinations in Change Management, and added practitioner courses in 2010.
- In 2011, the Association of Change Management Professionals (ACMP®) (www.acmpglobal.org) was incorporated as a non–profit organization with a remit similar to the CMI. The ACMP® has its own credential for Change Management professionals.

Interestingly, both PROSCI® and the newly established ACMP approach Change Management with an explicit focus on 'individual and organization level interventions', a notion that would fit Western cultures that focus more on the individual, but not Eastern cultures that focus more on the group. While ideas and change start with the individual, it is teams that get things done in organization, and transitioning teams through change is quite a different challenge from transitioning individuals. A comprehensive approach to organizational change for both Change Management and OD practitioners addresses the individual, the team and the organization. To learn more about managing teams through change turn to sections 4.2.25 and 4.2.26.

2010s

In this current decade, the push to understand how Project Management and Change Management can complement each other on projects has gained momentum.

- *Second Generation Frameworks* have emerged depicting Change Management processes and activities more closely aligned with Project Management activities and 'integrated' to some extent on various 'above the surface' levels such as structure, governance, roles and responsibilities.
- *Third Generation Frameworks,* the first of which is presented in this book, integrate Project Management and Change Management both 'above the surface' and 'below the surface' throughout the project lifecycle, incorporating that hidden subterranean cultural dimension that dictates how things get done in everyday operations.

2017–

- A unique feature of the above-mentioned third generation approach is creating a culture of partnership between Project Management and Change Management. PCP methodology, presented herein, is based on specific cultural assumptions that address those universal problems that the project organization faces. This represents a genuine revolution in thinking about how Project Management and Change Management can come together to both implement and embed change, and is sure to be a new growth area.

4.2 The Change Management Service Proposition

The Change Management value proposition is about ensuring that the business and end-users embrace and adopt change so that aspirational business benefits are realized. This is achieved via an array of services that are captured in the Change Management service proposition (see Figure 4.3). An appreciation of the Change Management service proposition will enable Change Management practitioners to understand the scope of their own role and position themselves appropriately, so that Project Managers see them as partners and trusted advisers. It will enable Project Managers to better understand the breadth and depth of the Change Management service proposition and the value that the Change Management team brings to the table.

Timing	Capability	Description
Before project cycle	**Organize culture analysis**	Diagnose current state culture (future state and gap to be diagnosed during project lifecycle once solution is confirmed).
During project cycle	**Change impact analysis**	Diagnose and analyse high-level change impacts on systems, processes and end users (granular impacts to be assessed during early stages of project).
	Change strategy development	Develop strategy and high-level plan, underpinning approach with Change Management theories, models and tools.
	Culture Adjustment Plan	Assess culture shift required based on solution, develop plan and implement.
	Change readiness assessment	Assess readiness for change at organizational, team and individual levels.
	Sponsor coaching	Regularly meet with executive sponsor, coaching them on their role and responsibilities and hold them to account.
	Project team culture analysis (new)	Diagnose culture on project team to assess and progress opportunities for alignment with a PCP culture.
	Change planning and execution	Co-develop and execute project plan.
	Stakeholder management	Identify, analyze profile and manage stakeholders. Track and mitigate risks, issues and concerns.
	Business change adoption Managers	Galvanize, train and lead a network of local leaders who will drive change adoption locally.
	Change champions	Galvanize, train and lead a network of champions who will support end users.
	Change communications	Design and implement communication strategies and plans that incorporate Change Management models.
	Training as a change agent	Design and implement training strategies and plans that incorporate Change Management models.
	Change benefits measurement	Track user adoption and progress and outcomes of change programmes based on evidence, data and insights so as to sustain change post-migration/deployment.
Not tied to a given project or phase	**Change capability development**	Assess organizational capability to support change. Develop strategy to increase capability.

Figure 4.3 The Change Management service proposition

While traditionally the Change Manager has owned other deliverables (such as the development of the Change Management Roadmap, Change Management Project Plan and team-building activities for their own direct reports), it is recommended that these activities are jointly owned and delivered with the Project Manager, as demonstrated in Chapter 9. The scope and scale of a given project will determine which Change Management services will be employed.

4.3 Theories, models and tools

Over the decades, a proliferation of Change Management theories, models and tools has emerged, and while the material can be of great interest to anyone concerned with the field, it can prove exceedingly difficult to navigate. A framework that organizes the disparate material in a meaningful way would be a very useful aid indeed. The 'Typology of Change Management' below organizes change theories, models and tools on three levels: 'change and the organization'; 'change and the team'; 'change and the individual'. Within these three levels, 28 subcategories frame dimensions of Change Management and a great many more theories, models and tools that inform us on how change occurs, and how it can be introduced and managed in the organizational context. Shaded areas relate (either wholly or predominantly) to non-human elements of change, while non-shaded areas relate more to the human elements of change.

Change and the organization			
1 The nature of change	2 The change process	3 The speed of change	4 The scope of change
5 The scale of change	6 How change occurs	7 Change drivers	8 The levels of change
9 Change levers	10 Change focus and content	11 The change context	12 Sequencing of change
13 Change project roadmap	14 Change goals, and benefits and measures	15 Change impacts	16 Politics and engagement
17 OCM maturity	18 Communicating change	19 Change readiness	20 Change leadership
21 Change and culture	22 Training as a change enabler	23 Change roles and governance	24 Sustaining change
Change and the team			
25 Team appetite for change		26 Team resistance to change	
Change and the individual			
27 Individual's appetite for change		28 The individual and resistance to change	

Figure 4.4 A Typology of Change Management

Below, each of the 28 dimensions of Change Management is introduced by a question that is informed by those key design decisions that leaders need to make about organizational change, while circa 50 theories, models and tools are used to shape answers. These questions and answers can help leadership teams make decisions on when and how to manage organizational change.

In Part II of this book, this typology of Change Management is used for reference purposes when describing Change Management activities and work packages for each phase of the project lifecycle. It is meant as a starting point and is not definitive.

4.3.1 The nature of change

What is change and what purpose does it serve in the organization?
Change is a natural phenomenon and is integral to the process of renewal and remaining relevant. Change is important for any organization because, without change, we have stagnation. Organizations benefit from change that results in new ways of looking at customer needs and expectations, new ways of delivering customer service, new ways of strengthening customer relationships, and new products and services that increase market share. Creating a culture that embraces change has to be a strategic imperative for any organization that wants to survive and thrive in an increasingly unstable world.

4.3.2 The change process

How does change behave, and how can the organization's approach to introducing change complement the natural change process?
To answer this question, we must first understand what the natural change process looks like. Different perspectives have been put forward.

A linear model

The Ice Cube Model (Lewin, 1947) is the classic linear model of planned change and underpins many of the subsequent models of change. This model consists of a sequence of three phases:

Figure 4.5 The Ice Cube Model

- *Unfreezing the status quo* – Lewin argued that the equilibrium needs to be unfrozen before old behaviour can be unlearnt and new behaviour successfully adopted. He advises that individuals must be encouraged to examine current processes with a critical eye and be open to the possibility that a new process may produce a better outcome.
- *Change* – This phase is about making the change happen. Once individuals accept that current processes could be improved and there are potential solutions to the problems, move to the new state by implementing the change. A long-term view is essential for maintaining confidence and morale.
- *Refreezing* – This stage seeks to stabilize the group at a new quasi-stationary equilibrium in order to refreeze the new state and ensure that the new behaviours are relatively safe from regression.

Any strategic change is most likely to be based on a linear Project Management framework (also known as the 'Waterfall' approach) where there is a specific starting point (unfreeze), a series of successive phases that work towards achieving goals and a specific end point (refreeze). Supporters of the linear approach believe that if the steps are followed the change project will be successful while detractors argue that life is messy, unfolding in an iterative fashion. The truth probably lies somewhere in between.

A cyclical model

Linear change models assume that change in a particular direction induces change in the same direction, while cyclical change models assume that change in a particular direction creates the conditions for change in another direction. Prochaska and DiClemente (1992) put forward a cyclical model (see Figure 4.6) that postulates a series of stages that people go through in their journey to change health-related behaviours:

- *Pre-contemplation (not ready to change)* – Exists where an individual has a blind spot about the problem, or fails to acknowledge it, and is not ready to take action. Individuals at this stage have no intention of changing their behaviour and may insist that it is normal;
- *Contemplation (thinking about changing)* – Occurs when the individual becomes aware of the issue. Individuals in this stage are thinking about changing their behaviour, but they are not ready to commit to action;
- *Preparation (ready to change)* – When the individual is ready to change their behaviour and makes plans to do so;

- *Action (making change happen)* – The individual engages in activities to modify their behaviour and demonstrate an increased ability to cope with behavioural change;
- *Maintenance (staying on track)* – The new behaviour is established and action is taken to reinforce the change as part of the individual's day-to-day lifestyle;
- *Relapse (regression to old behaviours)* – Occurs when the individual falls back into the old pattern of behaviour.

In this model, the individual can leave the process at any time and, even if they relapse into old behaviours, can revisit the contemplation stage and prepare for future action.

Linear and cyclical models of change are based on different assumptions about how to get things done. Marshak (1993) compared those assumptions underpinning Lewin's North American model with the assumptions underpinning an Asian model of change. He found that in Lewin's North American 'Ice Cube' model change is linear, progressive, and managed by people intent on achieving goals, while in the Asian model, change is 'cyclical, processional, journey orientated, associated with equilibrium, and managed in a way that is designed to create universal harmony'.

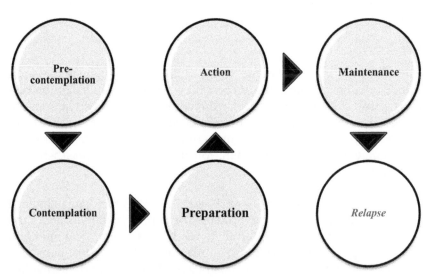

Figure 4.6 A cyclical model of the stages of change

Adapted from Stages of change, J. O. Prochaska and C. C. DiClemente (1992) In search of how people change: Applications to addictive behaviours. *American Psychologist*, 47: 1102–14.

A systems model

A system is a set of elements connected together which form a whole, thereby possessing properties of the whole rather than the component parts (Checkland, 1981). Change in any of the elements affects system activity and has an inevitable knock-on effect on the other elements. In *The Fifth Discipline*, Senge (1990) points out that the kinds of system thinking that explain why different tree seeds grow to different heights, shapes and states of health – or not at all – can be applied to change. According to Senge, to understand how profound change can be nurtured and sustained requires an understanding of the many self-reinforcing growth processes that will support and enable change, and those limiting processes that, if not addressed, will stunt or kill it.

Having considered different ideas on how the natural change process occurs, we can now turn our minds to how the organizational approach to introducing change can complement the natural change process. As established in Chapter 1, projects are the preferred approach to intro-ducing organizational change. Project Management approaches are typically linear in approach – a succession of work packages and other deliverables. Change Management approaches increasingly try to align with this approach but meet a challenge because of the emergent nature of change, particularly when one considers the political landscape, the ups and downs of stakeholder engagement and managing resistance to change. At best, change is a bumpy ride; at worst, it is a rollercoaster journey. Therefore, the approach to organizational change recom-mended herein is to embrace both the linear and the emergent, providing both structure and flexibility. It also involves fostering a supportive culture to make change stick and identifying processes that will either support or restrict change, promoting the former while eliminating the latter.

4.3.3 The speed of change

How is the rate of change increasing, and how can it impact consumer preferences and the business model?

Much has been said about the speed or pace of change accelerating 'at an unprecedented rate', but what exactly does that mean in real terms? According to a study by French economist George Anderlo and cited by Robertson (2011), if we assumed that all the scientific knowledge that mankind had accumulated by the year 1 AD equalled one unit of information, it took 1,500 years to double. The next doubling of know-ledge from two units of information to four took only 250 years, taking us to 1750 AD. By 1900, only 150 years later, knowledge had doubled again to 8 units. The speed at which information is doubling is getting faster and faster and, in this age of technology, now doubles every 1–2 years. Staying current in one's own area of expertise is challenge enough. There is a growing trend for more knowledge expertise and specialization as organizations grapple with the maze of information that is required to run a modern company.

Anderlo's example illustrates that once change occurs, it can gather momentum like a snowball rolling downhill. When the hill is fairly flat, momentum takes time to build and we have time to decide how to respond – the more adventurous of us can dive straight into the snowball for fun, others might poke at it as it passes, while the more cautious may side-step it altogether to avoid any impact. When the hill is steep, however, momentum builds rapidly and we can be buried under an avalanche of change before we even know what hit us.

4.3.4 The scope of change

What is the magnitude of the change being planned or implemented?

Levy and Merry (1986) introduced the concept of two degrees of organizational change – first order and second order:

- *First order* – Invoke minor, cosmetic, superficial and non-structural modifications while the core of the organization remains the same;
- *Second order* – A multidimensional, multilevel, qualitative, discontinuous, radical organizational change involving a paradigm shift.

In the 1990s, a refinement in thinking led to the identification of three degrees of organizational change:

- *Incremental change* (also known as 'organic', 'emergent' and 'developmental' change) 'starts from the assumption that change is not a linear process or a one-off isolated event but a continuous, openended, cumulative and unpredictable process of aligning and re-aligning an organisation to its changing environment' (Orlikowski, 1996). Incremental change deals with everyday contingencies, breakdowns and opportunities, and it is the preferred approach to continuous improvement.
- *Transitional change* involves the implementation of a known new state and the management of an interim state over a controlled period of time.
- *Transformational change*, also known as 'radical' change, involves a new way of doing things rather than improving the current way of doing things. Here, the new way is an unknown.

These three approaches are illustrated in Figure 4.7.

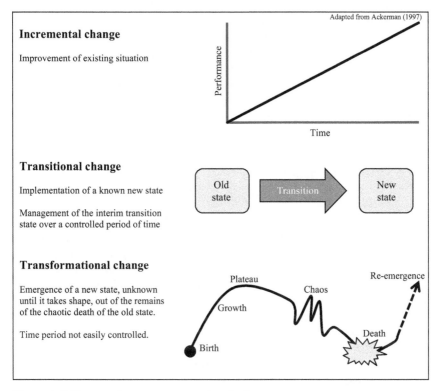

Figure 4.7 Perspectives on organizational change

From V. Iles and K. Sutherland (2001) Organisational Change: A review for Health Care Managers, professionals and researchers, NCCSDO (reproduced with permission).

4.3.5 The scale of change

What is the physical reach of the change across the organization, and how will this inform decisions on where responsibility for the change sits in the organization?

According to Caldwell (2003), the scale of strategic change can be:

1 *Organization specific* (or subsystem change), such as a new information system;
2 *Generic, organization-wide* change programmes such as Business Process Reengineering (BPR),[1] culture transformation, major restructuring, or the introduction of a single system that will replace all others and be used by all users across the organization;
3 *Generic, multi-organizational* change programmes – for example, mergers and acquisitions.

Caldwell recommends that responsibility for organization-specific change, such as the introduction of a new system or process for a particular department, should be placed as far down the organization as possible. Primary responsibility over organization-wide change is best placed from the lowest management levels on up to the executive and board level, while primary responsibility for generic multi-organizational change programmes, such as mergers and acquisition, is best placed with the CEO and a small team of senior Change Managers and Project Managers.

4.3.6 How change occurs

How does change occur in the organization?

Change can be planned or unplanned. *Planned change* allows for a proactive response to business opportunities and threats, and can minimize disruption to the business. Examples include new products and services, new systems and changes in organizational structures. Contrary to what one might expect, planned change does not necessarily occur in a highly organized fashion, and can be chaotic and disruptive, particularly when strategies and plans are poorly conceived, where general management skills are poor, and/or where environmental factors play a part.

Unplanned change (also known as imposed or reactive change) descends upon the organization with little warning. It can come from outside or from within, and often it can feel like 'fire fighting'. For example, the sudden departure of a key leader is sure to be immediately disruptive even if the best efforts are made to reassure the workforce and minimize impacts. Other unplanned changes can include shifts in government policies and regulations, shifting demographics, the emergence of new competitors and acts of terror. It is the business of leaders to have an eye to the future and make sense of the environmental context and pressures, so that change can be planned for where possible. As the organization is an open system and subject to external influences, planned change typically occurs within the context of unplanned change.

4.3.7 Change drivers

What are the environmental forces shaping the need for change in the organization?

The PESTLER mnemonic below outlines those external forces that impact organizations:

- *Political* – Because of the balance between systems of control and free markets, politics plays an important role in business;

- *Economic* – Economic factors measure the health of a region and will change over the lifetime of the organization;
- *Social* – Social factors assess demographics in a given market, and inform thinking on how an economy might react to certain changes;
- *Technological* – Advancements can optimize internal efficiency and help create new products and services;
- *Legal* – Understanding the law in your region is critical for avoiding unnecessary legal penalties;
- *Environmental* – Impact on the environment is a rising concern, and stakeholders (general public, government, media) penalize firms for having adverse effect on the environment;
- *Regulatory* – Understanding the regulations in your region is critical for avoiding regulatory infringements by your company.

Examples of major environmental forces that are currently shaping business strategies and projects include the following:

- As a result of the UK's political decision to leave the European Union (aka 'Brexit') many global organizations are moving staff and their headquarters out of the UK.
- The recent reversal in USA policy change on climate change will have repercussions for many industries at home and abroad. New environmental policies can impact anything from product contents, to product packaging, to product delivery and distribution.

Internal forces for change also play a part. These can be divided into the inert (e.g. technology, policies, processes, structures and strategies) and the human (e.g. leadership changes, industrial relations, employee engagement/climate and culture). It is important to differentiate between external and internal forces for change, with the key difference being that the organization, and leaders, may have little if any control over external factors while internal forces do fall within the powers of the business. At any one time, some or all of the forces for change will be exerting different degrees of pressure on the organization, and it is those forces that are exerting the most pressure that should inform strategies and plans.

Kurt Lewin believes that equal and opposing forces hold the organization system in equilibrium. His *Force-field Theory of Change* (1947) demonstrates that organizational equilibrium is constantly being challenged by forces for and against change. According to Lewin, 'An issue is held in balance by the interaction of two opposing sets of forces – those seeking to promote change (driving forces) and those attempting to maintain the status quo (restraining forces)'. When the sum of these forces are equal, they cancel each other out, resulting in equilibrium – i.e. a steady state. However, when the forces driving change are greater

Driving forces   **Restraining forces**

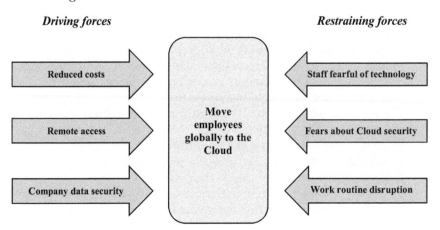

Figure 4.8 Force field analysis: moving to the Cloud

than the forces of resistance (either by the driving forces increasing or the restraining forces decreasing), then change will occur, and the organization will inevitably change and move to a new steady state.

Lewin recommends using his 'Force Field Analysis' model to weigh up the positives against the negatives of a likely change. In the example above, the organization is planning to move employees globally to the Cloud (hosted technology services delivered over the internet). Forces that make the change attractive are reduced costs, remote access for workers and increased company data security. Forces that make the change unattractive include a fear of technology, fears about Cloud security and disruption to daily operations and work routines.

Success will be achieved by either strengthening the driving forces, and/or weakening the restraining forces that make the change unattractive. As the increasing of new driving forces can add to tensions, targeting and removing restraining forces and resistance can be a more productive route to take.

4.3.8 Levels of change

What level of change is being introduced to the organization?

Forces for change impact the organization on four levels. Changes at the individual level (knowledge, skills, attitudes) and team level (climate and culture) create change within the organizational social system. Change at the organization level (policies, processes, systems) creates changes in the organization inert structures, while change in the external environment or market change creates change in the industry.

The level of the organization being impacted will inform strategies and plans.

Figure 4.9 The levels of change

4.3.9 Change levers

What are those elements of the organization that can be influenced to support organizational change?

The McKinsey & Company 7-S model (Waterman *et al.*, 2006) is based on seven elements that are mutually reinforcing and need to be aligned for productive organizational change:

1   *Strategy* – Actions planned to enhance the organization's competitive edge, and in response to or anticipation of external change;
2   *Structure* – Relates to the formal and information organization, how activities are divided, coordinated and integrated;
3   *Systems* – Procedures and processes that are carried out every day to get things done (resource allocation, reward, measurement etc.);
4   *Shared values* – The core beliefs and guiding concepts and aspirations of an organization, and their impact on different stakeholders;
5   *Style (Culture)* – Patterns of behaviour of key groups – e.g. supervisors;
6   Staff – Workforce categories and profile (educational, demographic, attitudes);
7   *Skills* – Competencies and capabilities.

Each of the elements can be isolated and used as a lever to promote change. In Figure 4.10 overleaf the model helps identify where any of the elements (or Ss) harmonize with the others, and highlights why change in one area must be planned along with supporting changes in the other elements.

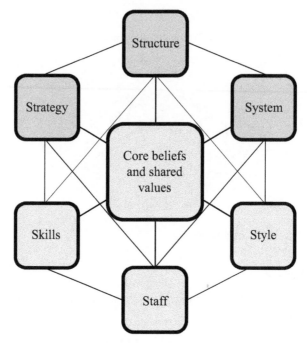

Figure 4.10 McKinsey's 7-S Model

4.3.10 Change focus and content

What is the main focus of the project and how is this shaping the content?

Is the project solution *technical in nature* and with a view to driving short-to medium-term financial benefit, and concerning the introduction of new structures, systems, technology and processes, or is it *people-focused,* concerned with building a culture that will meet the evolving needs of customers, and building adaptability in the face of change to help ensure longer term profit and survival. Looking across the portfolio of change being introduced and managed by the organization, is there evidence of a balanced approach that will derive value on both fronts? A strong leaning towards technical projects focused on short- to medium-term benefit should be cause for concern.

4.3.11 Change context

Is the change happening in isolation or in parallel with other strategic change? Caldwell (2013) argues that change should be understood from a changing organization perspective, which places multiple, simultaneous adaptive demands upon employees from many forces within the organization, many of which are not planned for.

Think about a current project you are familiar with and consider any other change projects that are being implemented in parallel. Some will be new, some will be ending, but all will be impacting on each other. How many are there? What is their scope and have employee impacts been defined to an appropriate level? In the case of multiple parallel rollouts, has the impact of the different solutions on each other been scoped, especially from an end-user perspective? How much change is the typical employee expected to cope with as they go about their daily business? A portfolio governance team is likely to be overseeing and coordinating the various change projects in your scenario, and will have a responsibility to coordinate work on impacts and protect business operations and productivity levels. As a given project unfolds, the context may well change and create the need for continuous adaptations to plans.

4.3.12 Sequencing of change

What is the logical sequence for introducing changes?

Where a number of change projects are in the pipeline, the sequencing of rollout should be informed by a clear view of how the different changes will impact on each other and impact on the end-user. This is particularly true for technology deployments, as the features of different applications being rolled out may conflict with each other and cause unexpected problems.

Should change be introduced in one fell swoop or is a staggered approach better?

Change can be introduced to an organization all at once or it can be staggered in phases. Factors that determine the best approach include the following:

- The urgency of the implementation.
- The resources required versus those available.
- The sequencing of other changes.
- The impact on the end-user and overall productivity.
- How experienced the project team is in implementing that particular change and how much they might need to learn from a phased rollout.

Either approach has implications for the organization and for how soon benefits can be achieved, so all factors need to be considered before making a decision.

How should end-users' perception of the change shape its introduction?

When engaging end-users, one needs to match the approach to end-users' perceptions of the change. Below, Dibella (2007) identifies four possible responses when engaging change recipients, based on how end-users perceive the appeal and the likelihood of the change occurring:

1   Where participants view the change as desirable and consider it inevitable, the Change Manager should expedite the change;
2   Where participants view the change as desirable but are not convinced it will happen, the Change Manager should plan for small victories based on 'low-hanging fruit';
3   Where participants do not view the change as desirable but consider it inevitable, the Change Manager should reframe the change to make it more appealing, or modify the change to make it more appealing;
4   Where participants perceive the change as undesirable and unlikely to happen, additional options open to the Change Manager include recruiting champions and removing resistors.

Likelihood change will occur

		High	**Low**
Appeal	**High**	**1 Expedite** Specify tasks and time frame to ensure nothing is missed	**2 Encourage and empower** Target 'low-hanging fruit' to ensure quick wins and build credibility
	Low	**3 Reframe** Increase appeal by communicating a compelling vision and/or modifying the change	**4 Revitalize or retrench** Increase appeal by communicating a compelling vision or modifying the change and/or make it inevitable by modifying the circumstances

Figure 4.11 Change participants' perceptions of the appeal and likelihood of change

From Anthony J. Dibella (2007) Critical perceptions of organisational change, *Journal of Change Management*, 1 September (reprinted by permission of the publisher, Taylor & Francis, www.tandfonline.com).

4.3.13 The change roadmap

What are the steps change leaders should take on the change journey?

Three prescriptive approaches, made up of a series of linear steps, were introduced in the 1990s:

- General Electric's Change Acceleration Process model (CAP);
- Jick's 10 steps;
- Kotter's 8 steps.

General Electric's Change Acceleration Project (CAP) model consists of a series of activities and, like many other change models, is underpinned by Lewin's Ice Cube model.

These activities are explained below:

1 *Leading change* – Authentic, committed leadership is critical throughout the duration of the initiative and is essential for its success.
2 *Creating a shared need* – There must be a compelling reason to change that resonates with all stakeholders.
3 *Shaping a vision* – Leadership must communicate a clear and legitimate vision of the 'improved state', after the change initiative concludes. The end-state must be described in observable, measurable terms.

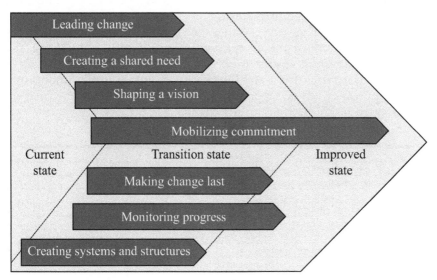

Figure 4.12 General Electric's Change Acceleration Project (CAP) model

4   *Mobilizing commitment* – Leverage friendly 'early adopters' to pilot the change before any official rollout, so that lessons can be learnt and incorporated into the final configuration and plans.
5   *Making change last* – Assess what is helping and hindering the change rollout and act on that feedback.
6   *Monitoring progress* – Set benchmarks and KPIs, and realize them. Celebrate achievements and create accountability for any failures.
7   *Changing systems and structures* – Identify underlying systems that must be changed in some way to support the desired future state of the business.

Jick (1991) developed an alternative 10-step blueprint for organizations embarking on change.

1   *Analyse the organization and its need for change* – The preliminary analysis should be sound so that it informs plans that enable the organization to achieve its goals. This will involve an organization assessment, impacts analysis and change readiness assessment; all will inform an effective execution plan.
2   *Create vision and common direction* – The vision should reflect the company ethos and help employees at all levels of the organization to understand the direction of the organization. An effective vision will guide behaviour and help the organization to achieve its goals.
3   *Separate from the past* – Disengaging from the past is critical to embracing a new way of doing things. For the new vision to be embraced, ways of working that no longer work need to be isolated, while aspects that add value to the vision are retained.
4   *Create a sense of urgency* – When the reasons for change are obvious (e.g. damaged brand or serious financial loss), convincing the organization that change is necessary will be like pushing an open door. But when the need for change is not generally understood or appreciated, it is important to create a sense of urgency based on facts, to build momentum for change.

1	Analyse the organization and its need for change
2	Create a shared vision and a common direction
3	Separate from the past
4	Create a sense of urgency
5	Support a strong leader role
6	Line up political sponsorship
7	Craft an implementation plan
8	Develop enabling structures
9	Communicate, involve people and be honest
10	Reinforce and institutionalize the change

Figure 4.13 Jick's 10-Step Change model

5 *Support a strong leader role* – Large-scale change must have a leader advocate to inspire, guide and drive it. This change advocate plays a central role in shaping the vision, motivating employees to embrace that vision and creating a supportive environment.

6 *Line up political sponsorship* – A change effort must have broad support throughout an organization for it to succeed. This will include managers and end-users of the change. Seek the backing of informal leaders and identify whose sponsorship is critical to the change project's success.

7 *Craft an implementation plan* – To enable delivery of the vision, a plan is needed to map what needs to be done, when and by whom, and when the organization expects to achieve its change goals. The plan should be kept flexible, a kind of living document that is open to revision.

8 *Develop enabling structures* – Design and align change-enabling structures so that they create a supportive environment for the change.

9 *Communicate, involve people and be honest* – When possible, change leaders should adopt an open and honest approach to communicating with the organization and to build and maintain trust. This will go a long way to overcoming resistance.

10 *Reinforce and institutionalize the change* – Reward and recognize behaviours that support the change. Reinforce the new ways of doing things, affirm the importance of the change and hasten its acceptance.

Kotter's ideas on managing change were set out in a Harvard Business Review seminal article (Kotter, 1995) where he identified eight common errors that organizations make when trying to undertake major changes. This was followed by his book *Leading Change* (2012 [1996]), in which he elaborated upon his eight steps below. Each step was an antidote to one of the errors he identified that organizations make when managing change.

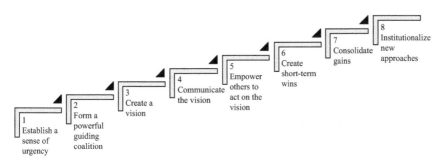

Figure 4.14 Kotter's 8-Step model

Below, we see how these three popular Change Roadmaps compare with one another. Clearly, there are strong similarities in a number of areas with the three models proving to be mutually reinforcing. Distinguishing features include Jick's steps to 'analyse the organization and its need for change', 'separate from the past', 'craft an implementation plan', and be honest in communications; GE's CAP model includes a step to 'measure progress', while Kotter calls out the need to 'generate short term wins'.

Thinking on Change Management has evolved since these early roadmaps emerged. Perhaps it is now more useful to consider these important activities not as a series of steps, but as pointers on 'critical success factors' (CSFs) which must be met when implementing change. For more on CSFs, see Chapter 2, section 2.6.

	Jick (1991)	*GE CAP Model (1992)*	*Kotter (1995)*
1	Analyse the organization and its need for change		
2	Create a shared vision and common direction	2 Establish the vision	3 Develop a vision and strategy 4 Communicate the vision
3	Separate from the past		
4	Create a strong sense of urgency	1 Explain the reason for the change 4 Mobilize the workforce	1 Establish a sense of urgency
5	Support a strong leader role	3 Line up leadership	2 Create a guiding coalition
6	Line up political sponsorship		
7	Craft an implementation plan		
8	Develop enabling structures	7 Change systems and structures	5 Empower employees for broad-based action
9	Communicate, involve people and be honest		4 Communicate the vision
10	Reinforce and institutionalize change	5 Measure the progress 6 Stay on course	6 Generate short-term wins 7 Consolidate gains to produce deeper change 8 Institutionalise new approaches

Figure 4.15 Comparison of early roadmaps on change

4.3.14 Change goals, benefits and measures

What are the strategic goals of the change project and what should they be?

Beer and Nohria (2000) studied the nature of corporate change for more than forty years and identified two archetypes that describe *corporate change goals*. Theory E change strategy they call the 'hard approach' to change, with shareholder value being the only legitimate measure of corporate success. Theory O change is the 'soft approach' to change and involves developing the corporate culture and human capability through individual and organizational learning. Companies that use the Theory O approach typically have strong, long-held, commitment-based *psychological contracts* (see section 4.3.27) with their employees.

Project success goals derive from corporate success goals and project success and business success are inextricably linked. Nowadays, more progressive project leadership teams are supplementing those traditional measures of project success – 'on time', 'on budget', 'on scope' – with new ones such as 'business adoption' and 'end-user proficiency'. This broader set of measures makes the project responsible not just for

Dimensions of change	Theory E	Theory O	Theories E and O combined
Business benefits, goals and measures	Deliver economic value	Build organizational capabilities	Explicitly embrace the paradox between economic value and organizational capability
Leadership	Manage change from the top down	Manage change from the bottom up	Set direction from the top and engage the people from the bottom up
Focus	Emphasize structure and systems	Foster supportive corporate culture (employee shared assumptions and resulting attitudes and behaviours)	Focus simultaneously on the tangible (structures and systems) and the intangible (corporate culture)
Process	Plan and establish programmes	Experiment and evolve	Provide structure and flexibility
Reward and recognition system	Motivate through financial incentives	Motivate through job satisfaction and build commitment – use total reward as fair exchange	Use incentives to reinforce change but not to drive it
Use of consultants	Consultants own problem analyse solutions design	Consultants guide and empower management to shape their own solutions	Consultants are subject matter experts who empower management and employees

Figure 4.16 Comparing theories of change

From M. Beer and N. Nohria (2000) *Cracking the Code of Change*. Boston, MA: Harvard Business Review Press.

building the solution but for ensuring that the organization adopts it and realizes those benefits that provide return on investment (ROI). To deliver on this broader remit, Project Management needs to partner with Change Management.

4.3.15 Change impacts

What is the impact of the change on the individual?

Change projects cause ripples through the organization, and a User Impact Analysis (UIA) can unearth the layers and levels of the organization that the change project will affect. To commence analysis, capture the current state and future state with input from subject-matter-experts (SMEs) and stakeholders, using a variety of approaches such as interviews and workshops. This analysis will expose the delta caused by the change and inform impacts. Impacts in turn can be defined and categorized according to their nature, and then prioritized in terms of agreed criteria – for example, frequency, criticality, complexity, time involved, number of business areas impacted, positions impacted and difficulty of implementation. Impacts can also be graded as 'low', 'medium' or 'high' impact with clear criteria applied to each rating. In the example below, two end-user impacts caused by a move from Oracle® employee time-tracking processes to Workday® processes are given.

Current state	Future state	Summary impact	Date	Rating	User group
Shift workers receiving shift rates must select a separate value in Oracle for each shift rate % applicable to them (10%, 15%, 20%) and the shift they have worked.	Shift workers will submit start and end times and workday will automatically calculate the appropriate shift rate.	Workday automatically works out shift rates for employees, making the transaction process simplified and easier.	March 2015	Medium +	Shift workers
Set-up of security and delegation rules required for new employee users of timekeeping system. Administrators make manual requests.	Workday system configuration determines inherited security roles for new users.	Reduced overhead of operational processes for HR shared services teams.	March 2015	High +	HR

Figure 4.17 User Impact Analysis: moving from Oracle® to Workday® time-tracking

A robust impact assessment will reveal the overall degree of disruption to be expected and inform mitigation plans.

What is the impact of the change on the organization?

To develop a broader line of sight of impacts, an Organizational Impact Assessment is required. This exercise measures impacts according to pre-defined categories which can be informed by those mentioned in section 4.3.9. An Organizational Impact Assessment can be used to understand which different organization elements will be impacted and how, and how impact in one area can impact other areas. Such an assessment will advise what else needs to change and inform plans on how to affect that change.

4.3.16 Politics and engagement

How does the political landscape affect the success of change?

As the project is a vehicle for introducing change, it is an inherently political environment. As such, the Change Manager will inevitably be involved in politics, promoting change in the face of adversity. This is why it is critical that the Change Manager is positioned for success as outlined in the Change Triad governance structure in section 9.1, p. 156. The Change Manager will need to be politically astute, with the knowledge, skills and disposition to navigate the political landscape. The political landscape refers to the current state of things (agendas, stakeholders, stakeholder interests and concerns, and where power and influence sits) as well as how things will look in the future. It is a dynamic environment. Political behaviour is driven by agendas and either promotes or blocks change. According to McNulty (2003), some may be motivated to defend the status quo, whereas others may perceive change as an opportunity to improve their position. Nadler (1987) argues that political behaviour tends to be more intense in times of change because individuals and groups perceive the possibility of upsetting the existing balance of power. This is where good stakeholder engagement can make a difference.

How much of the change should be leader-led and how much of it should be led from the grassroots up?

Dr William Ouchi (1981) of UCLA developed 'Theory Z' to answer this question. According to Ouchi:

*   *Top-down change* is leader-led and typical in 'parental' or 'command-and-control' type cultures. It can be introduced quickly but there

is no guarantee at all that the change will stick, as it may be rejected by the workforce if they feel excluded from the plans.

- *Bottom-up change* is led from the grass-roots up. It can take longer to make decisions as there are more views to consider, and it is at the risk of going off-track without strategic insight from leaders.
- A mixed 'top-down, bottom-up' approach allows for strategic direction while empowering those on the front-line to shape and own the change.

4.3.17 Organizational Change Management maturity

What is the organization's Change Management maturity level, and what does this mean for any proposed change initiative?

Management in general is a competency that can be developed from an initial level of capability to full optimization. It is an important lever for building organizational adaptability. The Change Management maturity level of an organization will impact how Change Management expertise will be received and utilized on projects and across the organization, and to what degree change implemented sticks. There are a number of different tools on the market developed to assess Change Management Maturity (CMM). PROSCI'S model has five levels, from 'Ad Hoc Change Management' (Level 1) to the highest level where Change Management is an 'Organizational Competency' (Level 5). In PROSCI'S *Best Practices in Change Management* (2012), roughly half of participant organizations (49 per cent) rated themselves at Level 1 (ad hoc or absent Change Management) or Level 2 (Change Management on isolated projects). Only 14 per cent rated themselves at the more advanced Level 4 or 5. This means that there are many Change Management teams out there trying to drive change readiness and adoption in a project environment that does not understand or support Change Management to a degree that will help ensure that organizational change sticks.

4.3.18 Communicating change

Is it clear to the organization what the consequences are if the change being implemented is unsuccessful?

As we saw earlier when reviewing those early Change Roadmaps, developing a sense of urgency is a key step in the process of managing change. In 1993, author Daryl Conner coined the term 'burning platform' for leadership communication on why a change was necessary. The term was inspired by the story of the Piper Alpha oil-rig disaster, which is summarized overleaf.

The Piper Alpha oil-rig disaster

At 09:30 on 6 July 1988 the Piper Alpha oil-rig in the North Sea exploded. 166 crew and two rescue servicemen died. It was the largest offshore disaster ever, caused by a failure to check some basic systems that had worked faultlessly for the previous decade. When disaster struck, flames from the blaze shot 90 metres into the sky and could be seen 100 km away. Initially, workers locked themselves into a room – hoping the fire would burn out or that emergency systems would kick in. Eventually, three men concluded that this wouldn't work, and made for the edge of the platform. There, they stood staring into one of the coldest and roughest oceans in the world. They had a choice – to stay where they were, and hope for possible rescue from the flames, or to jump fifteen stories into the freezing ocean and risk almost certain death from hypothermia. Two men chose to jump and, despite terrible injuries, they were rescued at sea and lived. The third man who didn't jump sadly perished, as air rescue helicopters failed to make it in time.

The Piper Alpha story contains some powerful lessons about the need to respond positively and proactively to serious challenges. Doing things the same old way is to risk probable failure, while sometimes a radical and risky approach is essential for basic survival. In his research, Conner identified four types of burning platforms that organizations face:

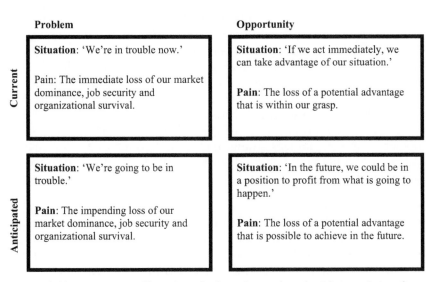

Figure 4.18 Four types of burning platform (reproduced with permission from Darryl Conner)

In his message to employees, Elop pointed to a number of problems in Nokia:

- Stock is moving on to 'negative credit watch' with rating agency Standard & Poor's, following Moody's last week, indicating that it might downgrade its creditworthiness because they are concerned about its competitiveness.
- The battle of devices has become a 'war of ecosystems' (such as Apple's App Store and Google's Marketplace) and 'our competitors aren't taking our market share with devices; they are taking our market share with an entire ecosystem. This means we're going to have to decide how we either build, catalyze or join an ecosystem'.
- 'Google has become a gravitational force, drawing much of the industry's innovation to its core.'
- 'We have multiple points of scorching heat that are fuelling a blazing fire around us' – from Apple, Android and from Chinese competitors who can produce a device 'much faster than', as one Nokia employee said only partially in jest, 'the time that it takes us to polish a PowerPoint presentation. They are fast, they are cheap and they are challenging us.'
- 'We're not fighting with the right weapons. We are still too often trying to approach each price range on a device-to-device basis.'

Figure 4.19 Summary of Nokia's burning platform statement

From Nokia's chief executive to staff (2011): 'we are standing on a burning platform' (www.theguardian.com)

Basically, the situation the organization finds itself in, and the level of pain attached to the situation, will determine whether the organization is facing a problem or an opportunity. It will inform subsequent communications.

The 'Burning Platform Statement' is a communication tool that articulates the organization's impetus for change. Above is a summary of the Burning Platform Statement created in 2011 by Nokia's new Chief Executive, Stephen Elop, for Nokia employees. Microsoft® was facing intense competition from Apple® and Google® and had fallen behind in the race to dominate the market. Looking at Conner's model on 'Four Types of Burning Platform', can you guess which of the four types of burning platform it is based on?

In essence, communicating change is concerned with creating stakeholder awareness, understanding, buy-in and commitment for change. According to Jicks (1991), good change-related communication has the following features:

- Is brief and concise;
- Describes where the organization is now, where it needs to go and how it will get to the desired state;
- Identifies who will implement and who will be affected by the change;
- Addresses timing and pacing issues regarding implementation;
- Explains the change's success criteria, the intended evaluation process and the related rewards;

- Identifies the things that will not be changing;
- Predicts some of the negative aspects that targets should anticipate;
- Conveys the sponsor's commitment to the change;
- Explains how people will be kept informed throughout the change process;
- Is presented in such a manner that it capitalizes on the diversity of the communication styles of the audience.

4.3.19 Change readiness

Is the organization ready for change?

The greater the complexity of any proposed change, the greater the need to understand if the organization is ready or not. Also, the success or failure of previously implemented change will have a residual effect that could work for, or against, any newly proposed change. Therefore, before introducing change, it is essential to carry out an Organizational Readiness Assessment. Such an assessment will cover three areas: perceptions on organizational readiness for change, individual and team readiness for change, and the perceived personal impact of the proposed change. Example statements that can be used to assess readiness for change are shared below.

Organizational readiness for change
• Most changes implemented in my organization have successfully adopted.
• Our leadership team are visible and active change leaders and sponsors.
• Middle managers have been advocates for previously implemented change.
• This organization rewards and celebrates successful change.
• This organization takes care of employees adversely impacted by change.
Individual and team readiness
• I think I have the knowledge and skills to cope with this change.
• I think my team has the knowledge and skills to cope with this change.
• I understand what this change involves and am bought into it.
• My team understands what this change involves and is bought into it.
Focus on Personal Impact
• The impending change supports my career plans and goals.
• The change will improve my financial position.
• I will not have to relocate to support this change.
• I do not view my job at risk with this change.
• This change will ultimately benefit my family.

Figure 4.20 Readiness for change

To gather meaningful data, questions about individual and team readiness and personal impact must be timed carefully so that people are informed appropriately on the change and are able to respond.

4.3.20 Change leadership

Change leadership has been described as 'the ability to influence and enthuse others through personal advocacy, vision and drive, and access resources to build a solid platform for change' (Higgs and Rowland, 2000). It is an essential skill for the change sponsor and broader leadership team. Earlier, we established that change can be implemented in the organization through ongoing improvements in business-as-usual or via change projects with discrete start and end dates. In both contexts, the role of change leadership is essentially the same:

*   *Providing strategy and direction* – Based on sound interpretation of the business environment, and identified strengths, weaknesses, opportunities and threats to the business;
*   *Making decisions* – Using insights and position to move project along towards goals;
*   *Creating a sense of urgency* – Galvanizing the workforce;
*   *Aligning all behind a vision* – Articulating the vision and strategic goals, how they will be achieved, and the role of the individual;
*   *Culture leadership* – Fostering the particular culture that will enable the change (both internal to the projects environment and across the organization), rewarding attitudes and behaviours that are aligned while dealing with those that are not, and reinforcing organizational mechanisms that are supportive while pruning those that are not;
*   *Visible advocate for change* – Use every opportunity to promote change with peers, selling the benefits, listening to concerns and encouraging them to promote the change in their own organizations;
*   *Supporting* – Oversee change and provide guidance to the programme management team.
*   *Meeting failure well* – Act with grace, get back on the horse and practise continuous learning;
*   *Good stewardship* of the resources entrusted to support the employers end of the 'employee contract' – Provide reasonable pay and conditions, proper treatment of workers, and career progression opportunities.
*   *A long-term view* – rather than a focus on short-term results;
*   *Remove obstacles to change* – Identify and deal with resistance, whether it derives from inert systems or people;
*   *Maintaining momentum and celebrating wins* – Plan for and reward short-term wins.

4.3.21 Culture and change

To what extent will change impact the organizational culture?

Change that requires a new way of doing things for a given group will always require some degree of culture shift as old assumptions are let go of and replaced with new ones:

- *Culture evolution* – Where incremental change is being introduced and the assumptions being replaced are lightly held and easily replaced or have a greater degree of personal ownership, this amounts to culture evolution. Individuals and teams either don't much care about the change, or they can make the transition to a new known state in their own time. Culture evolution is played out in daily operations, not in the project context, and is not under immediate time pressure.
- *Culture transition* – Where change to a new known state is being introduced via a project, this requires culture transition. Time pressure is added to the equation, so the level of pain involved, as the individual comes to terms with new replacement assumptions, increases. In this scenario, assumptions being replaced may be lightly held or subject to a greater degree of ownership, but deeply held assumptions (e.g. about the main purpose of the business) will not be challenged.
- *Culture revolution* – Where transformational change is being introduced and deeply held assumptions are being challenged across the organization, this requires culture revolution. Lightly held, and

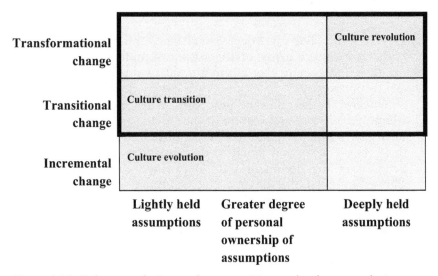

Figure 4.21 Culture evolution, culture transition and culture revolution

` not so lightly held assumptions may also be challenged but will not determine the overall nature of the culture shift. This scenario will be played out in the projects context where the transformation is planned using the project vehicle. A good degree of pain will be involved and culture revolution will need to be planned for and carefully managed to get the right outcomes and results.

In summary, how strongly a shift in the culture is felt will depend on the nature of those assumptions that must change, and the element of time pressure involved. All cultural assumptions are not equal. To change deeply help assumptions can greatly upset a person's understanding of their world, their role and how they should navigate their environment. It is a recipe for fierce resistance when people come together to reject change and must be carefully planned for.

How can two different cultures be brought together?

At this point we have to consider our broad strategy for bringing the two different Project Management and Change Management cultures together. The Project Management and Change Management disciplines and professions are at different stages of cohesion and maturity. Each comes from its own epistemic culture, or way or viewing the world, which affects how things get done day-to-day on projects. In this book, the bringing together of these two cultures is recommended as conducive to promoting synergies and maximizing benefits. This process is called 'acculturation'.

Nahavandi and Malekzadeh (1988) conducted studies on acculturation in the M&A context and identified four ways in which process can be carried out:

- *Integration:* Involves some degree of change for both units but allows both to maintain many of the basic assumptions, beliefs, work practices and systems that are important to them and make them feel distinctive;
- *Assimilation:* Is the unilateral process in which one group willingly adopts the identity and culture of the other;
- *Separation:* Involves members of the acquired unit seeking to preserve their own culture and practices by remaining separate and independent of the dominant unit, department or organization. If allowed to do so, the acquired unit will function as a separate unit under the financial umbrella of the acquiring unit;
- *Deculturation:* Involves unit members rejecting cultural contact with both their own and the other unit. It occurs when members of the acquired unit do not value their own culture (maybe because they feel that their work group, department or organization has failed) and do not want to be assimilated into the acquiring unit.

Integration, as defined above, is the strategy recommended in this book for the integration of Project Management and Change Management ways of working with all team members signing up to that set of prescribed assumptions that define a PCP culture and are summarized in Chapter 2. Integration, based on the principles of interdependence and partnership, does not involve the loss of cultural identity for either Project Management or Change Management and has the best chance of success. On any given project, the greater the gap between Project Management and Change Management cultures, the greater the integration challenge will be and the greater the effort will be to develop a culture of partnership and ensure that change sticks.

How will efforts to evolve the project team culture impact on project operations and project success rates?

Three possible approaches to project team culture evolution are identified here:

- *An incremental approach* – Will not be difficult for the team to digest, as it will involve ongoing continuous improvement as breakdowns occur. It will not impact project operations, but it will greatly hamper project success rates, as improvements in how Project Management and Change Management partner slowly emerge;
- *A transitional approach* – Involves implementing a known new state (e.g. a PCP culture) over the lifecycle of projects. This will involve some degree of impact on project operations as the project team proactively develop a shared culture under the guidance of the Change Manager and the broader management team. The transitional approach allows for planned change to a known new state. It will improve success rates over the short to medium to long term;
- *A transformational approach* – This involves waiting for a new, unknown state to emerge out of the chaos and the demise of current state project delivery approaches, which will be brought about by ongoing consumer dissatisfaction with dismal project success rates.

4.3.22 Training as a change enabler

How can training support change?

For training to be an effective change enabler in the projects context, a clear understanding of the project vision and goals is required, together with a strong connection with the workplace. This requires support from strategic management, a close relationship with operations, effective leadership, trainers and facilitators who keep current in their profession and abreast with change on the front line, and training programmes that cater for different learning styles and drive up change adoption. Training must be viewed by the organization as a means for achieving change and methodologies used must be modern and either match or exceed those technologies used by the workforce. Anything less could lead to under-utilization of training solutions and impede change adoption.

4.3.23 Change roles and governance

What are the essential change roles that need to be resourced?

The *Executive Sponsor* is accountable for the success of the change initiative, with the position and authority to sponsor the change effectively. The sponsor is responsible for allocating resources to the project, visibly advocating the change, walking the talk, being the face of the project and communications and removing obstacles. A sponsor who leads a customer facing part of the business and understands the impact of the change on the customer and on the business will be more effective than a sponsor who is leading a support function. The sponsor may appoint a deputy to delegate some of the role, some of the time, but the sponsor must retain overall accountability. The deputy is most likely to be a senior executive with a direct reporting line to the sponsor in day-to-day operations. The effectiveness of the sponsor can make or break a change initiative.

The *Project Manager* is responsible for the end-to-end project delivery and will focus on the technical aspects particularly. The Project Manager will lead a team that can include Project Leads, Project Analysts and Solution Designers and Developers.

The *Change Manager* is responsible for creating, resourcing and implementing a strategy and plan that takes the organization on the change journey, maximizing support and adoption, and minimizing resistance to change. The Change Manager will lead an interdisciplinary team of Change Leads and Change Analysts – for a sample Change Manager job description, see the Appendix at the end of the book. In the programme context, it is recommended that the Change Manager reports into a *Change Director* who sits at programme board level.

The *Change Lead* is an experienced Change Management practitioner who reports to the Change Manager and leads on particular deliverables, based on their skillset and/or project requirements. The Change Lead liaises directly with stakeholders on behalf of the Change Manager.

The *Change Communications Lead, Training Lead and Culture Lead* are specialists who have expertise delivering in the change and projects context. They will report to the Change Manager.

The *Change Analyst* is a Change Management practitioner who analyses the delta between current state and desired state to identify organizational and end-user impacts that need to be planned for. The Change Analyst will report to the Change Manager.

The *Business Change Adoption Manager* is a leader or manager from business-as-usual who has a role driving up change adoption in their part of the business. This individual will be a person with considerable gravitas who interacts with local line management as part of his or her normal duties. The Business Change Adoption Manager will report into business operations and have a dotted line into the Executive Sponsor, and work closely with the Change Manager.

The *Change Champion* is an individual who can complement the efforts of the Business Change Adoption Manager to drive up adoption of change. He or she will report into business operations and may have a dotted line into the Change Manager. All too often, Change Champions are junior or part-time colleagues who have little influence. In one client organization, anyone could set up a champions network (and many did to expand their own influence), resulting in considerable brand damage to the concept of the change champion.

A 'change agent' is recognizable not necessarily for their job title but more for their ability to build momentum for change. Any one of the above can be considered a change agent as they have a formal role in driving change. Others who informally drive change (preferably in the desired company direction) can also be considered change agents. Internal change agents are essential to the task of managing change.

4.3.24 Sustaining change

How can change be sustained and built on?

Buchanan and Fitzgerald (2006) conducted extensive research and identified ten recurring problems that organizations meet when trying to make change stick, offering practical solutions:

1 *Change initiators move on to another organization.*

    • Retain key change agents by redesigning reward and recognition and career development policies, making it attractive from them to stay on;
    • Choose successors who have a similar profile.

2 *Accountability for development becomes diffused over time.*

    • Establish effective reporting lines, and clear roles, responsibilities and accountabilities;
    • Ensure appropriate and visible reward and recognition for those responsible for driving change.

3 *Turnover results in a loss of knowledge, experience and new practices.*
   - Develop employee retention strategies to minimize such losses;
   - Involve outgoing change initiators in the induction and training of new staff.

4 *Old habits are imported with recruits.*

   - Make 'new world' and 'old world' attitudes and behaviours explicit in induction and training programmes.

5 *The drivers for change are no longer visible.*

   - Keep the issues that triggered the change and the rationale for the change visible by strong communications;
   - Identify any new issues and pressures that support the change agenda.

6 *New managers have their own agendas.*

   - Support new agendas as appropriate but give new managers an explicit remit to work with and not dismantle particular changes introduced by their predecessors.

7 *Powerful stakeholders are using counter-implementation strategies to block progress.*

   - When reason fails, develop a 'counter-counter-implementation' strategy to reduce their influence. Address stakeholder concerns within reason and remove obstacles where possible.

8 *Pump-priming funds run out.*

   - Start to revise budget allocation well in advance, so that the extra costs of new working practices can be absorbed gradually in a phased manner.

9 *Other priorities come on stream, diverting attention and resources.*

   - Do not divert resources until change is embedded;
   - Develop a time-phased change implementation strategy to provide periods of planned stability between change projects.

10 *Staff at all levels suffer change fatigue and enthusiasm for change falters.*

   - Beware the 'bicycle effect' where a lack of forward momentum leads to a crash. Maintain momentum and keep focus, themes and goals front-of-mind with stakeholders.

Edgar Schein (2010) identified twelve mechanisms that will lead to sustainable change. Primary embedding mechanisms should be aligned with change first and foremost, and include:

- What leaders pay attention to, measure and control;
- Leaders' reactions to critical incidents and organizational crisis;
- How leaders allocate resources;
- Deliberate role-modelling, teaching and coaching;
- How leaders allocate rewards and status;
- How leaders recruit, select, promote and excommunicate.

Schein advises that secondary articulation and reinforcement mechanisms (below) only work if they are consistent with the primary embedding mechanisms. This suggests that, where there is misalignment, the processes below won't stick and will be overridden by informal ways of doing things. It reminds me of a conversation I had with the manager of a local retail outlet in my hometown recently. When I admired the new layout, which now made it possible for anyone under 6 feet tall to reach some of the garments, the manager advised that her team had reorganized it based on customer feedback, but would 'return it to "corporate standard" prior to any visit by area management'. She said they had 'given up trying to get management to listen'!

- Organizational design and structure;
- Organizational systems and procedures;
- Rites and rituals of the organization;
- Design of physical space, façade and buildings;
- Stories about important events and people;
- Formal statements of organizational philosophy, creeds and charters.

All of the mechanisms above will reinforce culture. The job of leaders and the Change Manager is to ensure that they are listening to the end-user and reinforcing the desired culture, not the old way of doing things or any unofficial 'work-arounds'.

4.3.25 *The team's appetite for change*

What are the factors that bear on the team's relationship with change?

Factors that come to bear on a team's relationship with change include the team manager's attitude towards change, team relationships, shared interests that lead to collusion against change, and collective learning anxiety and survival anxiety.

Team manager attitude towards change

The team manager sets the tone for their direct and indirect reports on how to respond to change. If the team manager is hostile to the change, they can make it in the interests of their team members to toe the line, even if team members want to embrace the change.

Team relationships

If change is going to impact a particular team member who is part of the established order, the whole team can collude to undermine the adoption of change that has been sanctioned by the business.

Shared interests

Collusion is also likely to occur where change will impact those team members who are good at catering for the self-interest of other team members, where change might impact the reputation of the team, or where it might threaten the very survival of the team.

Collective learning anxiety and survival anxiety

Learning anxiety and survival anxiety take on a new dimension in the team context because fears are amplified and reinforced, and the group share their fears and concerns. When the whole team lacks the skills and competencies needed to deliver in the new world, or when they fear that roles will be impacted, this can damage team morale and productivity.

4.3.26 The team's resistance to change

How does resistance to change manifest on teams and how can it be managed?

Earlier, we explored external and internal forces for and against change. In the internal environment, resistance to change presents itself in workforce attitudes and behaviours such as a lack of cooperation, hostility, work to rule, negativity, challenging questions, etc. Resistance to change has a bad name and is often assumed to be value-destroying, but resistance can be value-adding when an informed workforce can see holes in the planned future state and are being challenging for the right reasons.

What are the options available for dealing with resistance to change?

Kotter and Schlesinger (1979) identified a number of strategies for dealing with resistance to change (see Figure 4.22 overleaf). They advise that the further down their list of proposed options one goes, the more coercive the approach and the less one tends to use the other approaches. The opposite is also true. This is probably because the strategies at either end of the list are based on different operating assumptions about how to treat people. If a leader is more inclined one particular way, they are not likely to consistently carry out policies that are the extreme opposite of what they believe in.

Kotter and Schlesinger (1979) also identified four factors that need to be considered when determining which strategies to adopt for dealing

Approach	Common uses	Pros	Cons
Education and communication	Where information or analysis is lacking	Once they understand and impacts are clear, people will often help with the implementation of change.	Can be resource intensive for large target populations.
Participation and involvement	Where the change initiators rely on stakeholders to help design the change, and where stakeholders have considerable power to resist.	Participation enables stakeholder ownership and commitment for change, as they get to shape the solution and how it is introduced.	Can be very time-consuming if the wrong decisions are made based on stakeholder input and result in an effective solution and/or poor execution.
Facilitation and support	Where people are not adopting change because of problems relating to adjustment.	No other approach works as well with adjustment problems.	Can encourage stakeholders to negotiate for compliance and impact deadlines.
Negotiation and agreement	Where stakeholders will clearly lose out because of the change and where they have considerable power to resist.	Sometimes it is a relatively easy way to avoid major resistance.	Can encourage stakeholders to negotiate for compliance and impact deadlines.
Manipulation and co-option	Where other tactics will not work or are too expensive.	It can be a relatively quick and inexpensive solution to resistance. Short-term impact is positive as change is implemented.	Long-term impact is negative. Will damage climate and culture and lead to future problems, as people will feel manipulated and bullied. Can leave stakeholders angry with the change initiators.
Explicit and implicit coercion	Where speed is essential and the change initiators possess considerable power.	It is speedy, and all obstacles can be removed and any resistance overpowered. Short-term impact is positive as change is implemented.	Long-term impact is negative. Will damage climate and culture and lead to future problems, as people will feel manipulated and bullied. Can leave stakeholders angry with the change initiators.

Figure 4.22 Methods for dealing with resistance to change

From J. P. Kotter and L. A. Schlesinger (1979) Choosing strategies for change, Harvard Business School Publishing Corporation

with resistance to change: the amount and kind of resistance that is anti-
cipated, the position of the initiator vis-à-vis the resisters (especially with
regard to power), the person who has the relevant data for designing the
change and the energy for implementing it, and the stakes involved. Other
factors to consider are whether employees are physically in attendance or
working remotely, and how different cultures will respond to the
different strategies. Neglecting these factors when considering the right
approach can result in increased – rather than decreased – resistance to
change.

When navigating a team through the change journey, it is important
to understand that individuals will be affected differently and this can
impact team dynamics. The team manager needs to understand these
dynamics and employ tactics that will maximize support and minimize
resistance:

- *Change advocates* – Reward and recognize change advocates and give
  them opportunity to influence the rest of the team;
- *Change passengers* – Acknowledge their efforts to come onboard with
  the change, reward and recognize their progress and pair them with
  change advocates so they have more responsibility for embedding
  the change;
- *Slow adopters* – Reassure them, listen to their concerns and provide
  them with opportunities to learn the skills and competencies they
  need to build confidence;
- *Uninformed resistors* – Inform them on the benefits of the change
  (especially personal benefits) and successes achieved by colleagues;
- *Informed resistors* – Minimize their influence on the rest of the team.

4.3.27 The individual's appetite for change

What are the factors that bear on the individual's relationship with change?

Factors that determine whether, and to what degree, an individual will
embrace change include whether they are 'hard-wired' for change or
not, the individual's sense of control as change impacts them, whether
the individual perceives that they will win or lose as a result of the
change, whether the individual feels equipped with the skills and competencies to deal with the change, the individual's work content and
work environment, and the psychological contract they hold with their
employer. Each of these factors can serve as motivators – or de-
motivators – for the individual to embrace change.

Psychometric profile and tolerance for change

How we are hard-wired affects our appetite for change. An array of psychometric tools is readily available to measure the individual's numeracy

skills, language skills and individual preferences when responding to situations.

The Kirton Adaptation Innovation Inventory (KAI) tool (www.kai centre.com) is particularly relevant here as it measures the individual's thinking style and preferences in the pursuit of change. KAI was developed in response to the findings of a study carried out to investigate how ideas, which led to radical organizational change, were developed and implemented. That study threw up a number of anomalies:

- *Delays in introducing change* – Some ideas could take years to be accepted as a possible course of action, while others were accepted almost immediately with just a basic level of supporting analysis.
- *Objections to new ideas* – Often, a new idea that eventually prevailed had originally been blocked by a series of well-argued and reasoned arguments, which were upheld until a 'precipitating event' occurred.
- *Rejection of individuals* – The majority of ideas opposed were put forward by managers who were outside or on the edge of the 'establishment' group. Conversely, the ideas of managers within the establishment were seen as more plausible. Where these ideas were later rejected or failed, managers from within the establishment were not seen as having personally failed. It was seen more as a case of 'brave effort' or 'bad luck'.

KAI was built to provide a linkage between these issues and to offer a solution. Based on their individual KAI score, everyone can be placed on a continuum that defines their relationship with change, ranging from 'highly adaptive' to 'highly innovative'. The 'adaptor' puts much of their effort in the pursuit of change in continuous improvement, while the 'innovator' reconstructs the problem, separating it from its existing paradigm and viewpoints.

Everett Rogers, in his book *Diffusion of Innovations* (2003), describes five profiles that categorize how individuals adopt innovations (see Figure 4.23 overleaf). Rogers used a 'bell curve' to illustrate the distribution of these five profiles across a given population (see Figure 4.24 overleaf). To secure 100 per cent adoption, the project must first secure adoption by 'innovators' (2.5 per cent), then 'early adopters' (13.5 per cent), followed by the 'early majority' (34 per cent) and then the 'late majority' (34 per cent). Using more 'pull' influencing methods and less 'push' influencing methods will be effective with these groups. Laggards, on the other hand, can be very hard-core and tenacious in their resistance, so getting them onboard might involve more 'push' interventions, such as removing their old tools. Once the project has secured adoption of 'laggards' (16 per cent), they will have secured full end-user adoption of change.

Category	Characteristics
Innovators	Somewhat obsessive about innovations. A necessary quality to be able to deal with a lack of instructions, ambiguity and setbacks if innovations are not adopted. Innovators proactively network and collaborate with other innovators regardless of physical location. Great innovation champions and super-users.
Early adopters	More concerned with practical use of innovations, judging the worthiness of an innovation before adopting it. The early adopters' networking and collation activities do not reach as far as those of innovators. They tend to be leaders and influencers and are respected by peers. Great innovation champions and super-users.
Early majority	Want to be sure that innovations are an improvement on current practices and tools. Adopt innovations before the average person. Rarely influence opinions. Tend to be followers rather than leaders.
Late majority	Adopt innovations after the average person. The Late Majority may find change difficult in general, they may be uncomfortable with technology, they may be swamped with change, or change embedding mechanisms and change adoption plans may not be in place to drive adoption.
Laggards	Adopt innovations after everyone else. Laggards may be fearful of change in general, they may be fearful of technology, or they may have the power and position to be able to reject change for political or personal reasons.

Figure 4.23 Categories and characteristics of innovation adopters

From E. Rogers (2003) *Diffusion of Innovations* (5th edn). New York: Simon & Schuster.

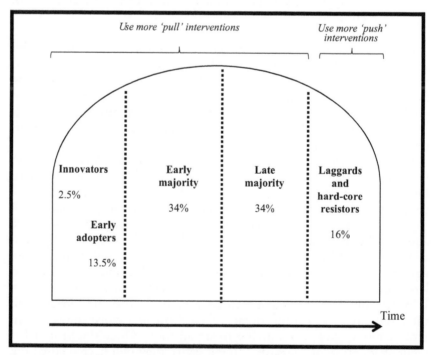

Figure 4.24 The Rogers Adoption/Innovation Curve

From E. Rogers (2003) Relationship between types of adopters classified by innovativeness and their location on the adoption curve.

Sense of control

One of the persisting myths about change is that it is human nature to resist change. People do not resist change per se. People resist change that is imposed on them, which takes away their sense of control over their own destinies, even if that change is in their interests. The person's sense of control can be more important to them than any benefits that change will bring.

Winner or loser

This factor requires no theory by way of explanation for it is common sense. As the individual considers the change they will come to conclusions as to whether or not the change is in their interests. To limit the possibility for misunderstandings and misinterpretations, communications about the change need to be as honest and transparent as possible. If information is not readily available to stakeholders, for whatever reason, stakeholders will fill in the gaps themselves and come to their own conclusions. This can lead to unnecessary complications.

Learning anxiety and survival anxiety

Fear about having the requisite knowledge, skills or competencies to cope can be another reason for resistance to change. Edgar Schein (1993) defines this as 'learning anxiety' and recommends that change plans aim to *decrease* it. Schein also recommends, as something of a last resort, that 'survival anxiety' is *increased* to deal with any complacency about change.

Work environment and work content

Many will be familiar with the work of Frederick Herzberg on job satisfaction. Herzberg (1987) found that 'dissatisfiers' were all about the context of the job (extrinsic), while the 'satisfiers' were built into the job itself (intrinsic).

How planned change impacts those dissatisfiers and motivators below for a particular individual will influence their attitude to change.

Dissatisfiers (hygiene factors)	Satisfiers (motivators)
Company policy and administration	Achievement
Supervision (technical)	Recognition
Relationship with supervisor	Job content
Working conditions	Responsibility
Salary	Advancement
Relationship with peers	Growth
Personal life	
Relationship with subordinates	
Status	
Security	

Figure 4.25 Hygiene factors and motivators

The psychological contract

This is the relationship between an employer and its employees, and is specifically concerned with mutual expectations regarding how the employee is treated by their employer and in relation to what the employee puts into the job. Effective Change Management increasingly depends on our ability to understand and manage the Psychological Contract and the drivers therein. People need to understand how change will impact them, while change leaders need to be as open and honest as possible so as to foster trust.

4.3.28 The individual's resistance to change

How does resistance to change manifest in the individual and how can it be managed?

To answer this, we need first to understand how the individual reacts to change that is imposed on them and behaviours they typically exhibit. Nelson and Quick (2012) suggest four possible reactions.

Strategies for dealing with the disengaged:

- Be an empathetic manager who encourages two-way dialogue.
- Name the behaviours in a non-confrontational way and encourage the employee to identify the causes and concerns they have.
- Address concerns and make sure the employee leaves the conversation feeling listened to and supported.

Strategies for dealing with disidentification:

- Encourage the employee to explore their feelings and what they liked about the old way of doing things; accept how individuals feel and do not try to persuade them to feel differently.
- Ensure the employee has the opportunity to learn the new skills and competencies required.
- Focus on the positive and remind the person of the benefits the change will bring them – e.g. career growth.

Strategies for dealing with the disenchanted:

- Encourage the constructive airing of issues. Where emotions run high, a trained facilitator can organize a session that takes the heat out of things.
- Acknowledge that anger is a normal and healthy human emotion and won't be held against them; accept how individuals feel and do not try to persuade them to feel differently.

1 Disengagement	
The employee appears to lose interest in the job.	• Physically present but mentally absent. • Lacks drive, initiative and commitment. • Difficult to locate. • Does the minimum. • Often says 'No problem' or 'This won't affect me.'
2 Disidentification	
Employee feels their identity has been threatened and is feeling vulnerable.	• Clings to the old way of doing things because of a sense of mastery over it and the security that gives. • Reminisces about the past. • Sad and worried looking. • Often says 'This is not the job I applied for' or 'I used to . . .'
3 Disenchantment	
Expressed by negativity or anger	• Realizes the past is gone. • Tries to enlist support of others by forming coalitions. • Sabotages and backstabs. • Bad-mouths and displays passive aggressive behaviour. • Often says 'this will never work' or 'I'm getting out of here . . .'
4 Disorientation	
Confusion and uncertainty	• Analysis-paralysis. • Appears to need a great deal of guidance and leave their work until all questions have been answered. • Often asks 'Now what do I do?' or 'What should I do first?'

Figure 4.26 How people react to change

- Capitalize on 'low-hanging fruit' and share successes to show that the new way can work and is working.

Strategies for dealing with confusion and uncertainty:

- Put the change in the context of the organization vision and mission, and explain how the role of the individual fits.
- Set clear goals and give unambiguous direction.

4.4 Trends and areas for development

So what next for Change Management? As an academic discipline, a profession, a practical skill set and a consumer product, Change Management is at varying levels of maturity as illustrated overleaf:

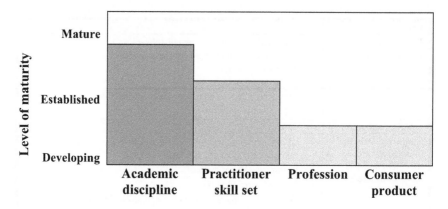

Figure 4.27 The faces of Change Management Maturity

4.4.1 Maturation of the academic discipline

As an area of study and research, Change Management is in the early advanced stages of development, with the subject now taught at undergraduate and postgraduate level in universities and colleges throughout the world, and backed by world-class faculties. Trends and areas for development include:

- Change Management is likely to see different strands of research develop to respond to the needs of different contexts – e.g. Technology Change Management, Construction Change Management.
- An ongoing refinement in thinking is required on how best to integrate Project Management and Change Management without diluting the value each brings to a joint value proposition.
- Increased appreciation and research on the role of culture on project teams.

4.4.2 Maturation of the profession

Change Management as a profession is in its infancy, with associations and first-generation standards and competencies only emerging in very recent years. Trends and areas for development include:

- Refinement in thinking on the scope and boundaries of Change Management allowing for the definition of touch-points with other disciplines and teams;
- Increasing professional development among change leaders and Change Management professionals;

- More robust certification programmes that require candidates to have a considerable number of hours' experience in Change Management; Change Management certification is big business and too many firms will trade you 'Change Management certification' in return for your minimal effort and a few thousand dollars.

4.4.3 Maturation of the practitioner skill set

Capabilities vary greatly across individuals with little clarity on what skills junior, intermediate and senior Change Management practioners should have. Collectively, the practitioner skill set is at best at the early intermediate stages of maturity only. Trends and areas for development include:

- Greater awareness of the Change Management Service Proposition;
- Greater mutual appreciation among Project Management and Change Management professionals on their complementary tool-kits and skill sets; it is becoming increasingly common for Change Management practitioners to learn Project Management skills as a secondary skill set;
- The ability to demonstrate attitudes and behaviours that express those cultural assumptions that will support a culture of partnership between Project Managers and Change Managers;
- In time, Change Managers are likely to hone their skill set to suit a particular context or goal – e.g. M&A Change Management, Technology Change Management, Culture Transition Management;
- Change Management will continue to incorporate the latest technology related to change, including back-end diagnostic tools and more front-end technology such as social media.

4.4.4 Maturation of the consumer product and consumer understanding

The Change Management Service Proposition offered to the business world varies greatly, depending on whom you are talking to. Too many consultancies position themselves as Change Management experts but offer little more than communications and training support to projects. This is especially true of Project Management consultancies, but even with the top management consultancies, there is evidence of Change Management being confused with Project Management. As Change Management is not a big earner for management consultancies, Change Management teams can be very small and staffed by junior workers. With industry still grappling with what Change Management is, consumer understanding of Change Management is too often elementary. Trends and areas for development include:

- Increased understanding among consumers as to what Change Management is, how it adds value, what the Change Manager does, and what to look for from a senior, middle-level and junior Change Management practitioners;
- A new growth area focused on cultivating a culture of partnership between Project Management and Change Management to secure successful delivery of change;
- The declining trend for Change Management to be positioned in Human Resources is making way for a new trend. More and more organizations are now positioning Change Management in project portfolio management as a central pool of resources who are 'loaned out' to programmes and projects who pay for their services;
- An increased focus on the end-user experience, particularly for complex, global technology deployments.

4.5 Chapter summary

While initially borrowing from other disciplines to help leaders respond to strategic challenges that could not be addressed by other methods, Change Management has emerged as a discipline in its own right with hundreds of books and university courses dedicated to the subject. Every major management consultancy has a Change Management practice, with interim managers and contractors providing the same services independently.

The proliferation of theories, models and tools on Change Management can be difficult to navigate, making their application to practical situations difficult and disjointed. To address this need, the 'Typology of Change Management' herein frames all such into three categories – 'change and the organization', 'change and the team' and 'change and the individual' – and 28 subcategories. The challenge for the Change Manager is to apply the material appropriately to create a strategy and plan that will meet the unique needs of their own organization and context.

Key trends and areas for development are evident on four fronts: Change Management as an academic discipline, as a practical skill set, a profession and as a consumer product. A central theme will continue to be the integration of Project Management and Change Management to better serve the needs of industry, while an emerging theme will be the role of culture on project delivery teams that adopt a joint value proposition.

Note

1   BPR: Business Process Re-engineering (BPR) – a business strategy, pioneered in the early 1990s, that focuses on the analysis and design of organizational workflows and business processes.

Bibliography

Books

Anderlo, G. (2011) Research as cited by Robertson J. *et al.* in *Unwrapping Increase, Destiny, Relationships, God and the Gifts of the Spirit*. Shippensburg, PA: DestinyImage.

Auglier, F. (1967) *Scanning the Business Environment*. New York: Macmillan.

Beer, M. and Nohria, N. (2000) *Cracking the Code of Change*. Boston, MA: Harvard Business Review Press.

Buchanan, D. A. and Fitzgerald, L. (2006) Improvement evaporation: Why do successful changes decay? In: *The Sustainability and Spread of Organizational Change*. D. A. Buchanan, L. Fitzgerald and D. Ketley (eds). London: Routledge.

Carnall, C. (2007) *Managing Change in Organisations* (5th edn). London: Prentice Hall, Financial Times.

Checkland, P. ([1981] 1999) *Systems Thinking, Systems Practice*. Chichester: Wiley.

Conner, D. (1993) *Managing at the Speed of Change*. Toronto: Random House.

French, W. and Bell, C. (1999) *Organization Development: Behavioral Science Interventions for Organization Improvement*. Upper Saddle River, NJ: Prentice-Hall.

Kotter, J. P. (2012) *Leading Change*. Boston, MA: Harvard Business Review Press.

Kotter, J. P. and Schlesinger, L. A. (1979) *Choosing Strategies for Change*. Boston, MA: Harvard Business School Publishing Corporation.

Levy, A. and Merry, U. (1986) *Organizational Transformational: Approaches, Strategies, Theories*. New York: Praeger.

Lewin, K. (1951) *Field Theory in Social Science*. New York: Harper & Row.

Nelson, D. L. and Quick, J. C. (2012) *Organizational Behavior* (8th edn). Cincinatti, OH: South-Western College.

Ouchi, W. (1981) *Theory Z: How American Management Can Meet the Japanese Challenge*. New York: Avon Books.

Peters, T. and Waterman, D. *et al.* (2006) *In Search of Excellence Reprint Edition*. New York: HarperBusiness.

Rogers, E. (2003) *Diffusion of Innovations* (5th edn). New York: Simon & Schuster.

Schein, E. (2010) *Organizational Culture and Leadership*. San Francisco, CA: The Jossey-Bass Business & Management Series.

Senge, P. (1990) *The Fifth Discipline*. New York: Doubleday/Currency.

Van Gennep, A. (1909) *The Rites of Passage*. Chicago: University of Chicago Press.

Weisbord, M. R. (1978) *Organizational Diagnosis: A Workbook of Theory and Practice*. New York: Basic Books.

Wendell, L. F. and Cecil, H. B. Jr (1999) *Organization Development Management: Behavioral Science Interventions for Organization Improvement* (6th edn). Upper Saddle River, NJ: Prentice Hall.

Journals and reports

Burke-Litwin (1992) A causal model of organisation performance and change. *Journal of Management*, 18 (3): 523–45.

Caldwell, R. (2003) Models of change agency: A fourfold classification. *British Journal of Management*, 14 (2): 131–42.

Caldwell, S. D. (2013) Are change readiness strategies overrated? A commentary on noundary conditions. *Journal of Change Management*, 13 (1): 9–35 (17).

Dibella, A. J. (2007) Critical Perceptions of Organizational Change. *Journal of Change Management*, 7(3/4): 231–42.

Herzberg, F. (1987) One more time: How do you motivate employees? *Harvard Business Review*, 65 (5): 109–20.

Higgs, M. and Rowland, D. (2000) What does it take to implement change successfully? A study of the behaviors of successful change leaders. *The Journal of Applied Behavioural Science*, 47 (3): 309–35.

Iles, V. and Sutherland, K. (2001) *Organizational Change: A Review for Healthcare Professionals and Researchers*. London: NCCSDO.

Jick, T. D. (1991) *Implementing Change*. Boston, MA: Harvard Business School.

Kotter, J. P. (1995) Leading change: Why transformation efforts fail. Boston, MA: *Harvard Business Review*, 73 (2): 59–67.

Lee, R. (1996) The 'pay-forward' view of training. *People Management*, 8 February, 30–2.

Lewin, K. (1947) Frontiers in group dynamics: Concept, method and reality in social science: Social equilibrium and social change. *Human Relations*, 1(36).

McNulty, T. (2003) Redesigning public services: Challenges of practice for policy. *British Journal of Management*, 14: S31–45.

Marshak, R. J. (1993) Lewin meets Confucius: A review of the OD Model of Change. *Journal of Applied Behavioral Science*, 29 (4): 393–415.

Nahavandi, A. and Malekzadeh, A. R. (1988) Acculturation in mergers and acquisitions, *Academy of Management Review*, 13 (1): 79–90.

Nalder, D. A. (1987) The Effective Management of Organizational Change. In J. W. Lorsch (ed.) *Handbook of Organizational Behaviour*. Englewood Cliffs, NJ: Prentice Hall.

Orlikowski, W. J. (1996) Improvising organizational transformation over time: A situated change perspective. *Information Systems Research*, 7(1): 63–92.

Prochaska, J. O. and DiClemente, C. C. (1992) In search of how people change. Applications to addictive behaviors. *American Psychologist*, 47: 1102–14.

Schein, E. H. (1993) How can organizations learn faster? The challenge of entering the green room. *Sloan Management Review*, 34(2), 85–92.

Schein, E. (2002) The anxiety of learning – The darker side of organizational learning. *Harvard Business Review*, March.

Todd, J. (April 1991) Implementing change: Note. *Harvard Business Review*.

Online

www.astd.org

www.connerpartners.com (Conner, 2012)

www.gecapital.com

www.theguardian.com (Nokia's Chief Executive to staff: 'we are standing on a burning platform', 2011)

www.ijhsdm.org

www.kaicentre.com

Nickols, F. (2000) *Change Management 101: A Primer*. Available at: http://home.att.net/- nickols/change.htm (accessed 19 November 2016).

5 Culture is the key to making change stick

So far, efforts to integrate Change Management and Project Management have focused only on those things that exist above the surface such as those processes and tools used. But it is what exists beneath the surface – culture – that will determine which processes and tools stick, so the cultural component has to be part of the solution to the problem.

5.1 The essence of culture

What exactly *is* culture? Culture has been variously defined as:

> The way we do things around here.
>
> (Bower, 1966)

> A pattern of basic assumptions – invented, discovered or developed by a given group as it learns to cope with its problems of external adaptation and internal integration – that has worked well enough to be considered valid, and therefore, to be taught to new members as the correct way to perceive, think and feel in relation to these problems.
>
> (Schein, 1996)

> An organic group phenomenon comprising shared assumptions and beliefs which are passed on to successive generations as the right way to do things. Newly incorporated assumptions and beliefs build capacity to evolve with a changing external environment. Culture is visible in shared attitudes, behaviours and artefacts and reflected in the outcomes and results the group achieves.
>
> (O'Donovan, 2006)

Each of these definitions complements the others and tells us a little more about the essence and dynamics of culture: Bower describes culture in a very handy catch-phrase that has us thinking about shared attitudes, behaviours and methods. Schein draws our attention to the very essence of culture (shared assumptions), while O'Donovan emphasizes the organic and evolutionary nature of culture, and the relationship between shared assumptions, attitudes and behaviours, and those outcomes and results the group achieves.

Culture has a dual nature. On one hand, it acts as a stabilizer, reinforcing the established way of doing things. But, at the same time, it is constantly reinventing itself as it faces new problems in a complex and ever changing world. An organization that is too mired in tradition becomes stagnant. Conversely, an organization that is changing for the sake of change, implementing more change than the business can cope with at any one time, and/or implementing change without embedding it, can weaken its very foundations.

5.2 How culture develops

When any group forms, it will have needs and the group will have to work together to meet those needs. In the organizational context, these needs will be entwined with the needs of the organization which can be baked down to two key functions – *to survive and thrive*. As the group solves problems presented by opportunities and threats in its environment, it develops a shared sense of what works and what doesn't work, and a collection of shared assumptions emerges based on that learning. Together, these assumptions form the essence (or content) of the group's culture. It is subconscious, for the most part, yet it acts as the group's survival toolkit and informs group members how to get things done on a day-to-day basis. The group culture finds expression in their shared attitudes and behaviours, and it is reflected in subsequent outcomes and results the group achieves.

While old hands pass on the established way of doing things, new recruits have an important role to play in the evolutionary side of culture. They bring with them an external perspective and new ways of working that can provide a dose of good medicine for a culture that has gone awry. With their fresh eyes, they can spot opportunities for improvement where employees might have a blind spot. For example, as a new member of the team in one organization, I found that the global meetings culture left a lot to be desired. Formal meeting agendas were unheard of, whole teams regularly attended where one representative would have sufficed, all members could be held waiting for a quarter of an hour if the host was running late, and it was common to be 'pinged' into a meeting (using instant messenger) to contribute on a topic that was well under discussion. It was simply impossible to come prepared, know what was expected of you, or manage your workload and schedule. Fortunately, the client was open to new insights and ways of doing things and soon all were signed up to a new meetings protocol and etiquette. This coincided with a global leader-led initiative to tackle the inefficient meetings culture.

Not all organizations are so amenable to feedback. Recruiters in particular are typically protective and even arrogant about their organizational culture, and strive to ensure that recruits will be a good 'cultural fit'. Yet for the most part, this is without any sound analysis of the culture, its strengths and weaknesses, and how new recruits with particular attributes can facilitate cultural evolution.

5.3 The cyclical nature of culture

Culture does not stand still. It evolves in response to forces for change (see section 4.3.7, p. 64) and this evolution is cyclical. As regulatory, political and other forces are felt by the organization, the group must solve new problems and come with ways of doing things to meet the needs of the organization and the group. As they experiment, they will find that some of their operating assumptions about how to do things just don't work any more. Where a learning culture exists, this input will result in new, shared, assumptions being incorporated into the culture, replacing those redundant ones. Related group attitudes and behaviours will see a resulting shift, as will subsequent outcomes

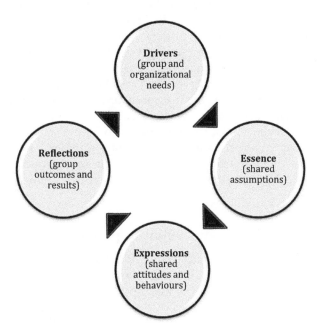

Figure 5.1 The culture cycle

and results. This cycle is continuous and, with each evolution, any given culture will become more or less of some aspect that defined it before. For example (and with a nod to some of those key cultural challenges that organizations face), a culture may become more, or less, customer-centric; more, or less, ethical; and/or more, or less, innovative.

As culture is constantly evolving, it is in the interests of the organization to actively manage this evolution so that the changing culture continues to adapt to the external environment. Culture management involves the mapping of the organization's cultural assumptions, reinforcing those assumptions that support strategies and benefits realization, and pruning those that are unproductive and lead to inefficiencies. It's a full-time job.

5.4 Assumptions in action

On any given project team, shared assumptions inform shared attitudes and behaviours, and impact what gets done and what doesn't. For example, if the team holds a shared assumption that successful measurement of project delivery is simply 'on time, on scope and on budget', they will not appreciate the need to secure end-user adoption of new ways of working, and are likely to see the work of Change Managers early on in the project cycle as little more than interference and a distraction. They may rationalize this mind-set by saying, 'If we don't have a system, we won't need users to be on board.' In this environment, strategies and plans that involve Project Managers' cooperation with Change Managers early in the project cycle (e.g. to agree user impacts) may prove difficult to implement. By way of further example, if Project Managers hold a shared assumption that Change Management priorities should play second fiddle to Project Management priorities, they will not be supportive of an integrated team structure that positions Change Managers as partners to Project Managers. In fact, they may vigorously sabotage such an arrangement. So before we can even think about choosing 'above the surface' interventions that will help us implement change, we need first to understand those assumptions at work in our change project teams and ensure they support any planned interventions.

5.5 Mapping culture and defining parameters

Culture is often said to be 'elusive' and 'difficult to pin down'. However, it doesn't have to be. The 'continuum approach' shared overleaf makes possible the mapping of cultural assumptions on a given issue (and/or a collection of issues) making positions, and any shifts in position, visible and trackable. In the example, the issue is the nature of the individual's value. On the continuum, two options are given – at one

The essence of the individual's value

_____ X ____

Useful to the job on hand   *Intrinsic to being human*

Each individual has intrinsic value by virtue of the fact that they are unique, human and precious and their value to the business goes far beyond their immediate usefulness to the job (or agenda) on hand. This has to be a fundamental core assumption of any civilized society. In *The New Alchemists*, management guru and writer Charles Handy states that while the world needs new ideas, new products, new kinds of associations and institutions, new initiatives, new art and new designs, seldom do these things come from established organizations. Rather, they come from individuals. When an organization considers individuals valuable only in terms of their usefulness to the job on hand, and when they are treated with derision and considered disposable, this has dire consequences for the integrity of the entire organizational community (O'Donovan, 2006).

extreme, the cultural assumption is that the essence of the individual's value is their usefulness to the job on hand, while at the other end it is that their usefulness is defined as intrinsic to being human. The optimal position is marked 'X'. Below the continuum, the assumption describing the optimal position is presented in italics, while the different positions are described thereafter.

Where a given culture stands on a given subject (and continuum) will vary from era to era, as shared assumptions evolve as the group learns in the face of new environmental challenges. Because mapping any given culture could be a never-ending task, it is essential to define the parameters of such work. Context is one such parameter and the context here is 'the integration of Project Management and Change Management methodologies for projects'. The other parameter I am employing is a three-part framework designed by Edgar Schein on those universal 'problems' or challenges that organizations face relating to external adaptation, internal integration and abstract issues – problems that are as relevant to change projects as they are to business-as-usual. The project is, after all, an organization, albeit a temporary one.

The first part of the framework focuses on those cultural assumptions that a group holds relating to their broader, macro environment (see Figure 5.3 overleaf). These deepest cultural assumptions concern matters where it is absolutely essential to get consensus for society to function – e.g. the nature of time and space. Cultural assumptions relating to these challenges will be deeply held.

- **The nature of life and change:** Every group must agree on how life and change evolve.
- **The nature of systems and environmental relationships:** Every working group must understand how their group and context relates to their broader context.
- **The nature of interdisciplinary relationships:** Every working group must understand how individual expertise and skills can complement group activities.
- **The nature of human relationships:** Every group needs to understand individual roles, how these interact with each other.
- **The nature of and value of gender roles and masculine and feminine ways of thinking** and how these impact how things are done.
- **The nature of epistemic cultures and how one can interact with the other:** Every working group needs to understand how individual disciplinary backgrounds inform the practitioner's thinking about fundamental things and their particular way of doing things.

Figure 5.2 Deepest assumptions about macro issues

The second part of the framework considers those challenges that the organization faces as it adapts to its external environment. My new additions added to Schein's original list include getting consensus on the 'shared approach to problem solving', and 'shared approach to risks and issues resolution' – challenges that are in the forefront for project leaders and teams.

- **Mission and strategy:** Obtaining a shared understanding of core mission, primary task, manifest functions and latent functions.
- **Goals:** Developing consensus on goals, as derived from the core mission.
- **Means:** Developing consensus about the means used to achieve goals, such as the organization structure, division of labour, rewards system and authority system.
- **Measurement:** Developing consensus on the criteria to be used in measuring how well the group is doing in achieving its goals, such as the information and control system.
- **Correction:** Developing consensus on the appropriate remedial or repair strategies to be used if goals are not met.
- **Problem-solving approach:** Developing consensus around how best to approach problem solving so as to build organization adaptability.
- **Risks and issues resolution:** Developing consensus on shared approach to risks and issues resolution so as to protect business benefits realization.

Figure 5.3 The problems of external adaptation and survival

Adapted from E. Schein (2010) *Organizational Culture and Leadership* (4th edn). John Wiley & Sons, San Francisco, CA.

- **Maximizing problem-solving capability:** A healthy appetite for diversity in thinking styles will maximize potential for creativity.
- **Openness to feedback:** A healthy appetite for feedback from all employees and customers, regardless of their rank or status, will accelerate learning and continuous improvement.
- **Creating a common language and conceptual categories:** If members do not have a common frame of reference and language to understand each other, a group is impossible by definition.
- **Defining group boundaries and criteria for inclusion and exclusion:** The group must be able to define itself. Who is in and who is out, and by what criteria is membership determined?
- **Distributing power, authority and status:** Every group must work out its pecking order, its criteria and rules for how someone gets, maintains, and loses power and authority. Consensus in this area is crucial to help members manage feelings of aggression.
- **Developing norms of trust, intimacy, friendship and love:** Every group must work out its 'rules of the game' for peer relationships, for relationships between the sexes and for the manner in which openness and intimacy are to be handled in the context of managing the organization's tasks. Consensus in this area is crucial to help members define trust and manage feelings of affection and love.
- **Defining and allocating of rewards and punishments:** Every group must know what its heroic and sinful behaviours are and must achieve consensus on what is a reward and what is a punishment.
- **Explaining the unexplainable:** Every group, like every society, faces unexplainable events that must be given meaning so that members can respond to them and avoid anxiety of dealing with the unexplainable and uncontrollable.

Figure 5.4 The problems of internal integration

Adapted from E. Schein (2010) *Organizational Culture and Leadership* (4th edn). John Wiley & Sons, San Francisco, CA.

The third part of the framework considers those universal problems that the organization faces in terms of internal integration (see above). Newly identified challenges added to Schein's original list include getting consensus on 'maximizing problem solving capability' and 'openness to feedback'.

While leaders may give considered thought to some or even all of the problems above when considering the larger organizational context, they rarely give these problems due attention in the temporary projects environment – and certainly not in terms of how they can define a network of cultural assumptions that will help resolve these issues. Therefore, these 21 challenges are an excellent reference point for doing just that, as they add a structured level of detail to that higher-level parameter of 'Change Management/Project Management integration'.

5.6 Defining a culture of partnership for project teams

In the following three chapters, I illustrate and articulate my vision for an occupational subculture of partnership between Change Managers and Project Managers:

- Figure 6.1 in Chapter 6 defines ten cultural assumptions relating to those problems the project organization faces that can be considered 'macro issues'
- Figure 7.1 in Chapter 7 defines twelve cultural assumptions relating to those problems the project organization faces in terms of 'adapting to the external environment'.
- Figure 8.1 in Chapter 8 defines nine cultural assumptions relating to the problems the project organization faces in terms of 'internal integration'.

Beneath each headline statement – e.g. 'The nature of the project' – any number of cultural assumptions could sit. For our purposes, the focus is a key problem that relates to change projects specifically. Often, the options are polar opposites and the optimal assumption that will support a culture of partnership is either one or the other. Other times, the optimal assumption is somewhere in the middle, or a balance of two or more alternatives. In the example 'Defining successful project delivery', three alternative assumptions are put forward – 'Change implemented', 'Change embedded', or 'Both' (implemented and embedded). 'Both' is the optimal position and this is denoted with an 'X'. Below each of the three diagrams mentioned above, cultural assumptions are described in turn.

The end result not only defines a sound culture to anchor any 'above the surface' interventions, but it defines an ideal occupational subculture for Change Managers and Project Managers alike, positioning them to work together to both implement, and embed, change. It also provides executive leaders with a unique reference guide that will help them drive culture evolution in their change projects environment.

5.7 Chapter summary

The essence of culture is a network of assumptions that are shared by a particular group to inform how they get things done. For the most part, those assumptions are unconscious and members of the group are not even aware how their attitudes and behaviours are shaped by the collective cultural mind-set.

Much like the individual's personality, culture has both constructive and destructive facets. It is the job of leaders to be aware of the nuances of their own organizational culture, and to shape and hone it so that it meets evolving business requirements. In the business-as-usual context, this is challenge enough, but in the project environment where a melting pot of employees, contractors and consultants are working alongside each other, the challenge is considerably greater. This creates all the more reason to identify and explore those cultural assumptions that are common in the projects space, and identify optimal ones that will create an ideal and shared subculture for both Project Managers and Change Managers.

Bibliography

Books

Bower, M. (1996) *The Will to Manage*. New York: McGraw-Hill.
O'Donovan, G. (2005) *The Corporate Culture Handbook*. Dublin: The Liffey Press.
Schein, E. (2010) *Organizational Culture and Leadership* (4th edn). The Jossey-Bass Business & Management Series. San Francisco, CA: John Wiley & Sons.

Part II

Implementing PCP methodology

(version 1.0)

Section A
Below the surface

6   Project team assumptions alignment

Macro concepts

Universal macro issues to be resolved for project teams relate not just to their project environment, but to the organizational and broader context that informs the workplace culture. These are fundamental issues that any group needs to agree on in order for the group to function. Macro-related issues that the project team needs to reach consensus on include:

- How life and change unfold in general, and in the projects environment;
- The nature of the project;
- How the project relates to its environment;
- How Change Management and Project Management will contribute to delivery;
- How the Change Manager and the Project Manager will cooperate;
- The roles of the Change Manager and Project Manager as separate to the core team who will report into these two key roles;
- Respecting differences in ways of thinking about project concepts, based on occupational subcultures and finding common ground;
- The nature and value of masculine versus feminine reasoning for managing organizational change;
- The nature and value of gender roles and what it means for project delivery.

Overleaf, Figure 6.1 maps specific cultural assumptions (both optimal and alternative) to each of these issues and identifies, with an 'X', the optimal cultural assumptions to hold for each. Any given team whose way of doing things is based on these optimal assumptions will be aligned on fundamental macro-level issues and build a good foundation for a culture of partnership.

The Nature of Life

	X_
Tidy	Messy

The Nature of the Project

	X	
Concrete set of linear tasks	Both	Series of activities arising from the needs of people and business

The Nature of the Relationship between the Project and the Organization

	X_
Separate from organisational realities	Inter-linked

The Nature of the Change Management/ Project Management Relationship

	X	
Independent	Inter-dependent	Dependent

The Nature of the Project Manager/ Project Manager Relationship

	X	
Independent	Inter-dependent	Dependent

The Role of the Project Managerand Change Manager as Separate to the Core Team

	X	
Getting plan and sticking to it	Both	Team leaders and integrating force

The Nature and Value of Masculine versus Feminine ways of Reasoning for Managing Organizational Change

	X	
Masculine Reasoning Superior	Equal Value	Feminine Reasoning Superior

The Nature and Value of Gender Roles

	X_
Stereotypical	Non-stereotypical

	X	
Male input more valued	Equally Valued	Female input more valued

The Nature of Change Management and Project Management Epistemic Cultures

_X		
Essentially Different	A Strong Degree of Sameness	Essentially the Same

Figure 6.1 PCP cultural assumptions continuum: macro issues

6.1 The nature of life

Life is messy and projects are messy too. The essential nature of life is that of renewal, brought about by evolutionary, transitional and transformational change. Some of that change is predictable, but a lot of it is not, making life a rather messy business with many a twist and turn. Projects are messy for this, and other, reasons too; they are typically a melting pot of employees, consultants and contractors and, as temporary environments, projects are perhaps more vulnerable than business-as-usual to political shifts, weak governance and poor general management practices. Take the following real life examples:

- Project/programme management overly dependent on a particular Project Management consultancy that used this power to hinder the best efforts of perceived competitors who were project team members;
- The new Project Manager who pushed out existing project team members, instated those of his own choosing and received backhanders from the recruitment agency that he was colluding with;
- Project and programme managers taking Friday afternoons off to play golf, with project team members sneaking out to the pub during their absence *en masse*;
- The project sponsor who signed off the project Statement of Work without consulting his direct reports, and had his plans for organizational structure change derailed as a result;
- The operations director who responded, 'We don't care; employees will do what they're told' when advised that a tiny Change Management team reporting into BAU could not support a global workforce for a technology project;
- The project director who went abroad on holiday during a critical and external stakeholder facing project activity because he feared it would fail (the Change Manager led the activity, although it was new to her too, and it was a resounding success);
- The project manager (note the small 'p' and 'm') for a global deployment who had never managed a project, project senior stakeholders or a Steering Committee before and was given the role of Project Manager as a 'stretch assignment';
- High project turnover among female team members, due to a culture of bullying, which went unnoticed in a constantly changing environment.

Any seasoned veteran in the projects space is likely to raise a wry smile and may even have some more examples to add. Yet, project and programme management literature, for the most part, seems to operate on the assumption that projects are neat and tidy, and come across as sanitized and academic. Such literature does not reflect the real world. Projects are messy environments indeed and, although addressing general management practices such as those listed above is beyond the scope of this book, it is worth bearing in mind that all members of the team – from both Project Management and Change Management disciplines – will have varying levels of general management skills that will impact teamwork. The same goes for project support partners working in business-as-usual. Behaviours in the projects space need to be subject to the same controls and good governance one would expect it the business-as-usual space, and it is for leaders to set the tone.

6.2 The nature of the project

The project is a series of linear and non-linear tasks and activities arising from the needs of the business. This cultural assumption recognizes both the consecutive and the emergent nature of project tasks and activities, while emphasizing the relationship between the product of the project and end-users. In a study on masculine and feminine logic systems in the projects environment, Thomas and Buckle-Henning (2007) found that the masculine way of thinking sees the project as a 'concrete linear set of tasks with a clear start and finish' and 'separate the project from its context'. The feminine way of thinking sees projects as 'a series of activities deeply embedded in a goal arising from the needs of the company's people and business' and emphasizes 'connectedness' and 'interdependence'. The recommended optimal assumption captures both these views to create common ground.

6.3 The nature of the relationship between the project and the organization

Projects don't exist in a vacuum; they emerge, exist and die in their host organizations. The relationship between the project and the organization has been the subject of much research. Grabher (2002) illustrates it by describing its different facets, which can be summarized as follows:

1 Projects are vehicles for introducing change and achieving organizational goals.
2 Projects are often hard to decompose into constituent tasks and such a (commonly agreed) discomposition is only possible when *stakeholders interrelate* with each other continually.
3 The contractor is the *lynchpin on whom trust is focused* (for our purposes, the contract will be the Project Manager and the Change Manager cooperating to bring change to the organization). The role of the manager is particularly important in projects on which team members do not have the time to get to know each other well.
4 The *contractor is also the wielder of organizational authority* as far as the project is concerned. He or she is, in this sense, a representative of the organization – a person whose presence underlines the fact that the project exists to achieve specified organizational goals.
5 The *final deadline* of a project culminates in the termination of the project and *serves as a connector* with the rest of the organization. As the project team disbands, the outputs of the project disperse into the wider organization.

6 Projects draw on organizational resources.
7 *Organizational culture* plays a role in determining how projects are governed, managed and run.
8 The project can serve as the lynchpin for strategic partnerships.
9 The *organization hosts a range of processes* that are needed to organize and run a project.
10 Projects present the *opportunity to enhance organizational learning*; however, as projects are typically high-pressure environments, there is little time for documenting knowledge.

Additional facets of the relationship between the project and the organization include *the political landscape* and *organizational climate*. Project progress, coordination and control are often hindered by organizational politics, and all the more so when project leadership is lacklustre and stakeholders in the business are not united behind a common purpose and objectives. Poor employee engagement in the larger organization can create a sense of inertia that can only increase the challenge faced by the project.

All of the points above support the operating assumption that the project and the organization are interlinked. However, it can be tempting for Project Managers to choose to operate from the alternative assumption that the project is isolated from its environment and not subject to organizational controls. With this mind-set, relationships and politics are seen as external to the project and problems relating to coordination and control are simpler to manage. The project team works, for the most part, in isolation to the host organization. My strongest first-hand experience of this assumption in action was when I worked as Change Manager for a successful M&A project where a firm was acquired by another. Our project team was located on a secure floor of the head office building and access to the floor was strictly limited. As we were dealing with highly sensitive information and liaising with legal advisers on a daily basis, we worked largely in isolation from the rest of the organization where there were, not untypically, strongly divided views on the best way forward. Politics could not but impact the project and the team members whose rewards and punishments were influenced not only by those who were for the change but also by those who were against it. In the real world, it is unrealistic to suppose that the project can operate in a vacuum and not be subject to organizational controls.

6.4 The nature of the Change Management and Project Management relationship

Project Management and Change Management are separate, but interdependent, disciplines. Project Management is concerned with end-to-end delivery of the change, with Change Management concerned about bringing stakeholders on the journey and ensuring that change meets the needs of the organization and is embedded. Each has its own distinctive service proposition and toolkit. When the project team operates on the assumption that one of the disciplines is dependent on the other, or to be assimilated by it, it is typically Project Management tools that dominate with the Change Management toolkit being used to a lesser degree. Alternatively, when the project team operates on the assumption that Project Management and Change Management disciplines are independent, they can overlook opportunities for synergies and the need to incorporate Change Management processes into project plans. An interdependent approach will reap the best results.

6.5 The nature of the Change Manager/Project Manager relationship

The Project Manager and Change Manager develop the plan, lead the team to deliver the plan, and work with stakeholders to integrate diverse perspectives. Traditionally, the Project Manager has been the central axis of project delivery. Carrying the weight of the responsibility, it is easy to see activities such as team leadership and interfacing with the organization being neglected as the demand to deal with technical matters presses. Where the Project Manager and Change Manager work together to develop a joint plan, co-lead with team on delivery, and utilize their respective strengths to manage the stakeholder equation, synergies are created and the burden is shared. Note that while the Change Manager will have facilitation and team-building skills, it is not the job of the Change Manager to make up for any weaknesses the Project Manager may have in terms of those tasks traditionally associated with female roles e.g. people management and performance management, as suggested in some quarters.

6.6 The role of the Project Manager and Change Manager as separate to the core team

The Project Manager and Change Manager are interdependent partners who together can implement – and embed – change. When the project team operates on the assumption that one of the managers/teams is dependent on the other, it is typically the Project Manager who wins out on the power-sharing agreement, and the Change Management team takes on a secondary and even administrative support role. Alternatively, when the project team operates on the assumption that the Project Manager and Change Manager best work independently, they miss important opportunities for synergies, and the results work in parallel to project team organizational structure, rather than in unison (see section 7.4 to learn more about the 'navel-gazing approach' and the 'parallel approach' to project team structure).

6.7 The nature and value of masculine versus feminine ways of reasoning for managing organizational change

Neither masculine nor feminine ways of reasoning are inherently superior to the other (Thomas and Buckle-Henning, 2007). In their study of masculine and feminine logic systems at work in Project Management, Thomas and Buckle-Henning describe the masculine way of thinking 'field independent' (detached from the individuals and situations they seek to understand), 'objective', 'impersonal', 'independent' and 'analytical', presenting in behaviours such as 'competitive', 'decisive', 'assertive', 'task-orientated' and 'directive'. Decisions are made with preference to conforming to predetermined project realities and tasks preferably executed according to predetermined views, regardless of the context. Feminine reasoning they described as 'field dependent', conceiving tasks and plans through emerging realities, relationships and information, and presenting in behaviours such as 'power sharing', 'collaborative sense making and working styles', 'information sharing' and 'empathy'. Thomas and Buckle-Henning argue that, as healthy adult life involves moving towards wholeness, both male and female Project Managers need to understand the differences inherent in masculine and feminine reasoning and ways of managing projects. They assert that 'neither style is the domain or liability of males or females' and that 'both sets of capacities are present in any healthy individual'. However, society still tends to view masculine behaviour as inappropriate for women and feminine behaviour as inappropriate for men. Wholeness and strength can be achieved for the individual, the organization (including the project organization), and society when both males and females claim the strengths of both approaches.

In their research, Thomas and Buckle-Henning found that in the PMBOK® 'hard masculine logic systems exert considerable influence on the "best practice" outlined in the PMBOK®. Softer feminine logic systems appear less influential and presumably less valued or trusted in the profession'. In essence, the culture of Project Management is inherently masculine and dominated by power relationships and a task orientation. This has serious implications for Change Management, and successful change adoption, as feminine reasoning and behaviours that focus on interpersonal relationships and process orientation are integral to the work of Change Managers who build stakeholder buy-in and embed change in the business.

6.8 The nature and value of gender roles

Male and female roles are not bound by stereotypes that are harmful to both, but to women in particular. Gender stereotypes stem from traditional male and female roles, depicting women as more communal (nurturing, relationships-focused and interdependent) and men as more agentic (ambitious, task-orientated and self-reliant). These stereotypes create expectations about how women should behave and how men should and should not behave, and they have shifted little, despite the growth of women in the workforce. Studies have shown that both males and females experience backlash when displaying non-stereotypical behaviour. But females face additional challenges and punitive behaviours. Rudman and Phelan (2008) conducted research on this topic and found that:

> because women are perceived to be less competent, ambitious, and competitive (i.e., less agentic) than men, they may be overlooked for leadership positions unless they present themselves as atypical women. However, the prescriptive nature of gender stereotypes can result in negative reactions to female agency and authority (i.e., backlash). This dilemma has serious consequences for gender parity, as it undermines women at every stage of their careers. It also has consequences for organizations, as it likely contributes to female managers' higher rates of job disaffection and turnover, relative to male counterparts.

The male and female contributions to the project are equally appreciated and respected. It will be no surprise to readers that often a macho culture reigns on projects. The project's environment is typically male- dominated, although this can vary in degree depending on the nature of the project (e.g. HR projects can have more female Project Managers than other types of projects), and how intergender relations present in the organizational and national culture. In *The Culture Code*, author Clotaire Raphialle provides perspective on the role of national culture on intergender relationships. Commenting on male bonding, and English culture in particular, Clotaire has this to say:

> The English men have a remarkably strong bond with one another, perhaps stronger than the relationship between men in any other culture. Because they truly believe that only other men can understand their feelings, all of their meaningful friendships are with other men . . . this understandably leads to a real disconnection from English women, who feel left out of the party.

The dominance of male versus female Project Managers (70 per cent to 30 per cent, respectively) suggests that more projects are run by men with more females playing a support role. Yet studies on gender in the projects environment strongly suggest that feminine reasoning is essential to the management of change. Author Charles Handy (1994) even goes as far as to say:

> They [organizations] want people who can juggle with several tasks and assignments at one time, who are more interested in making things happen than in what title or office they more, more concerned with power and influence than status. They want people who value instinct and rational, who can be tough but also tender, focused but friendly, people who can cope with these necessary contradictions. They want, therefore, as many women as they can get.

6.9 The nature of Change Management and Project Management epistemic cultures

Project Management and Change Management epistemic cultures fundamentally differ, attracting students and practitioners with different, but complimentary, interests and talents. Different thought worlds can lead to conflict over goals and methods, impending the collective action required to implement and embed successful change. As observed by Lehmann (2010), a huge gap exists between conceptualizations in Change Management and Project Management. Lehmann highlights the tendency for Project Management practitioners to focus on planning, control, processes and methodologies, while Change Management practitioners are more interested in 'change's objects and underlying mechanisms' and the behavioural aspects. Bresnen (2006) sees the two fields as representing two different approaches to the mechanisms of knowing, with Project Management bringing projects to the foreground (obscuring understanding of how projects dovetail with the wider organizational context), unlike Change Management which brings the organizational context to the fore. Differences in epistemic cultures become more rigid and entrenched if the change project is subject to external threat or failure and high stress levels prevail, as Project Managers and Change Managers will default to known behaviour that they are comfortable with.

6.10 Chapter summary

Universal macro issues that the project team needs to achieve consensus on include issues such as the relationship between the project and its broader environment, the nature of the Change Management and Project Management relationship, and the nature of the relationship between the Change Manager and the Project Manager.

Optimal cultural assumptions that support a culture of partnership between Project Managers and Change Mangers include the following:

life is messy and projects are messy too; the project is a series of linear and non-linear tasks and activities arising from the needs of people and the business; projects don't exist in a vacuum – they emerge, grow, decline and die in their host organizations; Project Management and Change Management are separate, but interdependent, disciplines; the Project Manager and Change Manager develop the plan, lead the team to deliver the plan, and work with stakeholders to integrate diverse perspectives; the Project Manager and Change Manager are inter-dependent partners who, together, can both implement – and embed – change; neither masculine nor feminine ways of reasoning are inher-ently superior to the other – male and female roles are not bound by stereotypes that are harmful to both but to women in particular; the male and female contributions to the project are equally appreciated and respected; Project Management and Change Management epistemic cultures fundamentally differ, attracting students and practitioners with difference, but complimentary, bias, interests and talents.

Bibliography

Books

Bresnen, M. (2006) Conflicting and conflated discourses? Project management, organisational change and learning. In Cicmil, S. and Hodgson, D. *Making Projects Critical*. New York: Palgrave Macmillan.

Handy, C. (1994) *The Empty Raincoat: Making Sense of the Future*. New York: Random House.

Raphialle, C. (2006) *The Culture Code*. New York: Random House.

Journals

Grabher, G. (2002) Cool projects, obring institutions: Temporary collaboration in the social context. *Regional Studies*, 36 (3): 205–14.

Lehmann, V. (2010) Connecting changes to projects using a historical perspective: Towards some new canvases for researchers. *International Journal of Project Management*, 28(4): 328–38.

Rudman, L. A. and Phelan, J. E. (2008) Backlash effects for disconfirming gender stereotypes in organizations. *Research in Organizational Behavior*, 28, 61–79.

Thomas, J. L. and Buckle-Henning, P. (2007). Dancing in the white spaces: Exploring gendered assumptions in successful project managers. *International Journal of Project Management*, 25: 552–59.

7 Project team assumptions alignment

External adaptation

At any point in time, a host of environmental forces are pressing on the organization. To ensure it survives and thrives in the face of this relentless onslaught, the leadership team must come up with the right strategies that will enable the organization to maximize opportunities and minimize the risks.

When deciding priorities and progressing with plans, project leadership will take learning from their broader organizational context on how to get things done, to achieve consensus on how to resolve those problems it faces relating to 'external survival':

- Core vision, mission and benefits to be realized;
- Goals and objectives to work towards;
- The division of labour in terms of expertise and skills sets, in particular of Change Management and Project Management expertise;
- Those methodologies and tools that will best meet the needs of the project;
- Project governance and organizational structure;
- The best approach to project problem solving;
- The best approach to risks identification and management, and issues resolution;
- What to measure and how;
- Tracking progress against plans;
- Appropriate remedial or repair strategies to be used if goals are not met.

Overleaf, Figure 7.1 maps specific cultural assumptions to each of these problems and identifies with an X the optimal cultural assumption for each. Optimal assumptions will facilitate a culture of partnership where Project Managers and Change Managers pool their expertise and skills effectively, to resolve problems relating to external adaptation.

The rest of this chapter is devoted to exploring each of these problems, with operating assumptions for each optimal position presented at the outset in italics.

The end game: Mission, strategy and benefits realization

	X	
Change implemented	Both	Change embedded

Goals and objectives

	X	
Project Management goals	Unified goals	Change Management goals

Means: Division of Project Management and Change Management labour

	X	
Project Managers dominant	Equitable resourcing	Change Managers dominant

Means: Methodologies and tools

	X	
Separate	Semi-integrated	Fused

Means: Project organizational structure

					X
'Head-in-sand'	'Navel-gazing'	'Bolt-on'	'BAU-Buddy'	'Parallel'	'Equal partner'

Problem-solving approach

	X	
Expert leadership	Both	Trial and error

Risks and issues identification and resolution

	X
Can be wholly identified upfront	Emergent in nature
	X
Off-the-record processes	Transparent processes

Agreeing what to measure and how

	X	
Traditional project measures	Both	Change Management measures
		X
Activity focused		Results focused

Tracking progress against plans

	X
Siloed processes	One shared PMO

Correcting course

	X
Absence of remedial action	Effective remedial action

Figure 7.1 PCP cultural assumptions continuum: external adaptation

7.1 The end game: mission, strategy and benefits

Project success is defined as successful implementation and embedding of the change, enabling the realization of business benefits. Organizational vision and mission statements define the purpose of an organization. They lead to strategies, and strategies lead to projects that are designed to deliver required changes to the organization. Any given project will, in turn, have its own 'statement of purpose' that should be aligned with business strategies. How such a statement is written will reflect shared assumptions held about how project success is defined and about the role of Change Management. Consider the following example statement-of-purpose for a global technology project, being rolled out to over 200,000 users: 'Introduce HR SaaS[1] technology to replace existing out-dated tech-nologies and processes.' Here, project success can be claimed with technical implementation alone and by meeting the traditional project success criteria 'on time, on scope, on budget'. With this shared view of how success will be measured, the project team focus is likely to be technology configuration and implementation, with little or no thought for stakeholders and end-users. This statement of purpose reflects the shared assumption of the project organization that it is enough to impose the change on the organization and trust that the rest will take care of itself. That might not be what is intended, but that is what this statement is communicating. Now consider this alternative statement of purpose that would support the optimal position that change is both implemented and embedded: 'Introduce intuitive, HR tools that will make life easier for end-users and achieve benefits realization for the organization.' Here, the end-user has entered into the equation. So too has the benefits the organization hopes to achieve as a result of the change. This project statement-of-purpose reflects a more strategic mind-set and the growing awareness that it is not enough just to implement change and hand it off to the organization on 'completion day'. Change must be implemented and then embedded in everyday practices by taking stakeholders, and end-users in particular, on the change journey. This will ensure that newly introduced technologies and processes are adopted and integrated as the new way of doing things by the organization, so that business benefits are realized.

7.2 Goals and objectives to aim for

Project goals and objectives must embrace both Project Management and Change Management perspectives. Project goals and objectives flow from the project statement-of-purpose. And, as illustrated above, having such a statement in place is no guarantee that it will reflect a rounded approach. Care needs to be taken when crafting goals and objectives to ensure they reflect not only Project Management priorities, but also Change

Management priorities such as 'maximize user adoption' and 'maximize user proficiency'. To focus on one perspective, to the detriment of the other, is a sure recipe for diminished returns.

7.3 Means: division of labour

Project resources need to be allocated equitably so that both Project Management and Change Management expertise and methods are utilized to deliver on the joint value proposition. Resourcing of the core team will vary across the project lifecycle, based on project demands and workforce availability. As demonstrated in Figure 4.3, Change Management provides a distinct service offering that was born of, and makes up for, the short comings of Project Management. An appropriately resourced Change Management team will be positioned to deliver across the project lifecycle. It is a scenario that is far from typical, but is becoming more commonplace.

7.4 Means: project organizational structure

Organizational structure defines how activities such as task allocation, coordination, problem-solving, decision-making and governance are all managed to enable the achievement of project goals and objectives. It determines how different roles and groups interact formally, who gets to participate in which decision-making processes, and to what extent their views shape the organization's actions. The three most common organizational structures are 'functional', 'matrixed' and 'projectized'. In the projectized structure, the Project Manager will always report into the executive sponsor and/or the project Steering Committee, but where the Change Manager reports can be anyone's guess. Where they land will impact a whole host of issues that determine the Change Manager's effectiveness. On any given project, the decision where to position the Change Manager is, in part, based on the assumptions held about the role of Change Management and the value it brings to the project. The decision will also be based on the executive sponsor's understanding of the pros and cons of various structures, and how to harness Change Management and Project Management expertise for a common purpose.

In the absence of a clear solution to the challenge of applying both Project Management and Change Management to any given project – organizations have applied their own approaches and some common trends have emerged. These approaches have different features and varying levels of effectiveness. These are represented in Figure 7.2, starting with the most effective 'Equal Partner' approach, and working down to the 'Head in Sand' approach – the point of diminishing returns. There is only one structure that allows the Change Manager role and status congruity – The 'Equal Partner' approach. All other structures position the Change Manager and team as second fiddle, one way or another.

	Project structure	CM and PM level of integration
1	Equal partner approach	Semi-integration of activities and deliverables to deliver a joint value proposition. Project Manager and Change Manager work interdependently.
2	Parallel approach	Some touchpoints around key milestones, but operate independently for the most part.
3	BAU Buddy approach	Similar to the parallel approach, but any divisions are compounded when Change Management reports into BAU and not into the project organization.
4	Bolt-on approach	Change Management operates separately to the project team, having joined the team in the later stages of the project lifecycle.
5	Navel-gazing approach	Change Management operates in a very limited administrative-type project support role. Very limited use of Change Management tools; main focus on inter-project communications.
6	Head-in-sand approach	Change Management expertise is not utilized for the project.

Figure 7.2 Change Management levels of inclusion on projects

On the following pages, each of these approaches is explored.

The Equal Partner Approach

Project and Change Managers are interdependent partners whose combined expertise can effectively implement and embed change. With this approach, the Change Manager and Project Manager are peers, with the Change Manager a fully fledged partner to the process. There is recognition at an executive level that Change Management makes up for the shortcomings of Project Management (and vice versa) and, together, the combined knowledge and skills will maximize business benefits realization. From the outset, the Change Manager and the Project Manager are inputting their respective expertise into the design and delivery of a solution that will meet the needs of the organization and end-users.

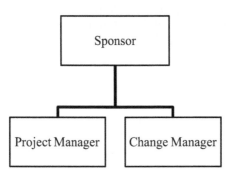

Figure 7.3 The Equal Partner project structure

FEATURES

- *Reporting line*: both the Change Manager and Project Manager report to the sponsor (the Change Manager will have a dotted line into the Project Manager).
- *Alignment*: there is one strategy, one plan and one team.
- *Influence:* both the Change Manager and the Project Manager attend Steering Committee Meetings and shape the strategic conversation and solutions.
- *CM role scope*: most, if not all, of the Change Management service proposition is employed, with Change Management expertise employed for the whole project lifecycle.
- *Inter-team engagement*: in addition to having touch-points around project milestones, there is ongoing engagement and synchronization of activities to support joint execution.
- *Creation of deliverables and execution of activities*: interdependent; the change team draft Change Management deliverables using their subject matter expertise for the input and refinement of the project team (and vice versa).
- *Measures*: success is measured by both Project and Change Management KPIs and measures that are unified as one set.
- *Progress tracking*: one PMO tracks both Project and Change Management deliverables.
- *Resource allocation*: resources are shared equitably between the Project Management and Change Management teams.

ADVANTAGES

This level of partnership will ensure that there is one shared vision, one shared plan and one jointly created set of project success measures. It also sets the scene for the clear division of responsibilities and joint accountability for delivering project benefits. The Change Manager can coach the sponsor and ensure that executives are aligned and supporting the change, while keeping a finger on the pulse of the organization. The project sponsor and broader project governance team benefit from balanced input that considers technical deployment, stakeholder engagement and the end-user experience. With the level of visibility afforded by this structure, the change team is more likely to be properly resourced and utilized than is currently the norm. This structure sets the stage for accelerated teamwork, communication and collaboration throughout the project lifecycle, building mutual respect and a strong team spirit. Synergies are maximized – e.g. collaboration on defining business benefits and end-user impacts. Change Management is subject to the same PMO tracking and measurement processes as Project Management. This helps to bring Change Management into the fold and gain credibility with Project Managers who can sometimes see Change Managers' work as 'unstructured'.

DISADVANTAGES

There will be a cost implication when the Change Management team is properly resourced, but this move will be value adding in the long run as change is not only implemented – but embedded – with business benefits realized. Also, until a culture of partnership between Change Managers and Project Managers becomes the norm, the new power-sharing agreement is likely to cause a few (necessary) headaches as Project Managers adjust to the new world order – short-term pain, long-term gain.

Note: It would be a misconception to suppose that, as a result of this specific organizational structure, sponsors would now have to manage two teams. With any approach or structure, the sponsor is managing both Project Management and Change Management specialists, but one team tends to be managed well while the other is neglected, with the value to be gained left untapped and under-utilized. The integrated approach above merely balances things out so that the Change Management team are brought into the fold. It is the job of the executive sponsor to bring the team together with a shared vision and objectives. This organizational structure will support such efforts.

The Parallel Approach

We'll just focus on our own bit and trust it will all come together in the end. The parallel approach exists where the change team and the project team have their own sets of plans and measures. They operate independently, for the most part, with communication and collaboration tending to centre around key milestones and plans that have gone awry. Perhaps the Change Managers don't understand the project subject matter and prefer to maintain a safe distance. Or maybe the project team doesn't understand the role of the Change Manager/team and, as a result, is marginalizing them. Whatever the reason for the disconnect, the result is poor alignment with project deliverables lacking Change Management input, and vice versa.

Figure 7.4 The Parallel Approach project structure

FEATURES

- *Reporting line*: the Change Manager may report to the Project Manager or a project director.
- *Alignment*: there are two strategies, two plans and two teams.
- *Influence*: the Change Manager does not get to shape the strategic conversations and influence solutions.
- *CM role scope*: how much of the Change Management service proposition is employed will vary greatly.
- *Interteam engagement*: collaboration touch-points are mainly around key milestones.
- *Creation of deliverables and execution of activities*: Change Managers and Project Managers work independently.
- *Measures*: success is likely to be measured by Project Management measures only.
- *Progress tracking*: Change Management may not be subject to PMO tracking and reporting processes.
- *Sharing of resources*: the change team is likely to be considerably less well resourced than the project team.

ADVANTAGES

As with any approach where Change Management is involved from the outset, good headway can be made in terms of securing stakeholder buy-in and maximizing user adoption of new ways of working. Both Project Managers and Change Managers are bringing their own expertise to bear on the project, and the project will benefit to some extent.

DISADVANTAGES

However, as the teams are operating independently, for the most part, this leads to poor communication and teamwork. The Change Manager and Project Manager have different interpretations of project requirements and appropriate solutions, and their own plans. It's a sure recipe for creating a 'them' and 'us' attitude. There is little co-operation evident and opportunities for synergy can be missed – e.g. jointly approaching key stakeholders.

The 'BAU Buddy' approach

Change Management is essentially communications and training, so our BAU colleagues can lead this activity. In this instance, Change Management reports into business-as-usual (BAU), typically to a communications or training team to provide operational level support only to the project. This is because the misconceived assumption held is that Change Management is, in essence, communications and training.

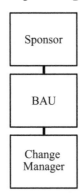

Figure 7.5 The BAU Buddy project structure

The Change Management team may or may not be financed by the project, but they will get their direction from the BAU team. They are not involved in the strategic project design phase and, working to different objectives, they try to work in parallel to the project team, connecting and communicating only sporadically.

FEATURES

- *Reporting line*: the Change Manager reports into a BAU team such as Corporate Communications or Training.
- *Alignment*: as the Change Manager sits outside the project structure, their work is not aligned with the project work.
- *Influence*: the Change Manager has no access to the Sponsor and cannot fulfil some of their key duties.
- *CM role scope*: the Change Manager provides operational level support to the project with Communications/Training providing the strategic input on Change Management.
- *Interteam engagement*: any engagement is limited, centring on Communications and Training deliverables.
- Creation of deliverables and execution of activities: Change Managers and Project Managers carry out their work in silos for the most part.
- *Measures*: 'Change Management' measures of success are likely to focus mostly on communication and training deliverables, rather than genuine Change Management deliverables.
- *Tracking progress*: progress against plans may or may not be tracked by the PMO.
- *Sharing of resources*: with Change Management expertise sitting outside the project, most resources will go to the project team.

ADVANTAGES

Where training and communication interventions play a bit role in the Change Management response, it makes sense to invite these functions to play a strategic role in project delivery. However, a more effective approach would be to invite them as members of the project Steering Committee where they could make a genuine contribution to the conversation, in line with their area of expertise.

DISADVANTAGES

At a strategic level, there is a Change Management skills gap and Change Management expertise does not shape the strategic conversation. The BAU function that is responsible for Change Management activity is likely to focus energies more on their own area of expertise (e.g. strategic communications), rather than the broader Change Management requirement. Project Managers are very unlikely to see Change Managers reporting into BAU as part of the team, creating a 'them' and 'us' mind-set.

The Bolt-on approach

Change management is essentially a sales function. Sometimes, the need for Change Management expertise is recognized post- deployment of the change (e.g. new tools and technologies) and Change Management is invited late to the party, either towards the end of or after deployment. At best, Change Managers will have 'merely' missed out on the opportunity to shape strategies and high-level plans. At worst, they will have been brought on-board after the project team has been disbanded. Reporting into a project representative in BAU, the Change Manager is employed to sell an often ill-conceived change to the business.

Figure 7.6 The Bolt-on project structure

FEATURES

- *Reporting line*: the Change Manager reports into a project representative sitting in BAU.
- *Alignment*: with the project team disbanded, or close to disbanding, there is almost no opportunity for alignment.
- *Influence*: the Change Manager has no strategic influence.
- *CM role scope*: the Change Manager provides operational level support only to secure end-user adoption of the change.
- *Interteam engagement*: there is little engagement among the team.
- *Creation of deliverables and execution of activities*: work is carried out largely independently.
- *Measures*: project measures of success are those traditional project measures 'on scope, on time, on budget', with change measures of success designed separately and at a later date.
- *Tracking progress*: Change Management progress tracking activity sits outside the project PMO.
- *Sharing of resources*: Project Management gobble up much of the resources and the Change Manager could well be a one-man band.

ADVANTAGES

With the need for Change Management identified late in the project, little budget is likely to be available to properly resource the team to meet the needs of the business. It may appear that money has been saved, but it is a false saving.

DISADVANTAGES

This approach lacks the benefit of the broader Change Management service proposition which would influence the design and implementation of the change from a people perspective, guide the sponsor on how best to maintain momentum and overcome resistance, and go beyond 'on-time, on-scope, on-budget' to optimize user adoption, and realize desired business benefits. The buy-in of executive stakeholders and the broader business has not been secured, and sponsorship, where it exists, is ineffective, leading to executive misalignment. The Change Manager lacks first-hand insights into strategic change issues and concerns, and feedback from executive forums may be piecemeal. Having not been involved during the development of the change, the Change Manager misses out on the opportunity to help build momentum for the change in the business. There is no end-user impact analysis to identify how the employee will experience the change, and the end product/solution may not meet the requirements of some or all end-users. There is potential role-scope creep for the Change Manager as the gap between the real need for Change Management expertise becomes apparent. The Change Management specialist often finds him- or herself 'wearing' two or even three 'hats' to try to cover the under-resourcing. The project is very likely to go over 'time', 'budget' and 'spec' due to poor stakeholder engagement and low rates of adoption. The inevitable poor user adoption rates are likely to be blamed on the change team.

The Navel-gazing approach

Change Management is a Project Management support role. Here, the Change Management service offering employment on a project is typically limited to administrative support and change communications, with the Change Manager reporting to the Project Manager. The focus is very much inwards looking, rather than outwards facing towards the broader impacted organization, and the Change Manager serves the needs of the project team. The Change Manager is likely to be early career, or he or she may have a marketing communications background and wish to develop a career in Change Management, and see communications are their route into the profession. Their role and responsibilities will fluctuate with the whims of the Project Manager.

FEATURES

* *Reporting line*: The Change Manager reports to a Project Manager.
* *Alignment*: The Project Managers and the Change Managers are aligned, but in an unhealthy inwards-looking way; the Change Manager provides little, if any, genuine Change Management expertise and input.

Figure 7.7 The Navel-gazing project structure

- *Influence*: The Change Manager is very unlikely to have strategic influence (unless she or he is a consultant and has a broader role than an employee or contractor might have in this post).
- *CM role scope*: The Change Manager provides operational level support only, and may spend a lot of time pulling presentations together to support meetings.
- *Inter-team engagement*: The Change Manager has been absorbed into the project team to support project activities and deliverables.
- *Creation of deliverables and execution of activities*: The Change Manager helps develop and deliver project deliverables rather than create and execute Change Management deliverables.
- *Measures*: Project success is measured by Project Management measures only.
- *Tracking progress:* The Change Manager's deliverables – e.g. communication materials for Project Managers and the steering committee – are not tracked by the PMO.
- *Sharing of resources*: The Change Management practitioners are absorbed into the project team as a Project Management resource.

ADVANTAGES

As this is not a bona fide Change Management role or arrangement, there are no advantages to be had for the business.

DISADVANTAGES

Broader stakeholder needs are neglected as Project Managers are more inclined to focus on the technical aspects of deployment. There is potential role-scope creep for the Change Manager as the gap between the reality for Change Management and what was provisioned for becomes apparent. For the organization, there is poor buy-in for implemented changes and low user adoption rates.

The Head in the Sand approach

Our Project Managers <u>are</u> Change Managers – we're covered. Here, the operation assumption is that Change Management does not add any value over Project Management. This stance may be due to a knowledge deficit; it may be prompted by a lack of funds or it may be due to a disregard for stakeholder and end-user concerns. In some organizations where the culture could be best described as 'command and control', the workforce may be assumed to do as they are told, regardless of how the change might impact individuals, teams and the organization.

ADVANTAGES

Needless to say, there are no advantages to be had from adopting a 'head in the sand' approach, although short-term cost savings achieved as a result of not employing Change Management expertise may seem a plus.

DISADVANTAGES

Medium- to long-term costs are incurred when new ways of working are rejected by stakeholders and end-users who were not engaged in the design process, and vote with their feet. The project is also very likely to run over time, over budget and over specification.

7.5 Means: methodologies and tools

Methodologies

Project Management and Change Management methodologies are semi-integrated to support overall alignment, while operating interdependently so as not to dilute the unique value each brings to the project. Project Management methodologies such as PRINCE2®, PMI® and MSP® typically consist of four to six process groups and a control system that together create a framework. Process groups typically include 'initiating', 'planning', 'executing', 'monitoring' and 'closing'. Mainstream Change Management methodologies have echoed this approach, with Change Management activities typically running in parallel to project activities. The trend now is for integration, and new and emerging methodologies recommend different levels of integration. With PCP methodology, semi-integration is recommended because to go for full integration would be to fuse or meld the two disciplines and lose what is unique and value adding with each. With this semi-integrated approach, Change Managers and Project Managers align their respective frameworks and operate interdependently, cooperating every step of the way.

Tools

Change Management and Project Management have their own toolkits that, for the most part, differ. As illustrated in Part I of this book, Change Management and Project Management employ their own particular theories, models and tools. That said, there is a small degree of crossover, with both disciplines including stakeholder analysis and communications plans in their toolkits (although how Change Managers and Project Managers develop and deploy such plans vary greatly given their respective biases and strengths). Crossover areas represent an opportunity for joint-enterprise. Other tools that sit in the Project Manager space but provide opportunity for joint enterprise include the initial Statement of Work, the Business Case development, Team Resourcing Plans, the Change Project Roadmap, the Project Plan, and those tools that are risks and issues related.

7.6 Approach to problem solving

Expert leadership, coupled with a culture of problem solving via a trial-and-error approach, maximizes adaptability to change. In his book *Adapt*, economist and author Tim Harford sets out a compelling argument on 'trial-and-error' as an alternative to 'expert leadership' for achieving economic success. Citing investigations that prove the transience of great companies and the limited effectiveness of leadership expertise, Harford advocates 'variation', 'selection' and 'survivability' – i.e. to seek out new ideas and try new things, do it on a scale where failure is survivable, seek out feedback and learn from your mistakes as you go along. By way of example, Harford portrays the former Soviet Union as the anti-thesis to this model. Based on expert leadership and uniformity, it demonstrated an abject inability to produce variation and selection, an inability to adapt, and feedback was ruthlessly suppressed. These shortcomings led directly to its ultimate downfall. However, while Harford's research showed leadership expertise to be significantly less effective than one might expect, those organizations that benefited from expert input fared better than those that did not. So it is a reasonable assumption that expert leadership does serve some good purpose, and we should be careful not to dismiss it completely.

7.7 Risks and issues identification and resolution

Risks can be identified in part upfront, but are largely emergent in nature and can be mitigated via information sharing, environmental scanning and collaboration, stakeholder analysis and attunement to the moment. In their research on gendered assumptions held by successful Project Managers, Thomas and Buckle-Henning (2007)[2] found that the masculine way of reasoning is to assume that it is 'appropriate and possible to accurately identify and assess risks at the initial planning stage of the project, and that things would not or should not change'. These researchers found that to masculine reasoning, risks represented a loss of control and a personal affront, and that the masculine logic that raises awareness of risks seems to have a limited repertoire of tools for handling it. Thomas and Buckle-Henning also found that feminine reasoning informs many of the behaviours required to mitigate risks as they occur. These include both listening to gain input from all and talking to raise awareness of risks (information sharing), using one's network to gain line of sight to emerging situations environmental scanning and collaboration), treading lighting when one first gets a foot in the door to understand stakeholders and the pressures leaders are under (stakeholder analysis), and improvising responses in real time (attunement to the moment).

Transparent processes and practices for risks and issues managements will ensure that information gets to the right people and that the right corrective action is taken. In the projects environment, progress against plans is tracked with due consideration to risks and issues that are actively gathered as part of the course for any major Project Management methodology. How risks and issues are managed can change the whole direction of a project for better or worse. Consensus needs to be reached on an appropriate level of visibility and how best to intervene for remedial action.

7.8 Agreeing what to measure and how

Successful change programmes begin with results (Thomson and Schaffer, 1992).[3] In their seminal article in *Harvard Business Review*, Thomson and Schaffer advise that most improvement efforts have as much impact on company performance as a rain dance has on the weather. They presented two alternative approaches to measurement activity, which are based on different underlying assumptions about what to measure – 'activity' or 'results'. Thomson and Schaffer point to organizations' ardent pursuit of activities that sound good, look good and allow managers to feel good, but which in fact contribute little or nothing to bottom-line performance. Features of such projects include no linkage to specific results, delusional measures (measures of activities carried out (e.g. number of training attendees, number of focus groups held) rather than business benefits achieved), large-scale and diffused, and driven by consultants and experts rather than operational teams. The alternative, and optimal, approach is to measure results, focusing on improvement processes that aim to achieve specific, measurable operational improvements where they are most urgently needed and within a short time frame.

The *what* informs the *how*. Well-articulated project benefits can translate into meaningful results-focused measures. These measures can form the basis of meaningful goals and objectives, and key performance indicators that will advise how the project is tracking against targets. Consensus must be reached on what to measure, how to track progress against plans and how to coordinate measurement activity. Where the team is dealing with constraints such as poor quality data, consensus must also be reached on whether it is reasonable to aim for perfection or if 'good enough' is more pragmatic.

A word of caution: external parties such as contractors and consultants tasked with the development of the measurement strategy are advised to get a clear steer from their team leader on the appetite the organization has for measurement. A light touch approach that measures activity could well be more palatable to 'the organization' than a robust measurement plan that focuses on results and benefits realized. Also, and on large projects, other functions may be engaging in measurement activity. Aim to have one measurement plan that is created with the input of anyone who has a role in project-related measurement activity. This will ensure alignment and optimize efficiencies. Avoid the situation where the different teams are developing their own measurement plans, and avoid at all costs the situation where any or all of the teams are carrying out this work in a vacuum with no line of sight to duplication of effort.

7.9 Agreeing how to track progress against plans

Both Project Management and Change Management deliverables are tracked by one Project Management Office (PMO), using key performance indicators (KPIs) that unify Project Management and Change Management priorities as one set. Because of factors such as the maturity level of the Change Management profession, and the disconnect between Project Management and Change Management, industry is in the process of figuring out what exactly Change Management has to offer projects and where it should be positioned. As we saw earlier (see section 7.4), a number of different project team structures have been used to position the Change Manager in relation to the rest of the team. Each has different implications for a number of matters, including how progress against plans is to be tracked. It is not unusual for the tracking of Change Management activities and deliverables to be carried largely in isolation to the tracking of Project Management activities and deliverables. This is not a good approach as it undermines alignment. The recommended approach, tracking progress against plans using one PMO, ensures that Change Management and Project Management are working to one set of shared goals, and that all activities and deliverables are subject to the same degree of rigour as progress against plans is tracked.

7.10 Correcting course

Effective remedial action depends on a good information flow and processes that ensure that any information is acted upon appropriately. While the context of projects will vary very considerably, the essential task of any project is the same – to develop and deliver a solution to a particular business challenge or opportunity that meets the needs of the business and is adopted by end-users. Gathering information on business and end-users' emergent needs and concerns is a critical and ongoing activity. The project team needs to agree how to gather information and in a way that is agreeable to stakeholders if at all possible. If the process is likely to get a stakeholder's back up, then have a rethink. Once information is gathered, it needs to be shared with the right parties, those individuals and teams who can incorporate the feedback. This may involve taking corrective action to the solution design, development or delivery, or it may relate to the broader organization. Where the information gathered identifies a weakness in project processes, consensus needs to be achieved on how to act (e.g. fire the manager, re-examine the approach, prepare lessons learnt, brush failure under the rug, resolve locally to avoid upward escalation or stop work on solution development). Once such action has been taken, new information must be gathered to determine whether results have improved or not.

7.11 Chapter summary

The organization is constantly facing pressures from the external environment. These forces for change can be political, economic, social, environmental and regulatory in nature. To meet the challenge, the organization must achieve consensus around some key areas such as mission and strategy, goals, means, problem-solving approach, risks and issues resolution, measurement and corrective action. The shared understanding reached on each of these critical matters determines the network of shared assumptions that will define how the group gets things done related to these areas on a day-to-day basis.

Optimal assumptions that support a culture of partnership include the following: project success is defined as successful implementation and embedding of the change, enabling the realization of business benefits; project goals and objectives must embrace both Project Management and Change Management perspectives, project resources need to be allocated equitably so that both Project Management and Change Management expertise and methods are utilized to deliver on the joint value proposition, Project Managers and Change Managers are interdependent partners whose combined expertise can effectively implement and embed change; Project Management and Change Management methodologies are semi-integrated to support overall alignment, while operating interdependently so as not to dilute the unique value propositions each brings to the project; Change Management and Project Management have their own toolkits that, for the most part, differ; expert leadership, coupled with a culture of problem solving via a trial-and-error approach, maximizes adaptability to change; transparent processes and practices for risks and issues managements will ensure that information gets to the right people and that the right corrective action is taken; successful change programmes being with results; both Project Management and Change Management deliverables are tracked by one Project Management Office (PMO), using key performance indicators (KPIs) that unify Project Management and Change Management priorities as one set; effective remedial action depends on a good information flow and processes that ensure that any information is acted upon appropriately.

Notes

1 Software as a Solution (SaaS).
2 Thomas and Buckle-Henning.
3 Thomson-Harvey, A. and Schaffer, R. H. (1992) Successful change programs being with results. *Harvard Business Review*, January–February.

Bibliography

Journals

Thomas, J. L. and Buckle-Henning, P. (2007) Dancing in the white spaces: Exploring gendered assumptions in successful project managers. *International Journal of Project Management*, 25, 552–59.

Thomson, Harvey A. and Schaffer, Robert H. (1992) Successful change programs being with results. *Harvard Business Review*, January–February.

8 Project team assumptions alignment

Internal integration

The internal orientated problems that the organization must face in parallel to those externally focused and abstract issues covered in the previous two chapters include:

- Maximizing problem solving approaches;
- Openness to feedback;
- Creating a common language;
- Agreeing conceptual categories;
- Defining group boundaries and criteria for inclusion and exclusion;
- Distributing power and status;
- Developing norms for relationships;
- Allocating rewards and punishments;
- Explaining the unexplainable.

Overleaf, Figure 8.1 maps specific cultural assumptions to these problems and identifies, with an X, the optimal cultural assumption to hold for each. Again, operating to optimal assumptions will facilitate a culture of partnership between Project Managers and Change Managers.

Below, each of these cultural assumptions is explained.

8.1 Maximizing problem-solving capability

We are all equally creative and each of us has an important role to play if overall team problem solving capability is to be maximized. In Chapter 4, we learnt about the Kirton Adaptation Innovation (KAI™) psychometric tool and one of its applications for Change Management (see section 4.3.27). According to extensive research conducted by the KAI™ team, we are all equally creative. Those of us who score as more 'adaptive' on a continuum, as measured by KAI™, approach problems within the given terms of reference and aim for improvements. By contrast, those of us who score as more 'innovative' on the continuum apply more lateral thinking and are liable to produce less expected solutions. The most effective problem-solving teams capitalize on diversity in thinking

Maximizing problem-solving capability

	X
Uniformity	Diversity

Openness to feedback

	X
Closed	Open

Language

	X
Different	Common

Conceptual categories

	X
Different	Common

Group boundaries and identity

	X
Fuzzy	Defined

Distributing power, authority and status

	X
Social processes	Formal and informal processes

Norms for relationships

	X
Unclear	Clear

Allocating rewards and punishment

	X
Random	Systematic and locally sensitive

Explaining the unexplainable

	X
Impossible	Possible

Figure 8.1 PCP cultural assumptions: internal integration

among team members as a strength and successfully deal with a wide range of problems.

8.2 Openness to feedback

Feedback ensures a good line of sight to project risk and issues, allows for moderation of ways to support project goals, and motivates goal attainment. A culture of transparency and openness to feedback maximizes the chance that information will get to the right people and be addressed appropriately. Hiding risk and issues, perhaps for fear of reprisal, can only magnify threats to the project and minimize opportunities. Project management cannot intervene and provide support with problems that they have no line of sight to. Feedback has come to be synonymous with bad news, but feedback can be positive too. We should remember to tell people what they are doing well and be open to feedback ourselves, regardless of our role and status. Empirical research shows that the performance-enhancing effort of setting a specific, high goal is greatly diminished when feedback relative to goal pursuit is not provided (Locke *et al.*, 1968). Feedback is critical to project teams because it provides them with the input they need to moderate their behaviours and processes. But when giving feedback up the project food chain, it is not advised to approach this impromptu. Write down what you want to say to help clarify your thoughts, approach the conversation in a professional manner, and be clear on how the current way of doing things is hampering goal attainment and what might need to change.

8.3 Language

One official project language permits the setting of goals, and interpreting and managing what is going on. When we think about project language, we think about project technical language – for example, the names of different methodologies (e.g. Agile, Waterfall, PRINCE2®), project acronyms, and system-related language. But the greatest confusion in the projects space is not caused by technical language but by general terms and, in particular, the use of the term 'change' in defining roles and expertise. Project Managers are called change managers, Programme Managers are called change managers, and 'Change Control' is called change management. This trend has muddied the field for us all working in the projects space, leading to a lot of confusion about who does what and when. Let's leave the term job title 'Change Manager' for those who are schooled in the discipline of Organizational Change Management (OCM) and bring that particular service proposition to the project.Alternatively, the term 'OCM Manager/Director' is appropriate. If the term 'change' wasn't so desirable to have on the project delivery resumé, mine would be an easy ask, but alas this is not the case. Clear role titles can make a valuable contribution to the development of a common understanding of who is doing what on project teams, while a glossary of terms can help develop a common language.

8.4 Conceptual categories

One official definition for conceptual categories supports the setting of goals, and interpreting and managing what is going on. Different conceptual categories among Project Managers and Change Managers is well documented in research such as that referenced in this book. It has resulted in separated 'Project Management' and 'Change Management' methodologies that have project team members working at cross-purposes with each other.

Building common means and a common language, through one shared 'project delivery' approach, which aligns activities and deliverables across both disciplines, will go a long way to delivering on this. PCP methodology is designed to that end.

8.5 Group boundaries and identity

Team boundaries and identity are clearly defined so the team can direct their energies towards delivering. For a group to function and develop, one of the most important areas for clear consensus is the perception of who is in the group, and who is not in the group (Schein, 2010). Mechanisms for clarifying group boundaries include physical means such as organizational structure, job titles and job descriptions, uniforms, language, communication rules, and rules on who is part of the team and who is not. It's very hard for the Change Management professional to understand that their place is on the team if they report outside the project governance are brought on long after others were, are not subject to PMO tracking and measurement, and are subject to creeping job scope. Earlier, we learnt what the optimal structure for a project team looks like. This structure will go a long way to building effective group boundaries and identity. Too often, it is the case that the change team is an afterthought, bolted on late in the project lifecycle. This has a negative impact on their integration into the project team and limits their voice in key decision-making processes. Earlier, we also learnt about the importance of having a common language and conceptual categories, and considered some key ones that can cause confusion in the change projects context. Developing a common language is another important mechanism for establishing group identity.

8.6 Distributing power, authority and status

Power, authority and status on our project team are determined by formal and informal processes, and not by social processes. Formal processes include seniority and job title, informal processes include knowledge, skills and talents, while social processes include family background, education, relationships and financial wealth. The beauty of formal and informal processes is that they are non-discriminatory, protect the project organization from any claims of discrimination, and support good inter-team relationships. Social processes for conferring power, authority and status are discriminatory; they expose the project organization to discrimination claims and create bad feeling on teams. It would seem like an easy call to make, but the class system and snob factor of the local culture will determine how much social processes are used.

8.7 Developing rules for relationships

Getting along with team members is important and it is reliant on a shared sense of how to behave with one another. From the very first day on the job, the new recruit is picking up cues on those rules that inform the functioning of the team they will join – how they address each other, what they wear, what they share about their personal lives, and how open or reserved they should be. Understanding these cues helps the new recruit understand their new team and moderate their behaviour in a way that is conducive to relationship building. Developing that insight into the team will be a challenge for remote team members who work in different time zones and are reliant on video-conference calling.

8.8 Allocating rewards and punishment

Sanctions for obeying or disobeying our cultural norms and rules need to ring true and be evident to the project team, with rewards and punishments appropriate to local cultures. Every project team has its own system for reinforcing desirable attitudes and behaviour, and punishing those that are not. This system is informed by the culture of the organization and by the values of the founding members of the project team. It guides team members on how to get things done on a day-to-day basis. To be effective, the system for allocating rewards and punishment must be aligned both formally and informally. We are all guilty of rewarding the wrong behaviours and punishing the desirable ones, be it in our personal lives or our work lives. Take the case of a global deployment where a culture of hiding risks and issues prevailed. In weekly meetings, the sponsor would often plead with project team members to raise risks and issues, promising 'not to get mad'. However, when a serious risk was raised the old blame game kicked in; those who created the problem were protected, while those who raised the alarm were punished. Such 'moments of truth' make bare to the project team what leadership is really made of and what they truly value, reinforcing the risk-adverse culture. Project teams are increasingly global and virtual. When designing a reward system, be aware that what works in one culture will not work in another, but that across all cultures people like to be thanked and have their work appreciated. No budget is required for a senior leader to simply thank an individual or team on internal social media, but such displays of praise can go a long way to motivate the ranks.

8.9 Explaining the unexplainable

Stories and myths can help explain the unexplainable. Project Managers and Change Managers have different appetites for dealing with issues that are not under their control. For the Project Managers, it is often *all about control* and any deviations from the plan are a problem. Change Managers, however, are drawn to their profession because of an interest in the dynamics of change and in helping people with the transition. They understand and even expect issues and events to occur at the organizational, team and individual level that might not be on the radar. That said, when things happen that we don't understand, every one of us can feel some level of alarm and feel threatened, and look around for explanations. According to Schein (2010), societies and organizations can turn to religion, superstition; stories and myths can help explain the unexplainable and provide reassurance. Our challenge, however, in the temporary project organization, is that corporate stories and myths may not have had much opportunity to take root, so the team will need to take some reference from stories and myths relating to their host organization. Stories and myths that will help the project team explain the unexplainable will centre around how crises were dealt with, and also how 'moments of truth' are dealt with, as these will demonstrate to the workforce what leaders value. When the unexpected occurs, employees will be able to take reference from how leaders behaved in the past.

8.10 Chapter summary

To gel as a group, project team members need to resolve issues relating to how they internally integrate. Cultural assumptions that will support them with this and help them to create a culture of partnership include the following: we are all equally creative and each of us has an important role to play if overall team problem-solving capability is to be maximized; feedback ensures a good line of sight to project risk and issues, allows for moderation of ways to support project goals and motivates goal attainment; one official project language permits the setting of goals, and interpreting and managing what is going on; one official definition for conceptual categories supports the setting of goals, and interpreting and managing what is going on; team boundaries and identity are clearly defined so the team can direct their energies towards delivering; power, authority and status on our project team are determined by formal and informal processes, and not by social processes; getting along with team members is important and it is reliant on a shared sense of how to behave with one another; sanctions for obeying or disobeying our cultural norms and rules need to ring true and be evident to the project team, with rewards and punishments appropriate to local cultures; stories and myths can help explain the unexplainable.

Bibliography

Book

Schein, E. (2010) *Organizational Culture and Leadership*. San Francisco, CA: The Jossey-Bass Business & Management Series.

Journal

Locke, E., Cartledge, N. and Keoppel, J. (1968) Motivational effects of knowledge of results: A goal setting phenomenon. *Psychological Bulletin*, 70: 474–85.

Section B

Above the surface

9 Partnership across every dimension and phase

Alignment and cooperation across every dimension of project operations will enable the Change Management and Project Management joint proposition to add value and raise those project success rates.

In this chapter, each of the six PCP project phases is taken in turn to demonstrate the integration of Project Management and Change Management across project lifecycle, team structure, culture, benefits and measures, expertise, activities, work packages and tools. This approach maximizes synergies while retaining the unique value that each discipline offers.

Both within the project and across the organization, culture alignment is achieved through the use of primary and secondary culture embedding mechanisms. Internally, the team will be working to embed a PCP methodology defined 'culture of partnership', while project planning will allow for a Culture Adjustment Plan to support end-users with the required shift in the organizational culture.

With PCP methodology, some project activities and work packages are owned and led by the Change Manager ('CM owned'), while others are owned by the Project Manager ('PM owned'). The remainder are owned by the Project Manager and Change Manager ('jointly owned') and, on occasion, by the project sponsor too ('Change Triad owned'). Where joint ownership exists, an activity leader is identified according to the expertise and authorities required for successful delivery. Because many project teams typically don't understand how to apply Change Management theories, models and tools to their projects, the relevant section/s of the Change Management Typology (Figure 4.4) is given for each work package, together with the relevant section in Chapter 4. This will enable both practitioner and reader to easily locate and apply Change Management, models and tools to their own projects. For example, Activity 1.01 on p. 157 is Change Triad owned/sponsor led, and the CM Typology reference numbers are 20 and 23, which relates to the topics of 'Change Leadership' (see section 4.3.20) and 'Change Roles' (see section 4.3.23). Also, because the Change Management profession is at an earlier stage of maturity to the Project Management profession,

Change Management activities and work packages are explained in more detail where deemed necessary. Where activities are repeated in subsequent phases, this is indicated to save duplication of activity descriptions.

9.1 Phase 1: Discover

Every project starts somewhere. It may be triggered by external events, such as the entry of a new competitor to the market, or by internal events such as industrial action. When a trigger for change presents itself, the commissioning agency (executive management or a programme management team) will communicate it, either verbally or in writing, thereby articulating the mandate for change. But before committing the organization and resources to a project to deliver on that mandate, it is important to determine if a real business challenge or opportunity exists, and if a project would be a worthwhile endeavour. It is also important to lay the foundations of project operations so that they are based on cultural assumptions that will promote an effective Project Management and Change Management partnership.

Success in the initial 'Discover' phase will be measured by:

- Clear determination as to whether or not there is a viable business challenge or opportunity that needs to be addressed;
- Development of a credible plan for Phase 2, which will see formal project kick off.

1.01 Establish the Change Triad
1.02 Develop project approach, outline business case and project brief
1.03 Develop change delivery roadmap
1.04 Develop Phase 1 Plan
1.05 Phase 1 stakeholder planning
1.06 Develop project charter
1.07 Develop team cultural assumptions and team protocols
1.08 Design, resource and align project team
1.09 Design, resource and align project governance boards
1.10 Assess organization change management maturity
1.11 Develop Phase 2 Plan
1.12 Gateway 1 review board meeting
1.13 Gateway 1 Steering Committee meeting
1.14 Review team performance and cultural assumptions
1.15 Wrap up Phase 1

Figure 9.1 PCP methodology: Phase 1 activities and work packages

Activity 1.01 **Establish the change triad**

Activity owner and leader	Output or deliverable	CM typology	
		Reference	Theories, models and tools
Change Triad owned/ sponsor led	1.01.01 Sponsorship and management model confirmed 1.01.02 Roles and responsibilities, structure and reporting lines agreed 1.01.03 Project Manager and Change Manager appointed	20 24	Section 4.3.20 Section 4.3.24

1.01.01 Sponsor management model confirmed

The project mandate should identify a potential sponsor. To get the wheels turning, the commissioning agency can confirm who is taking up this role. Once recruited, the sponsor will decide on their project management model. The 'Change Triad' model below recognizes the interdependency between Project Management and Change Management. It sets the foundation stone for a culture of partnership between these two bodies of work and lightens the workload of the sponsor. The Change Triad is based on a set of features and cultural assumptions that position the trio for success.

Figure 9.2 The Change Triad

Features

- The sponsor as overall project lead and owner sits at the top of the project hierarchy.
- The Change Manager and Project Manager with their different, but interdependent, expertise work together as partners and peers to ensure a balanced approach to execution; the Change Manager and Project Manager work on behalf of the sponsor, carrying the load of day-to-day activity.
- The Project Triad is supported by project governance committees that represent the business.

Cultural assumptions

- Project Management and Change Management are separate, but interdependent, disciplines that together can both implement and embed change.
- Project Management and Change Management epistemic cultures fundamentally differ, attracting those with different, but complementary, talents and interests that are needed by the project.
- The Project Manager and Change Manager develop the plan, lead the team to deliver the plan, and work with stakeholders to integrate diverse perspectives.
- Neither masculine nor feminine reasoning are inherently superior to the other.
- Male and female roles are not bound by stereotypes that are harmful to both, but to women in particular.

The Project Manager, Change Manager and sponsor responsible for upholding this model. Once the broader team is established, this management model must be communicated and documented, together with these requirements and cultural assumptions, so that the people do not apply their own conflicting interpretations.

1.01.02 Roles and responsibilities, structure and reporting lines agreed

Roles and responsibilities

The project sponsor will also familiarize him- or herself with the roles and responsibilities of the sponsor (see section 4.3.20), Project Manager and Change Manager (see section 4.3.23). Change Manager job descriptions (JDs) tend to be very poorly written, for a host of reasons not worth getting into here, but a well-written Change Manager JD, which is aligned with PCP philosophy, will clearly articulate:

- *The role* – To drive adoption and embedding of the change in the organization;
- *The Project Management model* – The Change Triad positions the Change Manager for success by giving him or her a platform for delivery;
- *Methodology* – for example, PCP methodology as a stand-alone, or to augment other methodologies;
- *Current project phase* – The earlier the Change Manager is recruited in the project lifecycle, the more effective he or she will be and the more successful the project will be;
- *Responsibilities* – Outlines the work packages and activities the Change Manager is expected to deliver, together with those that they are expected to jointly deliver with the Project Manager and/or the project sponsor;
- *Key knowledge and skills* – Outlines what the Change Manager is expected to know and be able to do, and what expertise they will need to recruit into their team;
- *Team size* – Resourcing should adequately reflect the business requirement. Too often, the size of the Change Management team is wholly inadequate to the remit of the team and results in role-scope creep as realities emerge;
- *Budget* – Funding for Change Management activities. This should come from the overall project budget and not the Project Management team element of the project budget.

Structure and reporting lines

In Chapter 7, we considered the common reporting organizational structures that projects use for Project Managers and Change Managers, together with the pros and cons of each approach. The 'Equal Partner' structure (see Figure 7.3) captures the recommended structure and reporting lines, and is aligned with the Change Triad model.

Later in Phase 1, the governance committees will be established – the strategically focused Steering Committee which will report to the Sponsor, and a Gateway Review Board which will report to the Steering Committee (see Activity 1.09 'Design, Resource and Align Governance Boards'). Both the Project Manager and the Change Manager *may* have a dotted line into the Steering Committee, but not a direct reporting line. This is to protect them from being potentially leaned on to facilitate individual committee members' agendas, at the expense of the broader project and organizational interests. One or more committee members may be chosen by the sponsor because they are resistant to the project, and not because they are supporters, in an attempt to bring them onboard with the change. For this and other reasons, neither the Project Manager nor the Change Manager will report to the Gateway Review

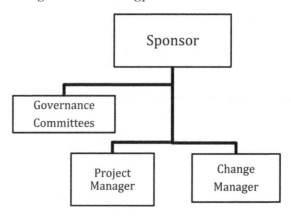

Figure 9.3 Project Management and governance structure

Board. That said, both governance committees are key stakeholders of the Project Triad.

1.01.03 Project Manager and Change Manager appointed

A distinguishing role of executive leaders is to develop and nurture their organizational culture to meet evolving business needs. That includes the internal projects environment. Projects are temporary organizations and face the same organizational challenges of adapting to their external environment and integrating internally. Change leaders and project sponsors need to set expectations at the outset on how Project Management and Change Management requirements, in particular, are to be resourced, and how the two disciplines will work together for a common purpose.

All the pieces are now in place for the sponsor to recruit the Project Manager and Change Manager. It may be that the Project Manager is recruited first, and then made party to the recruitment of the Change Manager (or vice versa) to ensure that these two key roles are a good fit in terms of chemistry, technical and interpersonal profiles. Alternatively, it may be that a recruitment activity is designed so that Project Manager and Change Manager candidates have to work together to develop a work package and present their joint product to the Sponsor and other recruiters. Whichever approach is taken, it should not happen that the Project Manager is excluded from the recruitment of the Change Manager (or vice versa) as this could create a bad situation that was not the making of the last recruit in. Too often, at this crucial stage, Change Management is seen through the lens of the Project Management discipline. A seasoned Change Manager will be able to influence discussions so that Change Management is woven throughout the complete project lifecycle, with the Change Manager and team positioned for success. Lessons learnt have shown that it makes sense for the same Project Manager to see the end-to-end cycle through. The same goes for the Change Manager role. Change Managers need to learn to walk away from roles where they are recruited too late in the lifecycle to ensure that business benefits are achieved, where they don't have the responsibility, authority and autonomy to deliver, or where Change Management is seen as 'a bit of Communications and Training'. At the very least, Change Managers need to go in with their eyes open and be very clear about what they can, and cannot, deliver.

Throughout the project, the sponsor will be responsible for ensuring that both Project Management and Change Management insights are heard and that a 'two-legged', or balanced, approach is taken to project execution. The sponsor has an important role in setting the tone and facilitating a culture of partnership from the top-down.

Activity 1.02 **Develop the project approach, outline business case and project brief**

Activity owner and leader	Output or deliverable	CM typology	
		Reference	Theories, models and tools
Jointly owned/ PM led	1.02.01 Initial project inputs 1.02.02 Project approach 1.02.03 Outline business case 1.02.04 Project brief	4, 5, 7, 14	Section 4.3.4 Section 4.3.5 Section 4.3.7 Section 4.3.14

1.02.01 Initial project inputs

To develop a robust preliminary view of why a solution (and project) is required by the organization, the Change Triad needs to gather information to help answer the following:

- *Change drivers* – What is the particular challenge the organization is facing? What is driving this challenge?
- *Change scope, scale and level* – What is the scope of the change? What is the scale of the change? What is the level of the change?
- *Change journey* – What does the current state look like? What might the high-level desired future state look like? What is the gap between desired future state and current state?
- *Solutions* – What are the possible options?
- *Business benefits* – What likely benefits are to be derived by different solutions? Ownership for benefits and measures identification sits with the Change Triad.
- *Timeline* – What are the likely start and end dates?

- *Stakeholders and concerns* – Who are the key stakeholders and what are their interests and concerns?
- *Project scope* – What is likely to be in and out of project scope?

The Change Manager can help shape the strategic conversation using Change Management theories, models and tools such as those shared in Chapter 4.

1.02.02 Project approach

Before commencing any planning activity, fundamental questions will also need to be answered concerning how the work of the project will be approached:

- Is the solution to be developed new or a modification of something existing in the business?
- Will the solution be developed internally or by external suppliers?
- Will the solution be a standard market product or unique?
- If it's an out-of-the-box solution, will be it possible to configure and customize it based on organizational requirements?

1.02.03 Outline business case

The purpose of this document is to establish whether a real business challenge exists that requires more in-depth consideration. The level of detail required will reflect the early project stage and required expenditure. At the very least, the outline business case should include an executive summary, vision and goals, the business challenge/opportunity and expected business benefits, change drivers, the scale, scope and levels of change involved, and critical success factors.

1.02.04 Project Brief

The Project Approach and outline business case will inform the development of the Project Brief. This document will give form to the project mandate and can include other items such as known stakeholders, the

Activity 1.03 **Develop Change Project Roadmap**

Activity owner and leader	Output or deliverable	CM typology	
		Reference	Theories, models and tools
Jointly owned/ PM led	1.03.01 Change Project Roadmap	13	Section 4.3.13

project management and governance models, role descriptions, constraints, risks, assumptions, issues, dependencies and tolerances.

The Change Triad will next design and develop their overall roadmap for completing Phase 1.

1.03.01 Change Project Roadmap

The 'Project Roadmap' used by Project Managers presents, using graphics and images, the high-level view of the project's goals, milestones and work packages for each work stream and against a timeline. It is a useful communication tool when engaging with senior stakeholder and setting expectations. The Change Manager's 'Change Roadmap' serves a different purpose, highlighting a series of steps to be followed that, in modern times, might be better construed as critical success factors (CSFs). Here, it is recommended that the Project Manager and Change Manager work together to come up with one Change Project Roadmap that follows the Project Management approach and incorporates Change Management 'swim lanes' for component parts such as 'Assessments', 'Change Advocates Network', 'Stakeholder Management', 'Training', 'Communications' and 'Change Adoption'.

Activity 1.04 **Develop Phase 1 Plan**

Activity owner and leader	Output or deliverable	CM typology	
		Reference	Theories, models and tools
Jointly owned/ PM led	1.04.01 Lessons learnt reviewed 1.04.02 Phase 1 Plan	N/A	N/A

1.04.01 Lessons learnt reviewed

Before getting to work on developing the Phase 1 Plan, ask whether the organization attempted this type of change before and, if so, what documentation exists in relation to it. What lessons have been learnt, and how can these be incorporated into strategies and plans?

1.04.02 Develop Phase 1 'Discover' Plan

The Phase 1 Plan is a presentation that is informed by the Change Project Roadmap, adding a new layer of detail focusing on Phase 1 specifically to describe the overall approach and detailing work packages, work package owners and leaders, resources required, and costs for both Project Management and Change Management. It will be supported by a basic Project Schedule that outlines those tasks required to deliver work packages together with expected durations, start and end dates (developing this schedule will be a discrete work package in Phase 2). Based on the size of the challenge facing the organization, the scale, scope and complexity of the project, and how educated the sponsor and Project Manager are about Change Management, the Change Manager will need to recommend, and possibly defend, essential Change Management work.

Activity 1.05 **Phase 1 Stakeholder Planning**

Activity owner and leader	Output or deliverable	CM typology	
		Reference	Theories, models and tools
Jointly owned/ CM led	1.05.01 Phase 1 Stakeholder Map 1.05.02 Phase 1 Stakeholder Analysis and Prioritization	16	Section 4.3.16

During Phase 1, when the project is just an idea being scoped and not yet approved to proceed, project stakeholders will be confined to a few key executives and decision makers. Between them, the Change Triad and members of their leadership team will be able to manage these Tier 1 stakeholders, and priority objectives will be to build relationships and solicit early thoughts on stakeholders' 'future state requirements'. However, once the project is confirmed, it will be critical that the Change Triad develops a strategic view of *all* stakeholders, and their likely interests, across *all* project lifecycle phases – not just the current phase. This will ensure that they have an end-to-end view of how stakeholders might behave over time and, critically, how events might unfold. As the Project Management team will be focused on building the solution, it makes sense for the Change Management team to lead on this.

Project stakeholders can be divided into four tiers who are engaged at different times of the project lifecycle:

Phase 1

- *Tier 1 stakeholders* are senior executives and are engaged at the outset.

Phase 2

- *Tier 2 stakeholders* are subject-matter experts and others who will provide input to help shape the solution to meet business.

Phase 3
- *Tier 3 stakeholders* are implementation partners who will develop plans to drive up adoption of the solution in the business post 'Go Live'.

Phase 4
- *Tier 4 stakeholders* are end-users, typically managers and employees and external third parties, who will need help and support before and after the rollout of change.

Phases 5 and 6
- Once the change is rolled out, Tiers 3 and 4 stakeholders will be engaged to a much greater extent than other stakeholders.

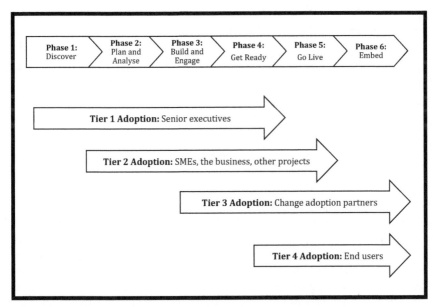

Figure 9.4 PCP methodology: the four levels of change adoption

For now, the project requirements are for a Phase 1 Stakeholder Map and for Phase 1 Stakeholder Analysis and Prioritizing.

1.05.01 Phase 1 Stakeholder Map

Using the guidance shared in Chapter 3 (see section 3.2.9), a draft Stakeholder Map can be developed. Mind-mapping tools can help one categorize and create different levels of detail where groups and sub-groups of stakeholders exist.

1.05.02 Phase 1 Stakeholder analysis and prioritizing

Once the Stakeholder Map is completed, stakeholders can be profiled in terms of agreed criteria – e.g. 'power', 'interest' and plotted on a Stakeholder Matrix relative to each other. This will crystallize for the Change Triad what their stakeholder engagement priorities are and where their focus needs to be.

While stakeholder engagement will evolve naturally during the early days, basic foundations are now in place to build a draft stakeholder management strategy and plan once the project is approved to proceed. With Phase 2 kick off, more planning will typically need to go into stakeholder identification and management, and that work is detailed in Activity 2.10. However, if the nature of a particular project requires more upfront planning than would be typical, Activity 2.10 can be executed earlier.

Activity 1.06 **Develop Project Charter**

Activity owner and leader	Output or deliverable	CM typology	
		Reference	Theories, models and tools
Jointly owned/ PM led	1.06.01 Project Charter	N/A	N/A

1.06.01 Project Charter

Developing a Project Charter to summarize the project team purpose is standard practice in the Project Management space (see section 3.2.8). It is not standard practice, however, for the Change Manager to input to the Project Charter. This needs to change. A jointly developed Project Charter sets the tone at the outset that this is a joint effort and makes transparent Change Management resources, deliverables etc. that will be of interest to key stakeholders and project team members. In Chapter 3, a template is shared that Project Managers and Change Managers can jointly use, and adapt, if required for their own projects (see Figure 3.8).

Activity 1.07 **Develop Team Cultural Assumptions and Team Protocols**

Activity owner and leader	Output or deliverable	CM typology	
		Reference	Theories, models and tools
CM owned and led	1.07.01 Team cultural assumptions agreed 1.07.02 Protocols agreed	21	Section 4.3.21

1.07.01 Team cultural assumptions agreed

Project team cultural assumptions define the shared mind-set that informs how the project team gets things done. Chapters 5–8 of this book detail, in considerable depth, those assumptions that are typically held by project teams and those that are conducive to a culture of partnership between Project Management and Change Management. These can be grouped, and documented, according to three categories (as illustrated in Chapter 2):

1 Cultural assumptions about 'macro issues' (Figure 2.2).
2 Cultural assumptions about 'external adaptation' (Figure 2.3).
3 Cultural assumptions about 'internal integration' (Figure 2.4).

As project team cultural assumptions inform attitudes and behaviours during day-to-day operations, they need to be agreed upon by the Change Triad up-front to ensure alignment, before any sharing with the broader team.

1.07.02 Project Team protocols agreed

Decisions will need to be made about how to get things done on a day-to-day basis – e.g. how will the team make decisions and what regular meetings will be held? Decisions made will define 'Team Protocols'. These can often reflect team cultural assumptions, so it is very important that the Change Manager checks for alignment between draft protocols and cultural assumptions agreed by the Change Triad, before any broader sharing of protocols with the project team.

Activity 1.08 **Design, Resource and Align Project Team**

Activity owner and leader	Output or deliverable	CM typology	
		Reference	Theories, models and tools
Jointly owned/ PM and sponsor led	1.08.01 Team number and budget 1.08.02 Resourced project team 1.08.03 Aligned project team	23	Section 4.3.23

1.08.01 Team number and budget

As Phase 1 progresses, the project team will expand beyond the Change Triad as additional knowledge and skills are required. This will mark an ongoing process of team expansion and contraction as project needs vary from phase to phase. The Change Manager's budget should be ring-fenced from the project Manager's budget, so that it does not fall foul to poor planning outside the control of the Change Management team – e.g. when a Project Manager 'forgets' to allocate financial resources to a particular activity that falls under their remit and raids the Change Management kitty to make up the difference.'

1.08.02 Resourced Phase 1 Project Team

The Change Triad will need a team who can execute Phase 1 activities. They will work together to develop a view of team resourcing requirements, required budget and whether individual roles will exist for a particular phase or be carried through other lifecycle phases. Most candidates will be recruited internally, unless there is a particular skill shortage that drives the recruitment process outside.

During 'Discover' phase, project team members are likely to work part-time on the project only, and hold other responsibilities, either in day-to-day operations or outside the organization.

1.08.03 Aligned Project Team

For Phase 1, the project team will be small, so a formal team kick-off event might be overkill. Self-study materials on the project and informal discussions can be a good alternative. Be approachable and encourage dialogue on project documentation to date, and in particular the Team Cultural Assumptions and Protocols. To ensure that the team are aligned on an ongoing basis, set up weekly meetings (face-to-face where possible) and make attendance mandatory. Discourage those who have to use conferencing facilities to dial in from multi-tasking, as attendees need to pay attention to important project developments and updates. During project team meetings use a standard dashboard-type reporting template (with 'Objectives', 'Activities', 'Progress' and 'Risks and Issues') for both Project Management and Change Management.

Activity 1.09 **Design, resource and align Project Governance Boards**

Activity owner and leader	Output or deliverable	CM typology	
		Reference	Theories, models and tools
PM owned and led	1.09.01 Resourced Steering Committee 1.09.02 Resourced Gateway Review Board 1.09.03 Aligned Governance Committees	N/A	N/A

In Activity 1.01.01, the project governance structure was outlined. Now, the two committees need to be resourced to reflect representation from all parts of the business being affected by the change.

1.09.01 Resourced Steering Committee

As the Phase 1 project team is being recruited, the Steering Committee needs to be resourced too. The role of the Steering Committee is first and foremost to ensure that the project outputs address the challenge faced by the organization, meeting the requirements of business stake-holders. Other responsibilities that support this overall objective include the following:

- Help Project Managers and Change Managers balance conflicting priorities and resources.
- Review project progress and provide guidance on project outputs.
- Consider ideas and issues raised when making decisions.
- Advocate and champion the project in the business, sharing project progress and achievements, and remove obstacles.
- Advise the Project Manager and Change Manager on strategic developments that will, or may, impact project plans.
- Check that the project is incorporating best practices and lessons learnt, from both within the organization and drawing from the external environment also.

As mentioned earlier, the project sponsor and chair of the Steering Committee will ideally be a leader in the external customer-facing organization, and understand the benefits and impacts of the proposed change on end-users, particular frontline workers. Steering Committee members will include leaders from both the customer-facing functions and support functions. Once membership has been agreed, get to work on defining those processes that will inform how this governance body will operate, by considering review and approval, risk escalation, project resourcing and funding. While the Steering Committee will meet frequently in later phases of the project, it may be that for now they meet just once to agree roles and responsibilities, and again for the gateway review process.

1.09.02 Resourced Gateway Review Board

In addition to the Steering Committee, a Gateway Review Board will be established to 1) make decisions on project deliverables (work packages) as presented for review at the gateway at the end of each project phase, and 2) make recommendations on project readiness to enter the next phase in the project lifecycle. The Gateway Review Board will consist of subject-matter experts and others with technical and other skills that can ensure informed decision-making. The Project Manager will work with the Steering Committee to clarify the Gateway Review Board role, responsibilities, expectations and time commitments.

1.09.03 Aligned governance committees

Once the governance boards are resourced, the Project Manager will disseminate the document to all members of the governance process to ensure alignment. Also, circulate the documents describing the Project Management model, Team Cultural Assumptions and Team Protocols.

Activity 1.10 **Assess Organizational Change Management Maturity**

Activity owner and leader	Output or deliverable	CM typology	
		Reference	Theories, models and tools
CM owned and led	1.10.01 Organizational Change Management Maturity assessed.	17	Section 4.2.17

1.10.01 Organizational Change Management Maturity assessed

During the recruitment process, a seasoned Change Manager will have prompted discussion within the Change Triad on Change Management maturity (CMM). They will have discussed how well the organization is currently utilizing Change Management tools and practices across projects, programmes and portfolios, as this will impact every facet of Change Management activity during the project. Now, a formal assessment can be carried out to gather facts to add substance to any initial impressions. The actual level of CMM will give the Project Triad some insight into the level of challenge they face incorporating Change Management into their approach to execution.

Activity 1.11 **Develop Phase 2 Plan**

Activity owner and leader	Output or deliverable	CM typology	
		Reference	Theories, models and tools
Jointly owned/ PM led	1.11.01 Phase 2 Plan	N/A	N/A

1.11.01 Phase 2 Plan

Towards the end of each phase of the project lifecycle, a plan for the following phase needs to be prepared for governance committees to review and approve. The Phase 2 Plan will require more effort than the Phase 1 Plan, and will need to be approached in a structured and thoughtful manner. The Phase 2 Plan will be informed by the Change Project Roadmap and developed in the same way as the Phase 1 Plan (Activity 1.04). Governance committee members will want to see a high-level view of topics that will be the subject of work packages and activity during Phase 2 – namely, Change Management related plans, benefits and measures management, risk management, quality management, and possibly configuration management and procurement management.

Activity 1.12 **Gateway 1 Review Board Meeting**

Activity owner and leader	Output or deliverable	CM typology	
		Reference	Theories, models and tools
Jointly owned/ PM led	1.12.01 Project team gateway readiness determined 1.12.02 Gateway 1 documentation assembled 1.12.03 Gateway 1 meeting logistics 1.12.04 Gateway 1 meeting pack 1.12.05 Board recommendation secured and documented	N/A	N/A

1.12.01 Project Team gateway readiness determined

Before the team can even think about planning for a phase gateway session, they must ensure that they are prepared as well as possible to best facilitate a 'Go' decision. This will help guard against rework and any related 'loss of face'. When the team is considering their readiness for a Gateway Review Board decision, the following questions can serve as useful discussion points:

* *Business case* – Have we clearly determined if there is a viable business case or do we need more information? Are the business benefits, and the achievement of them, realistic?
* *Stakeholders* – Did we engage with the right stakeholders and did we engage them appropriately? Do they understand the rationale for investment?

- *Risks and issues* – Did we appropriately identify and mitigate risks and issues?
- *Project governance* – Have we clearly established Terms of Reference and the right roles and responsibilities to steer project delivery? Can we demonstrate a culture of partnership between Project Management and Change Management?
- *Data and sources* – Is all of our data reliable? Are our sources credible and was our approach objective?
- *Readiness for the next phase* – Have we developed a clear and robust Phase 2 Plan that will provide governance committees with a good sense of Phase 2 objectives, work packages and activities? Have we established a Change Management function that will be accountable for the alignment of all organizational change activities, and working with business partners, to drive adoption of the capability offered by the project?

1.12.02 Gateway 1 documentation assembled

The Gateway 1 Documentation is a collation of project documentation that provides a foundation for Gateway Review Board decision-making. Inputs to this collation for Phase 1 will include the Project Approach, Project Brief, Change Project Roadmap, Phase 1 Plan, Project Roles and Governance and the updated outline Business Case.

1.12.03 Gateway 1 meeting logistics

Once the project team feels ready for a Phase 1 Gateway decision, the Project Manager will organize the meeting logistics and book attendees' diaries, giving plenty of advance notice for senior executives. Meeting logistics will include scheduling information, the agenda, materials and possibly dress code. Participants will include Gateway Review Board members, the Project Manager and the Change Manager. For this meeting, key roles will include:

- *Presenters*: Both the Project Manager and Change Manager are likely to be presenters; in fact, it is a great opportunity to show a united front. Both should be freed up to focus on representing their respective areas of expertise appropriately during Gateway sessions.
- *A designated facilitator* can ensure that key thoughts and ideas are periodically checked for understanding, any points of contention are captured and the meeting maintains momentum instead of getting bogged down in details irrelevant to the phase decision.
- *A timekeeper* can ensure that the session keeps to the agreed time.
- *A minute-taker* can ensure that key points, outstanding issues and decisions are captured appropriately.

1.12.04 Gateway 1 meeting pack

Before any governance committee meeting, a pre-read package will be circulated to attendees. This should be clearly marked main meeting material and supplementary pre-read material. Contents should include the following:

1 A summary note detailing the meeting logistics and objective/s.
2 The collation of Gateway 1 documents mentioned in Activity 1.12.03.
3 Recommendations on any outstanding scope-related issues.
4 The Phase 2 Plan, including the Change Triad Management Model and the PCP cultural assumptions.
5 An estimation of costs for the whole project.

The pack should be circulated by the Project Manager no less than five days before the gateway meeting, so participants have sufficient time to review the material. This window also allows the Change Triad time to deal with, offline, any queries or concerns the individual governance committee members may have.

Conduct a dry-run session with the project team to practise presenting those materials, identifying potential challenges, issues or concerns that the Project Review Board might pose, and agreeing the best responses.

1.12.05 Board recommendation secured and documented

During the Gateway Review Board Meeting, the Project Manager can lead discussion around the business case and project scope, with the Change Manager leading on organizational change and culture. Members will challenge whether a viable project exists, so have the answers to the questions below ready:

- Does the business case stand, or has it been eroded by developments in the business and marketplace?
- Has all the phase work been executed effectively? Is any rework required? Is it designed to ensure project delivery benefits from both Project Management and Change Management expertise?
- Do we have the right plan and resources in place for the next phase?
- Do we have alignment on the scope/purpose/objectives for the next phase of work?
- Is funding available for the whole project?

According to Cooper and Edgett (2012), during each phase gateway meeting, the Gateways Review Board will recommend one of the following:

1 *Go* – The business case looks strong enough for the project to proceed.
2 *Rework* – We are not sure if an opportunity worth pursuing exists. The project team needs to provide us with more information, or better information, before we can make a decision.
3 *Hold* – We need to temporarily suspend the project until we have resolved some other issues that are external to the project.
4 *Kill* – The business case is not strong enough for us to proceed.

Once the recommendation is made and the session concludes, the project team should debrief and document recommendations and any outstanding items.

Activity 1.13 **Gateway 1 Steering Committee Meeting (SCM)**

Activity owner and leader	Output or deliverable	CM typology	
		Reference	Theories, models and tools
Sponsor owned and led	1.13.01 Gateway 1 SCM logistics 1.13.02 Gateway 1 SCM meeting pack 1.13.03 Steering Committee decision secured and documented 1.13.04 Decision and next steps communicated	N/A	N/A

1.13.01 Gateway 1 SCM logistics

The Steering Committee will meet after the Project Gateway Session to consider the recommendation put forward and make the final decision.
    Logistics will be organized as per Activity 1.12.03. A basic agenda would include:

- Confirmation of minutes from the previous meeting;
- Review of the status of action items from previous meetings;
- Overall project status report on the status by the Project Manager and Change Manager;
- Discussion of any additional documents that need to be considered (e.g. Gateway Review Board recommendations and rationale);
- Discussion of any other business (AOB) that was not on the agenda and needs attention;
- Confirmation of logistics for the next meeting.

1.13.02 Gateway 1 SCM meeting package

The pre-read and presentation pack will be organized as per Activity 1.12.04, with the recommendation of the Gateway Review Board being the most important package input.

1.13.03 Steering Committee decision secured and documented

Having reviewed the recommendation put forward by the Gateway Review Board, together with any supporting evidence, the Steering Committee will make their decision on if and how the project should proceed. Where they are confirming successful completion of the current phase and a 'proceed' decision, they will also have to confirm the detail of Phase 2 Plan.

Once the Gateway 1 Steering Committee Meeting concludes, the team should debrief, documenting the decision made and any outstanding items.

1.13.04 Decision and next steps communicated

The decision made by the Steering Committee will determine next steps for the project team:

- *Go* – If the team is given the green light, the team should celebrate before getting to work on Phase 2.
- *Rework* – Have a more compelling business case prepared either by the original team, an expanded team which now includes some newly identified missing expertise, or a completely new team which will adopt a new approach to Phase 1 planning and execution.
- *Hold* – The action for the project team in this scenario is to wind up activities and ensure all documentation is stored properly and is easily accessible for future reference.
- *Kill* – A decision to terminate the project should only be made because the Business Case is not strong enough to proceed. When the decision is made to kill a project, the action for the team is to wind down all activities.

Whatever the judgement, stakeholders will need to be informed of the decision and the rationale. The Project Triad can decide among themselves who will inform individual stakeholders and stakeholder groups. As it is early days for the project, only those who have been involved and who will be impacted by the decision need to be informed.

Activity 1.14 **Team performance and cultural assumptions reviewed**

Activity owner and leader	Output or deliverable	CM typology	
		Reference	Theories, models and tools
PM owned and led	1.14.01 Team performance reviewed 1.14.02 Cultural assumptions realigned	21	Section 4.3.21

1.14.01 Team performance reviewed

During Phase 1, project team members will have had the opportunity to apply their knowledge and skills, and demonstrate what they bring to the project. Consolidate observations and share them with the team appropriately so that they can either continue to do what they are doing, or make some necessary adjustments to priorities and ways of working.

1.14.02 Cultural assumptions realigned

Cultural assumptions that promote a culture of partnership between Project Management and Change Management are at the heart of PCP methodology. 'Phase wrap-up' serves as an opportune checkpoint for reviewing team performance during the phase and revisiting operating cultural assumptions to ensure alignment with desired ones. Relate the learning from any performance-related issues to specific shared attitudes and behaviours, identify where the team might be out of sync with the agreed team cultural assumptions, and also where alignment or realignment is required. Focus on pain points and any incidences of conflict. Listen to what people have to say and use the discussion as an opportunity to build buy-in for a culture of partnership. Make sure team members understand what is expected of them collectively and individually. Reward and recognize a job well done to motivate the team and build momentum.

Activity 1.15 **Wrap-up: Phase 1**

Activity owner and leader	Output or deliverable	CM typology	
		Reference	Theories, models and tools
PM owned and led	1.15.01 Outstanding actions closed out 1.15.02 Lessons learnt documented	N/A	N/A

1.15.01 Outstanding actions closed out

At this point, outstanding actions must be closed out and anything that can impact the execution of the next phase must be documented and addressed.

1.15.02 Lessons learnt documented

Ensure that all lessons learned from Phase 1 been documented for easy application in the next phase/s. Don't forget to include any lessons learnt about team–operating culture assumptions versus the desired ones, and any realignment behaviours agreed.

9.2 Phase 2: Plan and Analyse

In Phase 2, the project needs to convince the governance committees that various solutions have been rigorously assessed and evaluated, and that the recommended solution is the right choice for the business.

2.01 Kick off Phase 2
2.02 Resource and align core project team
2.03 Develop project schedule
2.04 Develop viable solution options
2.05 Develop User Impact Analysis (UIA)
2.06 Complete user impacts disposition forms
2.07 Conduct user impact disposition workshop/s
2.08 Conduct organizational impact assessment
2.09 Identify recommended solution
2.10 Develop Change Management strategy and high-level plan
2.11 Project stakeholder planning
2.12 Develop technical plans
2.13 Secure steering committee approvals
2.14 Conduct 'Think Aloud' sessions and develop end-user profiles
2.15 Develop culture adjustment plan
2.16 Develop communications plan and initial collateral
2.17 Develop training plan
2.18 Develop change advocates network plan
2.19 Develop Phase 3 Plan
2.20 Gateway 2 review board meeting
2.21 Gateway 2 steering committee meeting
2.22 Review team performance and cultural assumptions
2.23 Wrap up Phase 2

Figure 9.5 PCP Methodology: Phase 2 activities and work packages

Resistance can strengthen during this phase, as the reality of organizational impacts and resource requirements become apparent. To fend against the risk of the project getting shelved, be prudent with project team resourcing costs, manage Phase 2 stakeholders carefully and develop credible plans that convince the governance committees.

Success for the 'Plan and Analyse' phase will be measured by:

- The establishment of the project organization, and the recruitment of both Project Management and Change Managment specialists.
- Thorough assessment of all viable solution options, and the recommendation of a business preferred solution that meets agreed evaluation criteria.

Activity 2.01 **Kick off Phase 2**

Activity owner and leader	Output or deliverable	CM typology	
		Reference	Theories, models and tools
PM owned and led	2.01.01 Phase 1 lessons learnt applied 2.01.02 Phase 2 plan finalized 2.01.03 Iterative documents updated	N/A	N/A

2.01.01 Phase 1 lessons learnt applied

In the previous phase, lessons learnt were documented during the wrap-up (Activity 1.15.01). Lessons are, in fact, only learnt when they are applied to real-life situations, to hopefully get a better result, so kick off Phase 2 by dusting off that document of insights and observations, and identify how Phase 1 learning can be applied in Phase 2.

2.01.02 Phase 2 Plan finalized

During the Gateway Review Board Meeting and the subsequent Steering Committee Meeting, feedback will have been given on the Phase 2 Plan. Finalize the plan now, incorporating this feedback as appropriate, and sharing it with the project team.

2.01.03 Iterative documents updated

While iterative documents should be reviewed and updated on an ongoing basis as required, it isn't always the case as project team members can be very busy elsewhere. Therefore, phase start-up is a good time to ensure that this work has been carried out. The input of the Gateway Review Board and the Steering Committee will still be fresh, and this activity now provides a link in the minds of the project team between the previous phase and the current phase. Iterative documents developed thus far will include:

- *The Business Case* – Did the recommendations of the Phase 1 Gateway session or subsequently the Steering Committee Meeting justify any change in the Business Case?
- *The Change Project Roadmap* – Have any changes been made to the overall project timeline, key milestones and work packages? If so, update the Project Roadmap accordingly.
- *The Project Brief* – Have any changes been made to how the project will be approached?
- *The Stakeholder Map and Stakeholder Analysis Document* – Have any new stakeholders been identified that are in need of profiling and documenting, or do any need to be removed from the picture?

Activity 2.02 **Resource and align core project team**

Activity owner and leader	Output or deliverable	CM typology	
		Reference	Theories, models and tools
Jointly owned and led	2.02.01 Project team resourced 2.02.02 Project team culture assessment 2.02.03 Project team aligned 2.02.04 Guidance on leading an international team	12 21	Section 4.3.12 Section 4.3.21

2.02.01 Project team resourced

Resourcing of the broader team can now commence. Individual roles may be recruited to deliver specific work packages for this current phase, or they may be recruited with the expectation that they will form part of the core team for subsequent phases also. Ideally, roles should be recruited for as and when the need presents itself so that no one is under-employed. An adequately resourced team allows individual team members to specialize according to their expertise, while a very lean team will need to juggle more and perhaps even stretch into areas where their expertise is limited or even non-existent.

The size of the Change Management team and how the workload is shared will depend very much on the size of the target stakeholder population, in particular the end-user population, and whether the project is adopting a 'big bang' or 'staggered', approach to rollout (see Chapter 4, section 4.3.12). These two factors will largely influence the size of the workload at a given point in time.

Prevailing (current) culture	
Structured	*Unstructured*
• Interview business leaders • Small focus groups • Questionnaires/ surveys* * Note: care needs to be taken distinguishing attitudes from underlying assumptions.	• *Desk research* (e.g. review language and tone used in internal memos, emails, speeches, social media, etc.; review organizational structure; review formal and informal networks, local context and national culture; evidence of diversity – or a lack of it; stories – who are the heroes and the villains?) • *Observation in the workplace* (in the office, at meetings, presentations, workshops), when socializing with colleagues, consider structures and layouts. • *Chat with workers*, particularly long-timers and new recruits.

Figure 9.6 Prevailing culture assessment: tools and techniques

2.02.02 *Project team culture assessment*

With the project team recruited, the Change Manager can now conduct a culture assessment to set a baseline on those assumptions this new project team holds. Some example methodologies for data collation activities are shared above. Completed assessment outputs can be used to identify team strengths and weaknesses in terms of creating a culture of partnership and areas for development.

For help assessing the culture of your project team using the new and innovative PCP Culture Assessment Tool, contact: gabrielle.o.donovan @icloud.com.

2.02.03 *Project team aligned*

Once the core project team has been recruited, bring them all together for a team-building event to ensure alignment.
   Logistics for a kick-off session will include:

- *Schedule* – Date of meeting, time, venue and equipment;
- *Agenda* – Topics to be covered and in what sequence (e.g. project background, roles and responsibilities, core values, team protocols, group dynamics, cultural assumptions and acculturation strategy;
- *Materials* – Project background and team information, project team culture assessment results, PCP Team Cultural Assumptions, Team Protocols;
- *Dress code* – formal or informal;
- *Participants* – All project team members and project sponsor;
- *Roles* – Key roles – e.g. presenter, facilitator, timekeeper, minute-taker.

During the workshop the Change Manager can lead on culture alignment activities:

- *Group dynamics:* Explain that teams go through four phases of development ('forming', 'storming', 'norming' and 'performing'). Acknowledge that a storming period will ensue as team members are new to each other and currently have different ways of doing things. Encourage the team to embrace the learning in such episodes, and reinforce 'One Team, One Vision'.
- *Cultural assumptions:* Share the results of the project team culture assessment conducted before the workshop, soliciting feedback and practical examples on areas of strength and areas to develop as they relate to the workplace. Share the draft PCP Team Cultural Assumptions and, to build buy-in, show how the Change Triad Project Management model and other processes and leader activities support these. Get the team to use that input to come up with an action plan for their own development areas. The PCP Team Cultural Assumptions will give them a language for challenging 'off-piste' attitudes and behaviours that conflict with the PCP Team Cultural Assumptions.
- *Protocols:* Socialize the team with the draft Team Protocols and finalize these with team input.
- *Acculturation:* The PCP methodology recommended strategy for Project Management and Change Management 'acculturation' (see Chapter 4, section 4.3.21) is *integration*. Where Project Managers and Change Managers express a preference in one of the other approaches below to acculturation, the following can be put to them:

  - *Assimilation* of one culture by the other would be to undermine the value and expertise the less dominant culture brings to the project.
  - *Separation*, or working in parallel, will undermine communication and opportunities for synergies.
  - *Deculturation* – working with no regard for each other's way of doing things – would make it very difficult to get anything done, especially as these two disciplines of Project Management and Change Management are mutually interdependent.

When this team-building activity is conducted effectively, it helps shorten the team 'storming phase', and speed up the 'norming phase' of team development, allowing the project team to focus on 'performing' and delivery. It also provides the team with a common language and common frame of reference for discussing culture, attitudes and behaviours. When team culture alignment is not a part of the team-building agenda, or when it is executed poorly, the project team can get stuck in that cycle of conflict that defines the early team 'storming' phase.

2.02.04 Guidance on leading an international team

For global deployments, the team is likely to be spread out across different time zones and if it is not, then perhaps it should. A centralized team based in head office suggests an inward-looking perspective that may not be appreciated in other jurisdictions. Guidance on leading an international team is as follows:

- *Time zones* – Be respectful of each other's time zones and demonstrate this when scheduling meetings.
- *Connectivity and collaboration* – Keep connected with conference-calling technologies and online collaboration tools.
- *Language* – A glossary of terms is a useful tool for explaining project terminology and abbreviations in particular.
- *Culture and social norms* – Get the team to challenge 'off-piste' attitudes and behaviours, and hold each other accountable for living up to agreed standards.
- *Holidays* – Public holidays will vary by location, so it is a good idea to have a shared calendar that captures all local holidays and factor these into plans. For example, a global deployment scheduled for January might prove problematic; December is largely a write-off in the UK and Ireland due to Christmas vacations and, even if you do corral the team to work and deploy pre-launch communications and training activities, there may be few end-users around to notice.
- *Teamwork* – To facilitate teamwork and team spirit, everyone should have their own deliverables plus those that they jointly deliver with those team members who they are co-located with.
- *The coalface of implementation* – Pre-deployment, the coalface of the programme, is where the project team is based. This will be a hub of activity where employees, contractors and consultants set to work. Team members who are operating in that space will have a very different experience from those operating remotely in different time zones who will be out of touch. For this reason, the Change Manager must be physically positioned with the project team.
- *Check assumptions* – Don't assume that remote teams have the tools and support they need to do their job. Check.

Activity 2.03 **Develop project schedule**

Activity owner and leader	Output or deliverable	CM typology	
		Reference	**Theories, models and tools**
Jointly owned/ PM led	2.03.01 Project schedule	N/A	N/A

During this 'Plan and Analyse' phase, the project team will be busy organizing their workload and resources – deciding what will be delivered, by whom, when and how – and organizing their inputs and outputs via the now established project/programme management office (PMO).

2.03.01 Project schedule

To commence Project Schedule development, gather the team together to create a first draft, using project-planning software, based on the chosen methodology/methodologies. Encourage all to contribute their best guess on work package activities, deliverables and timescales based on their own roles and responsibilities. This type of calibration encourages a joined-up view of the plan and joint ownership for its ongoing upkeep. By using Project Management tools and techniques, Change Managers will be speaking Project Manager's language, and have specific deliverables and milestones that tally with their own. Project Managers can complement this effort by embracing a holistic approach to Project Management that incorporates the end-user experience and adoption by the business of the solution. Store the draft Project Schedule in a shared online folder so that team members can update those items they own regularly as further project detail emerges. Then, revisit the Project Schedule together on a weekly basis to check progress with activities against agreed dates.

Activity 2.04 **Develop viable solution options**

Activity owner and leader	Output or deliverable	CM typology	
		Reference	Theories, models and tools
PM owned and led	2.04.01 Viable options identified 2.04.02 Viable options assessed 2.04.03 Testing process and preferred solution identified 2.04.04 Options documented	N/A	N/A

The work of collating high-level future state requirements (Activity 1.05) will continue into Phase 2. This output will inform the generation and assessment of potential solutions for the consideration of the governance committees. During discussions, business executives often have a view on possible solutions, or even their preferred solution. Don't commit to any one solution yet. A thorough analysis of the options will determine which solutions are viable, and which will best meet the needs of organization.

2.04.01 Viable options identified

The first task here is to brainstorm with the team and come up with a range of solutions. Then, weed out those that would not comply with company policies and standards (in particular those relating to procurement and vendor selection) to come up with a shortlist.

2.04.02 Viable options assessed

Next, focus on the three strongest options and refine them. What this process looks like will vary according to the nature of the project.

2.04.03 Testing process and recommended solution identified

Develop a rigorous testing process, so as to inspire the confidence of key stakeholders and governance committees in the recommended solution that will eventually be put forward. Again, the nature of the project will determine what the testing process looks like.

2.04.04 Options documented

Once the options are tested and refined, they need to be documented. This will be added to once the outputs of the next three activities are available, before being finalized for the Gateway Review Board.

Activity 2.05 **Develop User Impact Analysis (UIA)**

Activity owner and leader	Output or deliverable	CM typology	
		Reference	Theories, models and tools
Jointly owned/ CM led	2.05.01 User Impact Analysis	15	4.3.15

2.05.01 User Impact Analysis

Now it is time to start thinking about what the future state will look like for different users in the business, how people will be impacted by the change and how this information can be best captured so as to inform Change Management plans. While this activity is led by the Change Manager, it is recommended that it is jointly owned with the Project Manager to help ensure that solution configuration work does not override support for the identification of user impacts.

The User Impact Analysis (UIA) is a document that captures those user impacts that a particular project solution will create. Where the solution has different packages offering different functionality (e.g. software solutions for different capabilities/processes), there will be a UIA for each process, and a Change Lead and Project Lead should be appointed to each process.

Key categories of information on a UIA are as follows:

- *Project name* – e.g. 'Internal Recruit Onboarding' process;
- *Current state* – A description of a particular current state process (e.g. the new recruits pre-day one onboarding experience is conducted offline. The new recruit receives prescribed reading in the post and can either fax or email to HR confirmation of their start date);
- *Future state* – A description of the same process in future state (e.g. new recruits will log into new system pre-day one to access, read prescribed documents, acknowledge with electronic signature, confirm their start date and update their personal information. System credentials will be emailed to them by HR and to their personal email address);
- *Summary impact* – A description of how the delta between current and future state will affect the user (e.g. new recruits will move from offline to online processes);
- *Date* – The date when the change will kick in (e.g. deployment date);
- *Rating* – The weight of the rating (e.g. High, Medium, Low) based on agreed criteria. Alternatively, the symbol + can denote a positive impact, the symbol − can denote a negative impact and the symbol = can denote a neutral impact;
- *User group* – The specific user group that will be affected (e.g. internal recruits who will have experienced the previous onboarding process during previous recruitment processes);
- *Population size* – The number of people who will be impacted;
- *Region/country* – The geographical location of the impacted users (e.g. USA).

As user impacts emerge over time, the UIA spreadsheet could well extend down to 100+ lines. So while it may be tempting to dream up more categories and add more columns, it is best to keep the design of the UIA simple so that it is digestible for readers.

In principle, developing a robust UIA is straightforward enough, but in practice it can be anything but, as a host of issues can get in the way:

- *SMEs input is a critical dependency* for producing a quality UIA. Where your project is just one of a number of global projects being implemented, there can be a battle for SMEs time. Where the SME workload is ring-fenced to ensure that they are not overburdened and putting critical deliverables at risk, this can make it very difficult to secure the required input and deliver the UIA to the required standard.

- *No sight of the prototype solution*: For a technology deployment that involves the development of prototypes, the team will not have seen the product and it will be hard for them to imagine user impacts. They may look to upcoming 'Prototype1' (P1) workshops where they have first sight of the prototype tenant as the 'holy grail' that will answer all their questions about user impacts (alas, it won't). During P1 sessions it will become apparent that configuration and bug squashing is to take precedent, while post-P1 workshops, hundreds of scripts will need to be processed and prioritized.
- *Line of sight*: While the team will have a line of sight on what the future state will look like through the solution development processes, they may have little or no sight on current state processes, particularly where these vary by region and country.
- *Identifying user impacts proves to be a 'dark art'*: many Project Leads will be more comfortable with system configuration type work and try to wriggle out of this work.
- *Turnover on the project team*: Team members who were trained on UIA development can be replaced by new recruits who do not have the same training.
- *Other priorities*: During a global rollout, everything can seem important and, where the Project Manager is having difficulty prioritizing, UIA development might be pushed down the list.
- *Additional BAU activities* such as an unexpected internal audit will see resources redirected to support this work, putting the UIA on the backseat.

While it is important to give SMEs and Project Leads a bit of slack during the early stages of the project, and particularly before any solution development sessions, it is important to separate out genuine lack of sight of user impacts from lack of understanding or interest in what a user impact looks like. Good contracting upfront between the Project Triad and good risk mitigation planning can ensure that none of these issues emerge. For a project lasting eighteen months, with UIAs updates every two months, there will be nine iteration of each UIA, and UIA-related activities will be repeated throughout the following project phases to build up a clear picture.

Activity 2.06 **Complete Impact Disposition Forms**

Activity owner and leader	Output or deliverable	CM typology	
		Reference	Theories, models and tools
CM owned and led	2.06.01 Completed Impact Disposition Form/s (for each solution module)	15	Section 4.3.15

2.06.01 Completed Impact Disposition Form/s (for each solution module)

At agreed points in time, the Change Manager will submit their updated UIA/s to the Change Triad and, after each submission, the Change Manager will take the UIA output and use it as input to complete an Impacts Disposition Form. On this form, the Change Manager will identify high-level messages and/or skills that end-users will need, specific interventions recommended (e.g. communications, training), and appropriate delivery channels.

Impacts Disposition Form – Internal Recruit Onboarding UIA1							
Impact	*User group*	*Country/ region*	*Size of population*	*Rating*	*Message*	*Intervention type*	*Channel*

Figure 9.7 Template: Impacts Disposition Form

During upcoming Impacts Disposition Workshops, the Change Leads will use their UIAs and completed Impacts Disposition Forms to report to the Change Management team on their findings and recommendations, and calibrate to agree on specific Change Management interventions. This next level of output will inform official stakeholder engagement, communications and training plans respectively so that they have a sound basis.

Activity 2.07 **Conduct User Impact Disposition workshops**

Activity owner and leader	Output or deliverable	CM typology	
		Reference	**Theories, models and tools**
CM owned and led	2.07.01 Workshop logistics and agenda 2.07.02 Workshop/s delivered 2.07.03 Vetted and validated Change Management interventions (version 1) 2.07.04 Follow up	15	Section 4.3.15

2.07.01 *Workshop logistics and agenda*

Impacts Disposition Workshops are an opportunity to calibrate on user impacts across different processes and geographies and agree as a team on key messages, interventions and delivery channels.

Workshop logistics:

- *Scheduling* – Date of meeting, time, venue and equipment required;
- *Agenda* – UIA topics to be covered and in what sequence;
- *Materials* – A completed Impact Disposition Form for each UIA, and the latest version of each UIA;
- *Structure* – Presentations scheduled so as to balance the workload among the team;
- *Participants* – The Change Management team and the Project Manager; individual Project Leads and SMEs can be invited to slots relevant to them;
- *Roles* – Presenters, experts and question-takers, facilitator, timekeeper and minute-taker.

Like any group session, good forward planning of your Impacts Disposition workshops sets the right tone and reaps the best results. Below are some pointers.

Pre-workshops

- *Involve the team* in Impacts Disposition Form design and give them the opportunity to practise filling in the form, and giving and receiving peer feedback.
- *Give the team a clear brief* that has been agreed with any senior stakeholders who might be invited. For example, one presentation approach would be to get into user impacts on a very granular level, ask probing questions and then collectively consider Change Management interventions, while another approach would be to focus on recommended communications, training and engagement interventions with the detail on user impacts being a secondary focus. The first approach allows the team to 'get under the skin' of user impacts and jointly design the response, while the second approach allows the Change Lead to drive the discussion and solution. Whatever is deemed the best approach, do stick to it so that expectations are clear and individual Change Leads are aligned in their approach and set up for success. Any sudden change of tack can be disconcerting for the next presenter in line, particularly for early UIA iterations where the picture is still emerging.

2.07.02 *Workshop/s delivered*

During workshops:

- *Stick to the brief* and stay on track with the agreed approach unless the group agrees otherwise.
- *Accept that the presenter is closest to latest developments and hot-off-the-press items.* If such an item is shared and is counter to what is currently understood, accept that it is a new development with further detail to emerge. Do not challenge the presenter in front of their peers as this will undermine both the individual and team dynamics, and create anxiety among the team regarding their own presentations.
- *Acknowledge the critical dependency between the UIA and the Impacts Disposition Form.* If a particular UIA is in great shape with clearly articulated user impacts, the Change Lead will be able to play that back to their team and speak with confidence. If it is not, then quite simply they can't reasonably be expected to.
- *Adopt 'Chatter House Rules'* – Nothing said during the workshops should be repeated outside the workshop forum and particularly as the workshop is in session (e.g. using instant messenger to secretly inform a Project Lead that the UIA for their workstream has been found to lack the required level of visibility of user impacts), as this could negatively impact relationships and hinder future cooperation between a Change Lead and their Project Lead partner for a particular UIA. Formal processes should be used to communicate messages appropriately and in a timely manner, after the workshop session.

2.07.03 *Vetted and validated Change Management interventions (version 1)*

The main output of each Impacts Disposition Workshop will be a set of interventions that have been vetted and validated by the team. With each UIA iteration, a further level of detail will be added.

2.07.04 *Follow-up*

The Impacts Disposition Workshops add obvious value to the Change Management team as they serve to inform their plans. However, for senior management and sponsors, the process has added value in that the visibility to user impacts afforded by the sessions can serve as an early warning system if little progress is made between different iterations of the UIA, and project knowledge is not what it should be at any given point in time. In this regard, Impact Disposition Workshops act as mini-toll-gates.

Should a UIA be found to be below par, the issue can be escalated to the programme sponsor for resolution. An effective sponsor will ensure that road-blocks are removed and that the Change Manager has access to SME input and other tools.

Activity 2.08 **Conduct high-level Organizational Impacts assessment**

Activity owner and leader	Output or deliverable	CM typology	
		Reference	Theories, models and tools
Jointly owned/ CM led.	2.08.01 High level organizational impacts identified	15	Section 4.3.15

Before the project team can recommend a particular solution, they must have a line of sight into organizational and end-user impacts associated with each solution. Developing this line of sight will be the work of the Change Manager.

2.08.01 High-level Organizational Impacts identified

An Organizational Impact Assessment highlights, from different perspectives, how the organization will be impacted. Categories to be used can be shaped by tools such as McKinsey's 7-S Model, e.g.:

- *Strategy* – Is the solution in focus aligned with strategy? Does any particular strategy – e.g. the Workplace Digital Strategy need to be updated to reflect alignment with the solution?
- *Structure* – Will the change impact the organizational structure? If so, how?
- *Systems* – Will everyday workflows such as resource allocation, reward, measurement change, and if so, how?
- *Shared values* – Is the solution in focus in line with the core beliefs and guiding concepts and aspirations of an organization?
- *Style* – How will the solution in focus impact key workforce groups – e.g. line managers?
- *Staff* – Will the solution in focus suit the workforce profile (e.g. knowledge workers versus blue collar workers)?
- *Skills* – Will the solution require new competencies and capabilities?

The output of the High Level Organizational Impacts Assessment will inform final solution selection, as will the output of the UIA sessions.

Activity 2.09 **Identify recommended solution**

Activity owner and leader	Output or deliverable	CM typology	
		Reference	Theories, models and tools
PM owned and led	2.09.01 Evaluation criteria confirmed 2.09.02 High level requirements prioritized 2.09.03 Recommend solution identified	14	Section 4.3.14

2.09.01 Evaluation criteria confirmed

Once the project team has tested viable options, they will need to identify a solution that can be recommended to the Gateway Review Board. It is essential that standard evaluation criteria is used to assess options, so that a 'like-for-like' comparison is made. Evaluation criteria may include solution functionality, organizational impact, end-user impact, ease of implementation, speed of implementation, resources required to implement, expertise required, costs and future cost savings.

2.09.02 High-level requirements prioritized

High-level requirements gathered previously from stakeholders will need to be consolidated and prioritized to help identify the solution that will meet the needs of the organization. Is the top priority to plan for the future and increase organizational capability, reduce costs, or implement the solution as soon as possible to meet immediate needs (see section 4.3.14)?

Stakeholder requirements and expectations can vary greatly and need to be managed and balanced against the greater good. For example, for the building of Dublin Airport 'Terminal 2', budget airline Ryanair had a strong preference for a basic design solution that some stakeholders equated with a 'cattle shed'. The preferred terminal design solution was somewhat more sophisticated, leading an irate Michael O'Leary to complain to the media that Dublin Airport Authority (DAA) was building 'the Taj Mahal'. The project team led by DAA Director Mark Foley stuck to their guns and the recommended design option that best met the needs of the country won out. According to an article in the

Irish Independent newspaper, it would be found to be one of the most important pieces of infrastructure ever developed by the state ('Michael O'Leary Dubbed it the "Taj Mahal"', *Irish Independent*).

2.09.03 Recommend solution identified

Next, evaluate each of the solutions in terms of those requirements gathered to identify the best solution.

Activity 2.10 **Develop Change Management Strategy and High Level Plan**

Activity owner and leader	Output or deliverable	CM typology	
		Reference	Theories, models and tools
CM owned and led	2.10.01 Change Strategy and High Level Plan	Various	Sections 4.3.1 – 4.3.28

2.10.01 Change Management Strategy and High Level Plan

The Change Management Strategy and High Level Plan outlines the approach to making organizational change stick and answers:

- *Stakeholder engagement*: When and how will senior executives and decision makers, department/division heads, subject matter expert, super users, business change adoption leads, change champions and end-users be engaged?
- *Culture adjustment*: What shift in the culture does the preferred solution require? Is it transitional or transformational? How will it be managed?
- *Organizational alignment*: What policies and processes need to change to support workplace adoption of new attitudes and behaviours?
- *Readiness*: How will we assess and ensure readiness?
- *Change adoption*: What networks and embedding mechanisms will be used to drive up local adoption of the change?
- *Communication:* When will user impacts be known and available to inform the Communications Plan? What initial communications collateral needs to be developed? Which end-user languages need to be catered for and what translation work needs to be budgeted for?

- *Training*: What is the likely demand to be and how will it be met?
- *Managing resistance to change*: What strategies and tactics will be used to deal with resistance to change?
- *CMM:* What was the result of the Organizational Change Management maturity assessment? What actions need to be taken to mitigate any related risks?

Once the Change Management Strategy and High Level Plan are approved by the Steering Committee, the team will be able to progress with related deliverables.

Activity 2.11 **Project stakeholder planning**

Activity owner and leader	Output or deliverable	CM typology	
		Reference	Theories, models and tools
CM owned and led	2.11.01 Stakeholder workshop logistics 2.11.02 Workshop pre- read pack 2.11.03 Workshop delivery 2.11.04 Project stakeholder map and analysis 2.11.05 Project Stakeholder Governance Plan 2.11.06 Phase 2 Stakeholder Engagement Plan/s 2.11.07 Follow-up coaching sessions	N/A	N/A

In Phase 1, the focus for stakeholder management was on planning for managing senior executive stakeholders and their concerns. In Phase 2, the stakeholder engagement net will expand to include Tier 2 stakeholders such as SMEs, department heads and other functional or divisional leaders who are not currently in the loop but whose contribution is required to shape the solution.

Identifying and profiling stakeholders is very much a team activity for large and complex programmes. No one executive will have the full picture on the stakeholder challenge, and you want to avoid the situation where the project is mid-cycle and critical stakeholders and issues emerge out of the woodwork and blind-side you. A workshop attended by either Steering Committee members only, or both governance boards, is recommended.

2.11.01 Stakeholder workshop logistics and planning

This can be a challenging workshop to facilitate and upfront planning is very important. Organize the logistics first and foremost, and agree them with the sponsor:

- *Scheduling* – Date of workshop, time, venue and equipment required.
- *Agenda* – e.g. Introduction, Develop Project Stakeholder Map, Conduct Stakeholder Analysis and Prioritization, Develop Phase 1 Stakeholder Engagement Plans, Wrap-up.
- *Materials* – Stakeholder Map template, Stakeholder Matrix template, Stakeholder Engagement Plan template.
- *Inputs and outputs* – What, if any, preparation is required and what outputs or deliverables are expected as a result of the workshop?
- *Structure* – Formal or informal (this will inform attire to be worn).
- *Participants* – project governance committee members.
- *Roles* – facilitator, timekeeper and a minutes-taker.

The Change Manager should learn as much as possible about stakeholders upfront, and have prepared some useful questions that can move the discussion along. Also, as the project sponsor may be the most senior person in the room and prone to dominating discussions, plan ahead and contract with the sponsor upfront to prevent this happening.

2.11.02 Workshop pre-read pack

Pre-read materials disseminated before any type of meeting or workshop will give attendees the opportunity to understand what is expected of them, and can help them prepare in advance. It can also save any time being lost, during meeting or workshop delivery, should individuals find the subject matter difficult or terminology being used difficult to follow. This particular pre-read pack, which will be disseminated by the Change Manager, can include the following:

- Workshop objectives, inputs expected and outputs required;
- Version 1 of the Project Stakeholder Map, prepared by the Change Manager and based on project documentation and insights gained during day-to-day activities;
- Version 1 of the Stakeholder Governance Plan (see Figure 3.12), prepared in the same vein as the previous document;
- A Phase 2 Stakeholder Engagement Plan template (see Figure 3.13);
- An example completed Phase 2 Stakeholder Engagement Plan;
- A glossary of terms.

Agree the content of these documents with the sponsor and Project Manager before committing them to the pre-pack for circulation among workshop attendees. Allow five days between pack dissemination and the workshop.

2.11.03 Workshop delivery

The workshop will be delivered by the Change Manager who will be supported by project team members in the roles allocated to them. The following three activities explain how three key deliverables will be developed over the course of the workshop.

2.11.04 Project stakeholder map and analysis

During the workshop, the Change Manager will present the draft Project Stakeholder Map and validate the content with participants to encourage the identification of more stakeholders. Participant input should be noted and captured on the updated Project Stakeholder Map.

Next, a visual image of a 'Stakeholder Matrix' can be presented to the group either on a flipchart or whiteboard, and the model and terminology therein explained – e.g. 'power' and 'interest'. Participants will receive a worksheet that contains a blank Stakeholder Matrix only. The Change Manager will proceed to call out each stakeholder on the jointly created Stakeholder Map, and ask participants to plot, on their own worksheets, where they think that stakeholder should sit based on their own perception of the stakeholder power and interest. When all stakeholders have been plotted on the participant worksheets, the Change Manager can turn attention back to the unpopulated Stakeholder Matrix on the flipchart/whiteboard. Now, views will be solicited on where each stakeholder should sit on the Stakeholder Matrix. The previous preparation activity will have given workshop participants an opportunity to organize their own thoughts or come up with a view. As the plotting of stakeholders on the matrix progresses, the group will start to calibrate their thinking about stakeholder profiles, relative to where they have positioned other stakeholders on the matrix. Be prepared – they may have very different views and all must be heard so that as accurate a picture is created as possible.

2.11.05 Project Stakeholder Governance Plan

Based on the outputs of the previous exercise, the Project Stakeholder Governance Plan can now be populated. Have workshop participants agree who the 'Relationship Owners' and 'Interface Managers' will be for different stakeholders. A straightforward enough activity, one might think. Yet this can be one of the most politically charged activities of the governance committees, and there may be many iterations of the Project Stakeholder Governance Plan over the coming months. This can occur when Relationship Owners and Interface Managers for stakeholders already exist, perhaps informally and perhaps for years, but ownership and interface does not sit with the right parties (e.g. individuals whose role and expertise does not best match the stakeholder when compared to others) who can progress the project interests. Current opposite reason. The match might be made in heaven – on paper – but the Relationship Owner might be terrified of dealing with a stakeholder who is, for example, prone to run to the media with mis-leading information about the organization, or who is forever flanked by a team of challenging legal advisers. During the workshop, develop an initial draft and listen carefully to what is said about appropriate matches. The sponsor can use this input to approve the final Project Stakeholder Governance Plan with the Steering Committee.

2.11.06 Phase 2 Stakeholder Engagement Plan/s

The final workshop activity is for participants to develop their own Stakeholder Engagement Plans for Phase 2. The Change Manager will socialize Relationship Owners on their role and how to develop and execute a Stakeholder Engagement Plan. Then, participants will be allowed the opportunity to draft such a plan for one or two of their stakeholders. Some may take to it like a duck to water, while others may find it very hard going indeed. Do not push for completion there and then. Instead, the Change Manager should agree with Relationship Owners to follow up with each of them individually to help them develop their plans.

2.11.07 Follow-up coaching sessions

During follow-up sessions, expect a bit of push back about who owns which stakeholder and whether a particular individual should be managing any stakeholders at all. It may be that some perceive the Project Manager or the Change Manager as being the 'stakeholder manager' and expect them to carry all related duties. To counter this view, simply explain how it would be impossible for any one individual to have the 'stakeholder related' subject area expertise across a broad range of stakeholders, that such knowledge is held within the leadership team and has been accumulated over many years when history was created and relationships built.

Activity 2.12 **Develop technical plans**

Activity owner and leader	Output or deliverable	CM typology	
		Reference	Theories, models and tools
Jointly owned/ PM led	2.12.01 Risk Plan 2.12.02 Quality Plan 2.12.03 Procurement Plan 2.12.04 Benefits and Measures Plan	N/A	N/A

During Phase 1, project governance received a high level view of plans that feed the overall project plan, covering benefits and measures, risk, quality, procurement and configuration management.

2.12.01 Risk Plan

The Risk Management Plan is part of the overall project plan and outlines the risk methodology. It helps forecast risk and define responses to risks that come to pass (issues). Typically, the Risk Management Plan will include a risk assessment matrix such as that shared in section 3.2.16.

2.12.02 Quality Plan

The Quality Management Plan describes quality standards and how they will be achieved. It describes the overall strategy for managing quality and those tools and processes that will be used, including remedial training, and procedures for dealing with defects.

2.12.03 Procurement Plan

The Procurement Plan describes how the project organization will secure goods and services from external suppliers. It will help define the procurement requirement, describe the procurement process, schedule delivery timeframes and create sound justification (financial and otherwise) for decision-making.

2.12.04 Benefits and Measures Plan

In the outline business case, project goals, benefits and high level measures will have been outlined and agreed by project governance. Key performance indicators (KPIs) will need to be identified so as to capture eventual return-on-investment (ROI). KPIs must be based on quantifiable units such as time, cost, quality, user numbers and user proficiency. Before developing such a plan, see Chapter 7, section 7.8.

Engineering and technology projects in particular will need a Configuration Management, which establishes and maintains the consistency of a product's performance and attributes against requirements and other information throughout its life.

Activity 2.13 **Secure Steering Committee approvals**

Activity owner and leader	Output or deliverable	CM typology	
		Reference	Theories, models and tools
Jointly owned/ PM led	2.13.01 SCM conducted and approvals secured	N/A	N/A

2.13.01 Steering Committee meeting conducted and approvals secured

Once Phase 2 commences, the Steering Committee will meet on a frequent basis – e.g. every 4–6 weeks. The exact frequency will depend on project requirements and may be adjusted accordingly. As the Steering Committee meet early in Phase 2, they will consider strategies and plans that will be presented by the Project Manger and Change Manager for review and approval. The Change Management Strategy and High Level Plan needs to be approved before any work commences on related plans mentioned therein.

Activity 2.14 **Develop user profiles**

Activity owner and leader	Output or deliverable	CM typology	
		Reference	Theories, models and tools
CM owned and led	2.14.01 'Think Aloud' sessions delivered 2.14.02 User Profiles developed	25 – 28	Section 4.3.25 – 28

2.14.01 'Think Aloud' sessions delivered

In the modern workplace, where layer upon layer of change is being introduced within the same timeframe to any given employee population, protecting the 'employee experience' has become increasingly important. Before signing off the latest change, savvy organizations want to know how the preferred solution will impact productivity levels as different end-users get up to speed with new ways of working.

Think Aloud research helps develop this line of sight and can be used on change projects to gain valuable early insights into how well end-users are likely to master new tools and technologies. It can help the Change Management team develop different User Profiles and customize 'scenario-based' training and communications interventions. The 'Think Aloud' method involves a person vocalizing what they are thinking and those decisions they are making, while they attempt to complete a new task using a new tool or process. A designated observer looks on and documents comments, decisions and how well progress is made in comparison to other subjects. 'Think Aloud' research can be carried out remotely, using modern technology. For example, where the project solution is new technology for employees, a number of employees and managers from different parts of the business can be invited to partake in 'Think Aloud' research. Each volunteer will be allocated a different time to dial into a conference call and participate. When the volunteer's turn comes up, he or she will dial in and be briefed by a session facilitator who will ask the individual to go to a particular website and log in to a test site, before sharing their computer screen with conference call attendees (the facilitator and observer/note-taker). The session facilitator will invite the subject to attempt different test scenarios (e.g. fill in an online timesheet, update personal information) using the new technology, while an observer takes notes.

2.14.02 User Profiles developed

Once Think Aloud sessions have been completed, the Change Manager can consolidate the sessions outputs to develop separate 'User Profiles' based on the commonalities and differences between participants' approaches, comments and overall performance. As an extreme example, one User Profile might represent all those who found the technology easy to navigate, while another might represent those at the other extreme who found it particularly difficult and will need more help in adopting the change being rolled out.

Activity 2.15 **Culture Adjustment Plan**

Activity owner and leader	Output or deliverable	CM typology	
		Reference	Theories, models and tools
CM owned and led	2.15.01 Culture assessment 2.15.02 Culture Adjustment Plan	21 24 25–28	Section 4.3.21 Section 4.3.24 Sections 4.3.25–4.3.28

2.15.01 Culture assessment

The Change Triad will already have a sense of whether the culture adjustment required of the workforce at large is transitional or revolutionary (see Chapter 4, section 4.3.21). Now, a plan needs to be developed to support the workforce with that adjustment.

A number of structured and unstructured processes are available to the Change Manager/Culture Lead to identify cultural assumptions. Some examples of methodologies were shared in Activity 2.02. Desired cultural assumptions will be either explicit or implicit in formal vision and mission statements, values statements, policies and procedures, and methodologies and tools. Hopefully, they will also be reflected in that pattern of shared attitudes and behaviours that the workforce displays during daily operations. Where this is obviously not the case, and the desired culture is but an aspiration, the Change Manager/Culture Lead will need to use a variety of approaches to identify the prevailing culture. Once the prevailing culture has been assessed, the Change Manager/Culture Lead will conduct a gap analysis between the desired culture and the prevailing culture.

2.15.02 Culture Adjustment Plan

With the gap identified, a plan needs to be put in place to detail those interventions that will be used to support the workforce with the culture adjustment and create sustainable change. Such interventions will cover some or all of those 'embedding mechanisms' shared in Chapter 4, section 4.3.24. It will typically involve sharing the desired culture with the workforce and creating a supportive working environment that rewards desired attitudes and behaviours, and penalizes undesirable ones. Every project that requires a new collective way of doing things, some degree of culture adjustment, and every project should have such a plan in place to support the workforce with the culture shift.

Activity 2.16 **Develop Communications Plan and Initial Collateral**

Activity owner and leader	Output or deliverable	CM typology	
		Reference	Theories, models and tools
CM owned and led	2.16.01 Communications Plan 2.16.02 Vision and Objectives Statement 2.16.03 Burning Platform Statement 2.16.04 Elevator Pitch Statement	18 25–28	Section 4.3.18 Sections 4.3.25–4.3.28

The overall approach to Communications will have already been described as a subset of the Change Management Strategy and High Level. It will outline the strategic objective, goals challenges and key tactics for approval by the Steering Committee.

2.16.01 Communications Plan

A dilemma that communications professionals often face is premature demands for a Communications Plan. A Communications Plan does not exist in a vacuum. It is very dependent on input from the project on organizational and end-user impacts, as these inform those messages that need to be landed with key audiences. This is a critical dependency that will need to be tracked closely so that SMEs and others are supporting the UIA processes. To manage the expectations of impatient stakeholders, a three-pronged approach to Communications Plan development is recommended.

Part I: A cohesive story (format: presentation)

First, develop a short presentation-type document that creates a cohesive story of how the change being introduced by the project will link with other activities and changes that employees will experience around the same time period. Link the benefits the project will bring to daily worker transactions and develop a story. For example, where new tools/technologies are being introduced, the narrative might read 'make it easier for workers to understand the benefits and resources available to them', 'simplify the employee experience', 'help workers grow in their careers' and 'help workers manage their health and financial wellness'. Then, go down a level of detail and create a more personal narrative which outlines how specific tools, and tool modules, will facilitate each of these benefits in turn – e.g. 'a new HR web portal will provide a personalized view into my relationship with the organization'. A cohesive story is a great tool for sharing with executive stakeholders during Phase 2 and making them comfortable that there is a plan and that progress is being made.

Part II: The Central Communications Plan (format: presentation or excel)

As user impacts and user profiles emerge, develop the standard Communications Plan that schedules which audiences will get which key messages, when, and using which delivery channels. This operational level plan will inform execution activity, and will need to be aligned with the Corporate Communications plan.

Part III: The Local Communications Plan

Local communications will play a critical part in driving up end-user adoption of new ways of working. Well conceived and executed communications are a powerful way of raising awareness of team successes and celebrating wins so as to maintain momentum. Identify the local communications leads in the different parts of the business, and what support and guidance the project will provide them (e.g. briefing packs, posters, social media related materials).

2.16.02 Vision and Objectives Statement

The project vision and objectives will have been documented in the Business Case and shared with the project team during the team-building event. It is important that the broader team and stakeholders also have sight of the project vision and objectives to ensure alignment. A clear vision statement captures in a nutshell what the organization aspires to and should capture imaginations. Make it come alive by basing team performance objectives on them, and reinforcing the vision and objectives in team meetings and stakeholder communications.

2.16.03 Burning Platform Statement

It is not enough for members of the executive leadership team to have the 'burning platform' on their radar (see Chapter 4, section 4.3.18). This impetus for change must be articulated and communicated through the ranks to add weight to the support for change. In order for people to adopt change, they need to feel that it is important and necessary. So the Change Manager needs to think about how to generate that message and convey its urgency and importance. Be aware, however. The term 'burning platform' can raise the hairs on the neck of a project sponsor or Project Manager who is unfamiliar with Change Management terminology. Some might think that the Change Manager is suggesting large-scale radical action that will negatively impact the project. Explain clearly what the term means and why a 'Burning Platform Statement' is important. That said, I would discourage the sponsor or others from using this term when communicating with the broader organization.

2.16.04 Elevator Pitch Statement

The project 'Elevator Pitch' is another important communication tool that summarizes in a few short sentences what the project is about and helps sell it to stakeholders. It is based on the premise that, if a person is asked what their project is about, while in an elevator, they should be able to succinctly communicate their answer before the lift reaches the top floor. Busy executives are bombarded with proposals on an ongoing basis so, if they don't understand quickly what the idea is, they can quickly lose interest. A well-articulated elevator pitch is clear and concise, and communicates the unique selling proposition (USP) of the project.

Activity 2.17 **Develop Training Plan**

Activity owner and leader	Output or deliverable	CM typology	
		Reference	Theories, models and tools
CM owned and led	12.17.01 Training Plan	22	Section 4.3.22

The strategic approach to end-user capability development will have been prepared by the Change Manager (in conjunction with the Change Training Lead) and described in the Change Management Strategy and High Level Plan. This will have included resourcing and funding.

2.17.01 Training Plan

To develop a comprehensive Training Plan:

- *Set training goals*: A priority goal will be to get end-users up to speed as soon as possible so they can do their job at least as well as they could when using the old tools/way of doing things. The next goal will be to help users do their jobs faster and better than before.
- *Conduct end-user training needs analysis*: Tap into the output of the 'Think Aloud' sessions, which will have categorized the different technical skill levels, and different comfort levels, for different User Profile groups. Customized training will be required for each.
- *Cater for individual learning styles*: The training plan must cater for different learning styles and capabilities to be effective. With the rush to get to the Cloud and the pressure to reduce costs, many leaders have become caught in the trap of signing up for Cloud-based technologies that promise a 'modern and intuitive feel' that 'could be embraced by any worker' and require little training. The reality can be far from the truth.
- *Decide training delivery channels*: A combination of approaches will help meet the needs of different users – for example:

  - *One-to-one instruction* – suitable for VIPs (typically senior executives) and those with special needs.
  - *Seminar style group demonstrations* – suitable for dealing with groups who will use specialized functionality.

- *Classroom-style instructor-led training* (can be face-to-face or conducted via video conferencing) – can be effective for training large populations who prefer instructor-led learning.
- *On demand self-paced training* – training is broken down into bite-size chunks and made available via short (30-second to 2-minute) videos that are stored online and easily accessible by end-users.

- *Identify appropriate measures*: The five levels of training measurement are reaction, learning, behaviour, results and return-on-investment (ROI), with reaction to training being the weakest measure and ROI being the strongest.
- *Design learning experiences to engage hearts and minds* – emotion is what makes learning stick.

Activity 2.18 **Develop Change Advocates Network Plan**

Activity owner and leader	Output or deliverable	CM typology	
		Reference	Theories, models and tools
CM owned and led	2.18.01 Change Advocates Network Plan	23	Section 4.3.23

While Change Management is a critical enabler, for change to stick the business must own the success or failure of change adoption. To that end, a network of business change advocates will be established to work under the steer of the Change Manager who will provide them will guidance, support and tools. A well-designed Change Advocates Network has the gravitas and influence to embed and sustain change locally.

2.18.01 Change Advocates Network Plan

1 Network structure

Key network roles include the project sponsor, local Business Change Adoption Managers and functional champions (see Figure 9.8 over-leaf). While Business Change Adoption Managers will be local senior leaders with a primarily vertical reach in their department or part of the business, the Champions will sit in BAU functions such as OD, Human Resources, IT and Communications and have a horizontal reach across departmental boundaries.

Figure 9.8 Change Advocates Network Structure

2 Roles and responsibilities

The project needs to be clear about what they are expecting from the different role holders and how much time they are expected to commit.

Project sponsor

The project sponsor will provide leadership to the network via their normal project sponsor activities and will not have additional responsibilities other than perhaps to kick off a network session. He/she would be updated by the Change Manager on network 206progress against plans via project governance meetings.

Local Business Change Adoption Managers

Nominated by the Steering Committee, they will work with the local business sponsor to embed change locally, meeting regularly with the Change Manager to:

- Develop and execute a local Change Adoption Plan (see Phase 3, work package 3.12.02).
- Become early adopters and/or super-users.
- Report on local adoption rates and progress against plans.
- Understand the change the impact has on local employees.
- Understand the key project milestones and timeline.
- Understand the capability of their colleagues and suggest additional support interventions as appropriate.
- Identify local resistance to change and help address it.

Functional champions

Those who take up this role will also be required to do some, or all of, the following:

- Inform local Change Adoption Plans developed by Business Change Adoption Managers.
- Become early adopters and/or super-users.
- Attend focus group sessions for solution testing and training.
- Gather feedback on communications and training interventions.
- Assist in the training and support of their local end-users.
- Assist with the circulation of project communications locally.
- Provide ongoing support to colleagues during Phase 6 and beyond.

To recruit members of the Change Advocates Network, get the help of the project sponsor to invite them to participate and highlight how the role will be of value to the business and to them. Have on the plan some training or other interventions to deal with any skills gaps that present themselves among those who do sign up.

Organize for a Phase 3 network kick-off session to explain roles and responsibilities, and how to drive up local adoption of the change being rolled out.

A Change Advocates Network can have a ripple effect in the business and make a big difference in driving up local adoption of new ways of working. It can enable the centralized team to extend Change Management strategy execution to different parts of the business, translating messages and customizing plans to suit local needs. It emphasizes business ownership for the success of the change.

Activity 2.19 **Phase 3 Plan**

Activity owner and leader	Output or deliverable	CM typology	
		Reference	Theories, models and tools
PM owned and led	2.19.01 Phase 3 Plan	N/A	N/A

For Phase 2, this activity will be similar to Phase 1. For this particular plan, add detail around how the solution will be developed or built.

Activity 2.20 **Phase 1 Gateway Review Board**

Activity owner and leader	Output or deliverable	CM typology	
		Reference	Theories, models and tools
Jointly owned/PM led	2.20.01 Project team gateway readiness determined 2.20.02 Gateway 2 documentation assembled 2.20.03 Gateway 2 meeting logistics 2.20.04 Gateway 2 meeting pack 2.20.05 Board recommendation secured and documented	N/A	N/A

2.20.01 Project Team Gateway readiness determined

For Phase 2, this activity will be similar to Phase 1.

As the team gather to consider their level of readiness, some of the questions they can consider, to guide their decision-making, include the following:

- *Business case* – Has anything changed? Are we aware of any upcoming events that could impact the business case? Will the recommended solution meet the needs of the business?
- *Stakeholders* – During Phase 2 solution identification and design activities, did we engage with the right stakeholders?
- *Risks and issues* – Do we have an approach for risks and issues management?
- *Project governance* – Have we ensured that the team has the right skills sets?
- *Data and sources* – Is our data reliable and are our sources credible? Did we conduct a robust analysis of options and alternatives, and will we be able to support and defend our recommendation?
- *Objectivity* – Did we consider all of the possible solutions when coming to our recommendation, or did we only include those that the governance committee have expressed an interest in or preference for?
- *Readiness for next phase* – Have we developed a clear and robust Phase 3 Plan that will provide governance committees with a good sense of Phase 3 objectives, work packages and activities?

2.20.02 Gateway 2 documentation assembled

For Phase 2, this activity will be similar to Phase 1.

2.20.03 Gateway 2 meeting logistics

For Phase 2, this activity will be similar to Phase 1.

2.20.04 Gateway 2 meeting pack

In addition to those materials provided in the Phase 1 Gateway pre-read and presentation package, the Phase 2 Gateway pack will also include the information about the alternative solutions assessed in Phase 2 and more detail around the recommended solution.

2.20.05 Board recommendation secured and documented

For the Phase 2 Gateway meeting, the Project Manager can lead discussions around the solutions and recommendations, with the Change Manager leading discussions around potential organizational impacts. SMEs should be invited and available to answer any of the more technical questions relating to the solution itself and current ways of working. During the meeting, the Gateway Review Board will want to ensure that the following questions are answered well:

- Have we considered all the viable options?
- Did we agree the right criteria to screen in/out the various options?
- Did we choose the right solution?
- In the business case still strong enough to proceed with the recommended solution?
- Is the Phase 3 Plan robust and realistic?

Once queries and concerns have been addressed, the Gateway Review Board will be able to make their recommendation on if, and how, the project should proceed. The project team must document this and any other outstanding items.

Activity 2.21 **Gateway 2 Steering Committee Meeting (SCM)**

Activity owner and leader	Output or deliverable	CM typology	
		Reference	**Theories, models and tools**
Sponsor owned and led	2.21.01 Gateway 2 SCM logistics 2.21.02 Gateway 2 SCM pack 2.21.03 Steering Committee decision secured and documented 2.21.04 Next steps communicated	N/A	N/A

For Phase 2, this activity will be similar to Phase 1. The Steering Committee will want to know about any visible challenges that may surface during solution development, and how the team plans to deal with them. When the Steering Committee decides to proceed to the next phase, this is a big vote of confidence in the project team and is cause to celebrate.

Activity 2.22 **Team performance and cultural assumptions reviewed**

Activity owner and leader	Output or deliverable	CM typology	
		Reference	Theories, models and tools
CM owned and led	2.22.01 Team performance review documentation 2.22.02 Team cultural assumptions realigned	21	Section 4.3.21

For Phase 2, this activity will be similar to Phase 1. The team will have been assembled fairly recently and will probably still be in the 'storming phase', which is evidenced by conflict as different ways of doing things clash. Encourage the team to openly discuss these incidences. How the Project Triad react to problems and incidences of conflict reveal their own operating assumptions and are 'moments of truth'. The project team will expect the Project Triad to demonstrate attitudes and behaviours that are in alignment with the PCP Team Cultural Assumptions that everyone signed up to. Use any momentary lapses in that regard as stories to explore so that lessons are learnt and the culture of partnership strengthened.

Activity 2.23 **Phase 2: Wrap-up**

Activity owner and leader	Output or deliverable	CM typology	
		Reference	Theories, models and tools
PM owned and led	2.23.01 Outstanding issues closed out 2.23.02 Lessons learnt documented	N/A	N/A

For Phase 2, this activity will be similar to Phase 1.

9.3 Phase 3: Build and Engage

Successful delivery in this phase will require working with the business and SMEs to design plans that meet the needs of the business and the individual end-user. The Change Manager can lead on the identification of organizational and end-user impacts, while the Project Manager focuses on leading solution build.

Success for the 'Build and Engage' phase will be measured by:

- The development of design plans for the preferred solution.
- The building of the solution.
- Robust collation of stakeholder requirements and end-user impacts.
- The development of end-user support material and support networks.

3.01 Kick off Phase 3
3.02 Phase 3 stakeholder planning
3.03 Gather detailed requirements
3.04 Refine User Impact Analysis
3.05 Complete Phase 3 Impacts Disposition form/s
3.06 Conduct Phase 3 Impacts Disposition workshop/s
3.07 Conduct Change Readiness assessment
3.08 Refine designs and freeze scope
3.09 Develop communication material
3.10 Develop training material
3.11 Engage change advocates
3.12 Develop Phase 4 Plan
3.13 Gateway 3 Review Board Meeting
3.14 Gateway 3 Steering Committee Meeting
3.15 Review team performance and cultural assumptions
3.16 Wrap up Phase 3

Figure 9.9 PCP Methodology: Phase 3 activities and work packages

Activity 3.01 **Kick off Phase 3**

Activity owner and leader	Output or deliverable	CM typology	
		Reference	Theories, models and tools
PM owned and led	3.01.01 Phase 2 lessons learnt reviewed 3.01.02 Phase 3 Plan finalized 3.01.03 Iterative documents updated 3.01.04 Team kick off	N/A	N/A

3.01.01 Phase 2 lessons learnt reviewed

For Phase 3, this activity will be similar to Phase 2.

3.01.02 Phase 3 plan finalized

For Phase 3, this activity will be similar to Phase 2.

3.01.03 Iterative documents updated

The following iterative documents need to be reviewed and may need to be updated:

- The Business Case
- The Change Project Roadmap
- Culture Adjustment Plan
- Change Project Charter
- Communication Plan
- Training Plan
- The Lessons Learnt Document
- Stakeholder Management related
- The Risk Plan.

Once these documents have been updated, they should be combed for potential inputs to other documents that will be developed in Phase 3.

3.01.04 Team kick-off

This activity will be jointly led by the Project Manager and the Change Manager. Gather the team together to align all with Phase 3 goals and objectives, and lessons learnt from previous phases. Welcome any new team members and make sure that they feel part of the team. Reinforce team protocols and team cultural assumptions, giving positive reinforcement for successes achieved.

Activity 3.02 **Phase 3 Stakeholder Planning**

Activity owner and leader	Output or deliverable	CM typology	
		Reference	Theories, models and tools
CM owned and led	3.02.01 Phase 3 Stakeholder Map	N/A	N/A

For Phase 3, this activity will be similar to Phase 2, building on the output of Activity 2.10 with a focus on planning for Phase 3 stakeholders.

Activity 3.03 **Gather detailed requirements**

Activity owner and leader	Output or deliverable	CM typology	
		Reference	Theories, models and tools
Jointly owned/ PM led	3.03.01 Detailed requirements gathered	N/A	N/A

3.03.01 Detailed requirements gathered

From the outset, the Change Triad will have been engaging with stakeholders to understand their requirements. With the final solution now agreed, the focus shifts to ensuring that the chosen solution meets the needs of the organization. It can be tempting for the project to burrow into the development and refinement of design plans, assuming that they know best. That would be a big mistake, as without detailed and validated stakeholder input, the solution may fail to meet the business needs and fall flat.

The requirements gathering process will look different, depending on the nature of the project. It may involve dedicated workshops where stakeholder representatives try out the solution under development and feed into the design. Or for a major infrastructure development, it may involve organizing for stakeholders to tour similar facilities (e.g. airport terminal, production plant). Whatever the process used, the stakeholder requirements must be documented carefully and validated. In some contexts, they will be subjected to external audit.

Activity 3.04 **Refine User Impact Analyses (UIAs)**

Activity owner and leader	Output or deliverable	CM typology	
		Reference	Theories, models and tools
CM owned and led	3.04.01 Updated UIA/s	15	Section 4.3.15

For Phase 3, this activity will be similar to Phase 2. The Change Management team will work with SMEs and super-users to identify how the chosen solution will impact end-users with disparate profiles.

Activity 3.05 **Complete Phase 3 Impacts Disposition Form**

Activity owner and leader	Output or deliverable	CM typology	
		Reference	Theories, models and tools
CM owned and led	3.05.01 Phase 3 Impacts Disposition Form/s completed	15	Section 4.3.15

For Phase 3, this activity will be similar to Phase 2. End-user impacts will be logged and appropriate interventions identified to mitigate any negative impact on people and operations. Individual interventions may relate to stakeholder management activities, culture embedding mechanisms, communications or training.

Activity 3.06 **Conduct Phase 3 Impacts Disposition Workshops**

Activity owner and leader	Output or deliverable	CM typology	
		Reference	Theories, models and tools
CM owned and led	3.06.01 Phase 3 Impacts Disposition Workshops delivered	15	Section 4.3.15

For Phase 3, this activity will be similar to Phase 2. Good leadership and people management skills can ensure that these workshops result in strengthened team spirit (both within the Change Management team and across the broader project team), and that they have the support they need to identify end-user impacts.

Activity 3.07 **Conduct Change Readiness Assessment – Part 1**

Activity owner and leader	Output or deliverable	CM typology	
		Reference	Theories, models and tools
CM owned and led	3.07.01 Change Readiness Assessment – Part 1	19	Section 4.3.19

With the solution now confirmed and the substance of the change thereby defined, it is timely to conduct Part 1 of the Change Readiness Assessment, which will focus on organizational readiness only. Anything else would be premature.

3.07.01 Change Readiness Assessment: Part 1

An online questionnaire is the most popular tool used for change readiness, although this input can be supplemented with information from other sources such as interviews with managers and focus groups. A Change Readiness Assessment can:

- Identify sources of resistance to change and inform plans;
- Uncover risks so they can be mitigated quickly and effectively.

Assessment results, findings and recommendations will be put to the Steering Committee for their review and action to ensure that the organization is aligned to support the change.

In Phase 4 of the project lifecycle, Part 2 of the Change Readiness Assessment (which focuses on individual and team readiness, and perceptions of individual readiness) will be conducted. This can help improve workforce satisfaction levels by engaging them throughout the business transition.

Activity 3.08 **Refine designs and freeze scope**

Activity owner and leader	Output or deliverable	CM typology	
		Reference	Theories, models and tools
PM owned and led	3.08.01 Designs refined 3.08.02 Scope freeze	19	Section 4.3.19

3.08.01 Designs refined

At this point, ask those stakeholder representatives who shared their requirements to come together to vet the design plans and confirm that they are aligned with their requirements.

3.08.02 Scope freeze

Where it has not been possible to accommodate any individual requests, the project team should be ready to explain why and have a good rationale for their thinking. It may be that stakeholders push for a change in scope to accommodate their own interests. This will need to be brought to the attention of the Steering Committee, which may decide to freeze the scope to contain impact on costs and resources.

Activity 3.09 **Develop communication material**

Activity owner and leader	Output or deliverable	CM typology	
		Reference	Theories, models and tools
CM owned and led	3.09.01 Pre-launch material 3.09.02 Launch material 3.09.03 Post-launch material	18	Section 4.3.18

The strategic approach to Communications will have formed part of the Change Management Strategy and, at this stage, will be signed off. The Communications Plan and initial communications collateral will also have been developed and signed off in Activity 2.15. It is time now to develop the remainder of the communications materials on the plan, to support end-users through the change journey.

3.09.01 Pre-launch material

Before implementation of the change, stakeholders will need to be aware and informed of the following where it applies:

- *Limited transaction window* – Where existing tools and processes cannot be used for a window of time before the launch of the replacement tools, impacted users need to be informed in advance so they can make plans.
- *'Go Live' dates/s for all geographies* – The business will need to know when to expect the change to hit and the likely impact on operations. The project sponsor may address the workforce via the intranet and advise them to get ready for the impending change.
- *Frequently asked questions (FAQs)* – The business will appreciate some prepared answers to those frequently asked questions workers will have.
- *Early bird resources* – A library of video clips and tutorials will be a welcome aid to those who want to learn more about new tools.

3.09.02 Launch material

- Day 1 communications

On the day the change goes live in the business, the aim of communications is to reach all audiences regarding the change. A range of communications and resources will need to be available to all end-users – e.g. FAQs, video-clips and demonstrations.

3.09.03 Post-launch material

- Post-launch communications

After the official launch, the job is not done. End-users will take time to learn the new ways of working and post-launch communications can help them understand where they might be going wrong and how to apply new ways of working.

Activity 3.10 **Develop training material**

Activity owner and leader	Output or deliverable	CM typology	
		Reference	Theories, models and tools
CM owned and led	3.10.01 Pre-launch material 3.10.02 Launch material 3.10.03 Post-launch material	22	Section 4.3.22

While solution providers may also offer end-user training material, training content is more effective and memorable for end-users if it is customized to meet the needs of the organization and include:

- The purpose of the new tool/technology/processes;
- How it differs from legacy ways of working;
- Common problems users may encounter and how to resolve them;
- Frequently asked questions, together with the answers;
- Contact information for future help and support.

The Training Plan will determine what training materials need to be developed for 'pre-launch', the 'Go Live' date and 'post-launch'. Some particular training materials to be developed are given below.

3.10.01 Pre-launch material

- *One-to-one instruction for VIPs* (typically senior executives).
- *Seminar-style group demonstrations* – suitable for Super Users and the Change Advocates Network, and for dealing with specialist groups who will use specialized functionality.

3.10.02 Launch material

- *Classroom-style instructor-led training* (face-to-face or conducted via video conferencing) – Is effective for maintaining that personal touch some learners need.
- *On-demand self-paced training* – Short (30-second to 2-minute) videos that are stored in an online library and easily assessable by end-users.

3.10.03 Post-launch material

- *Corrective training* – Any post-launch revisions to the solution may require additional corrective training to be provided.

Activity 3.11 **Engage Change Advocates Network**

Activity owner and leader	Output or deliverable	CM typology	
		Reference	Theories, models and
tools CM owned and led	3.11.01 Kick-off Business Change Advocates Network 3.11.02 Local Change Adoption Plans secured	23 24	Section 4.3.23 Section 4.3.24

During Phase 2, the Change Advocates Network was designed. Now it is time to activate that group and secure local Change Adoption Plans that will outline how adoption will be driven up locally.

3.11.01 Kick off Business Change advocates network

During Phase 2, members of the network were recruited and a kick-off event designed. The project sponsor can be invited to conduct the opening speech to highlight the important role of the network and to drive home that the business owns the success or failure of adoption of the change. The Business Change Adoption Manager for each part of the business will work with the local sponsor, who is accountable for overseeing local efforts and results achieved. Much of the engagement with Business Change Adoption Managers will centre on their local Change Adoption Plan, which is described below and illustrated overleaf. Functional champions will also have been invited to join the network and, based on their area of expertise, will be able to advise Business Change Adoption Managers on their plans for local OD interventions, communications, training etc. It may be that a mix of global and local functional champions is invited to feed back on plans.

3.11.02 Local Change Adoption Plans secured

The Change Adoption Plan example shared overleaf outlines the plans of the business to drive up adoption rates and embed change. It is structured to focus on those 'primary embedding mechanisms' and 'secondary embedding mechanisms' described in Chapter 4, section 4.3.20.

Change Adoption Plan for technology deployment

Primary embedding mechanisms	What	How	When	Owner
What leaders pay attention to, measure and control on a regular basis.	Regular local tracking of adoption rates.	Dashboard report which captures local adoption rates and progress against targets set by Steering Committee.	Monthly Bi-weekly	Local change governance and local Business Change Adoption Manager
How leaders react to critical incidents, organizational crises and blatant non-cooperation.	Have courage and keep the change on track in the face of obstacles.	During 'moments of truth' where the change is tested, walk the talk of the change vision, mission, goals and philosophy. Stay on message. Input to 'Housekeeping Report' (led by Change Manager and fed to Steering) to demonstrate that processes are in place locally to drive adoption.	Ad hoc Phase x	Business Change Adoption Managers and local leaders Business Change Adoption Manager and Change Manager
Observed criteria by which leaders allocate scarce resources.	Demonstrate importance of change by allocating resources and support.	Senior Business Change Adoption Managers with gravitas and influence appointed locally and supported appropriately.	Phase 2	Local leader/s
Deliberate role modelling, teaching and coaching.	Local leaders visibly walking the talk.	One-to-one coaching for local leaders, EAs and PAs. Follow up to ensure that local leaders are proactively advocating change.	Phase 4 Phases 5/6	Local leader/s and Business Change Adoption Managers
Observed criteria by which leaders allocate rewards and status.	Ensure actual reward and recognition practices are constructive.	Reward and recognition for first teams in each function/department to adopt technology.	Ad hoc	Business Change Adoption Managers
Observed criteria by which leaders recruit, select, promote, retire and excommunicate organizational members.	Take into consideration the individual's ability and desire to use and advocate new technologies.	Align policies to favour individuals familiar with new technologies and who are visible advocates.	Phase 5	Local leader/s and Human Resources

Secondary embedding mechanisms	What	How	When	Owner
Organization design and structure	Ensure organizational design and structure support change adoption.	Establish appropriate local governance to oversee change deployment and adoption.	Phase 3	Local leadership team and local leader/s
Organizational systems and procedures	Remove tools used for old way of doing things.	Get buy-in of local leadership to remove old tools and practices as soon as is feasible without disrupting operations.	ASAP	Business Change Adoption Manager, local leaders and Operations/IT
Organizational rites and rituals	Leaders to use new technologies when addressing workforce particularly.	Ensure leaders are comfortable using technologies for employee facing events in particular; provide hands-on technical support for important conference calls and events.	ASAP	Local leaders, IT and Champions
Design of physical space, façades and buildings.	Ensure physical environment supports the change.	Equip local conference rooms with new technologies.	Phase 5	IT and Business Change Adoption Managers
Stories, legends and myths about people and events.	Public recognition for individuals and teams who achieve success with new tools.	Local leaders to use well utilized channels to recognize and reward individuals and teams. A simple 'thank you' or 'well done' from a leader can be more powerful than monetary rewards.	Phase 5 on	Business Change Adoption Manager and local leaders
Formal statements of project vision, goals and philosophy.	Incorporate the importance of embracing change and technology.	Project vision, mission, values, rationale and philosophy to be kept uppermost in people's minds.	Phase 5 on	Business Change Adoption Manager and local leaders
Other support	**What**	**How**	**When**	**Owner**
Local communications	Use local channels to reach different groups with different needs.	Local road-show, intranet stories, social media discussions etc. to raise awareness, understanding, buy-in and commitment for the change. Share local successes.	Phase 5	Local management and communications
Local training	Training in local language	Face-to-face training. Library of online, on-demand mini video clips showcasing technology functionality.	Phases 5 and 6	Business Change Adoption Manager and training

Figure 9.10 Change Adoption Plan

After explaining how to complete a Change Adoption Plan, give the Business Change Adoption Managers a deadline for submitting their own plan, and hold them to it.

After the Change Advocates Network kick-off event, the Change Manager will meet with each Business Change Adoption Manager on a regular basis to review their plans and progress against plans. These sessions are great coaching opportunities, and below are some tips:

- Take a supportive and encouraging stance – 'We're here to help'.
- Request for the local Change Adoption Plan to be shared as the session commences and work through it; some may try to distract from a lack of progress and hesitate to share the plan.
- Make sure no plan is heavy on Communications and Training interventions; these efforts target change in the individual alone, rather than change in the physical environment also. Make the term 'embedding mechanisms' part of everyday language (see first column of Figure 9.10).
- Keep notes of action points agreed and check that in follow-up sessions these have been addressed.
- Invite a member of the project team who has technical expertise regarding the solution, but don't allow the session to get bogged down in technical issues; if an issue cannot be addressed easily ask for it to be taken offline.
- Acknowledge progress and recognize high performers.

Give each Business Change Adoption Manager targets to work towards, and include submission status and progress against targets in the reporting dashboard for the Steering Committee. The regular sessions described above will give the Change Manager good insight into local issues and developments and identify where the Steering Committee might need to intervene to remove any blockages.

Activity 3.12 **Develop Phase 4 Plan**

Activity owner and leader	Output or deliverable	CM typology	
		Reference	Theories, models and tools
PM owned and led	3.12.01 Phase 4 Plan	N/A	N/A

For Phase 3, this activity will be similar to Phase 2.

Activity 3.13 **Gateway 3 Review Board Meeting**

Activity owner and leader	Output or deliverable	CM typology	
		Reference	Theories, models and tools
Jointly owned/ PM led	3.13.01 Project team Gateway readiness determined 3.13.02 Gateway 3 documentation assembled 3.13.03 Gateway 3 meeting logistics 3.13.04 Gateway 3 meeting pack 3.13.05 Board recommendation secured and documented	N/A	N/A

3.13.01 Project Team Gateway readiness determined

For Phase 3, this activity will be similar to Phase 2.

The following are some questions the team needs to ask themselves for a Phase Gateway 3 meeting:

- *Business case* – Will the solution meet the needs of the business and deliver expected benefits?
- *Stakeholders* – Have we engaged with the right stakeholders for reviews of the solution?
- *Risks and issues* – Have risks and resistance to change been minimized?
- *Project governance* – Have we the right roles and responsibilities resourced?
- *Data and sources* – Have we used credible sources for decision-making?
- *Objectivity* - Are we keeping impartial and building a solution that best meets the needs of the organization?
- *Readiness for next phase* – Have we developed a clear and robust Phase 4 Plan that will provide governance committees with a good sense of Phase 4 objectives, work packages and activities?

3.13.02 Gateway 3 documentation collated

For Phase 3, this activity will be similar to previous phases.

3.13.03 Gateway 3 meeting logistics

For Phase 3, this activity will be similar to previous phases.

3.13.04 Gateway 3 meeting pack

Create and distribute pre-read material.

The pre-read package for Phase 3 should contain materials similar to those prepared for previous phases, i.e. meeting logistics, the business case, project background information, the Phase 4 plan and an update on project spend against forecasts

3.13.05 Board recommendation secured and documented

For Phase 3, this activity will be similar to Phase 2.

Activity 3.14 **Gateway 3 Steering Committee Meeting (SCM)**

Activity owner and leader	Output or deliverable	CM typology	
		Reference	Theories, models and tools
Sponsor owned and led	3.14.01 Gateway 3 SCM logistics 3.14.02 Gateway 3 SCM Meeting Pack 3.14.03 Steering Committee decision secured and documented 3.14.04 Decision and next steps communicated	N/A	N/A

For Phase 3, this activity will be similar to previous phases. To proceed Phase 4, the committee will need to be convinced that good progress is being made and robust plans are in place for Phase 4.

Activity 3.15 **Review team performance and cultural assumptions**

Activity owner and leader	Output or deliverable	CM typology	
		Reference	Theories, models and tools
CM owned and led	3.15.01 Team performance review document 3.15.02 Cultural assumptions realigned document	21	Section 4.3.21

For Phase 3, this activity will be similar to previous phases.

Activity 3.16 **Wrap-up: Phase 3**

Activity owner and leader	Output or deliverable	CM typology	
		Reference	Theories, models and tools
PM owned and led	3.16.01 Outstanding issues closed out 3.16.02 Lessons learnt documented	N/A	N/A

For Phase 3, this activity will be similar to previous phases.

3.16.01 Outstanding issues closed out

For Phase 3, this activity will be similar to previous phases.

3.16.02 Lessons learnt documented

For Phase 3, this activity will be similar to previous phases.

9.4 Phase 4: Get Ready

In Phase 4, the development team continues their work to build, test and pilot a solution that meets the needs of the business. Tier 4 stakeholders will be engaged and end-user support materials will be finalized. Deployment plans will be shared with relevant project stakeholders, to identify possible deployment risks and to develop the necessary contingency plans to ensure that an acceptable level of productivity is maintained during the transition. Resistance to change will peak during this phase and can manifest in different ways. Above the board, expect to see requests for deferments or changes in scope while, below the board, be alert to efforts to sabotage the project so that it is abandoned.

Success in the 'Get Ready' phase will be measured by:

* The testing and piloting of the final solution.
* Final preparation of all deployment-related materials.
* Tier 4 stakeholders engaged appropriately and the business mobilized.
* End-users prepared for change.

4.01 Kick off Phase 4
4.02 Refine User Impact Analyses
4.03 Complete Phase 4 User Impacts Disposition form/s
4.04 Conduct Phase 4 User Impacts Disposition workshop/s
4.05 Change Readiness Assessment – Part 2
4.06 Test, pilot and refine solution
4.07 Vet and finalize end-user support material
4.08 Vet and finalize Go-Live Plan
4.09 Train change advocates network
4.10 Engage managers and employees
4.11 Launch limited transaction window communications
4.12 Develop Phase 5 Plan
4.13 Gateway 4 Review Board Meeting
4.14 Gateway 4 Steering Committee Meeting
4.15 Team performance and cultural assumptions review
4.16 Wrap up Phase 4

Figure 9.11 PCP methodology: Phase 4 activities and work packages

Activity 4.01 Kick off Phase 4

Activity owner and leader	Output or deliverable	CM typology	
		Reference	Theories, models and tools
PM owned and led	4.01.01 Phase 3 lessons learnt review 4.02.02 Phase 4 Plan finalized 4.03.03 Iterative documents updated 4.03.04 Team kick off	N/A	N/A

For Phase 4, kick-off processes will be similar to previous phases. All too often, the updating of project documentation falls below the radar and is deprioritized as other issues press on the team of the project team. This is bad practice and can have lots of knock-on effects. During the team kick-off session, it is important to remind everyone that updating documents is very important for alignment purposes. In everyday practice, Change Management specialists will often be a new addition to the project team, with Change Management added as a bolt-on to sell a solution that has not benefited from a robust Change Management approach. Change Management specialists will rely on project documentation being up-to-date, as they try to play catch-up. With PCP methodology, the Change Manager and team have been key partners from the outset.

Activity 4.02 **Refine user impact analyses**

Activity owner and leader	Output or deliverable	CM typology	
		Reference	Theories, models and tools
CM owned and led	4.02.01 Updated UIA/s	15	Section 4.3.15

For Phase 4, this activity will be similar to previous phases. By now, the team should have a clear line of sight on end-user impacts.

Activity 4.03 **Complete Phase 4 Impacts Disposition Form/s**

Activity owner and leader	Output or deliverable	CM typology	
		Reference	Theories, models and tools
CM owned and led	4.03.01 Phase 4 Impacts Disposition Form/s	15	Section 4.3.15

For Phase 4, this activity will be similar to Phase 3.

Activity 4.04 **Conduct Phase 4 Impacts Disposition Workshop/s**

Activity owner and leader	Output or deliverable	CM typology	
		Reference	Theories, models and tools
CM owned and led	4.04.01 Phase 4 Impacts Disposition Workshop/s	15	Section 4.3.15

For Phase 4, this activity will be similar to Phase 3.

By the end of this workshop/s, the Change Management team should be able to provide the executive leadership team with a good line of sight into end-user impacts, and share robust stakeholder management, communications and training plans that will counter such impacts. This will, of course, continue to be an evolving story, as tweaks may be made to the solution post-launch based on end-user feedback.

Activity 4.05 **Conduct Change Readiness Assessment: Part 2**

Activity owner and leader	Output or deliverable	CM typology	
		Reference	Theories, models and tools
PM owned and led	4.05.01 Change Readiness Assessment Part 2 completed	19	Section 4.3.19

4.05.01 Change Readiness Assessment: Part 2 completed

Now that managers and employees have been engaged in preperation work, they will have an understanding of the impending change and what it means for them. It is therefore timely to conduct Part 2 of the Change Readiness Assessment, which will gather information about workforce perceptions on individuals' and teams' readiness for change and perceived personal impact. The output of this exercise can be used to inform the final solution design and last-minute tweaks to end-user materials.

Activity 4.06 **Test, pilot and refine solution**

Activity owner and leader	Output or deliverable	CM typology	
		Reference	Theories, models and tools
PM owned and led	4.06.01 Solution tested 4.06.02 Solution piloted 4.06.03 Solution refined	N/A	N/A

Where possible, the product of the project should be tested and/or piloted before rolling out to the workforce. The bigger the intended audience, the more critical these activities will be.

4.06.01 Solution tested

For some projects, such as technology deployments, testing of solution veracity and integrity will be a must. The quality of the testing process is as important as the quality of the solution itself. To build a quality testing process, determine how close the test results will bear on real life use of the solution:

- What is being tested – the final product or a prototype?
- Where the solution has a number of modules, are all modules being tested?

- Will the testing involve a pilot in the real business environment?
- Are key stakeholder groups being represented in the tests?
- How will test outcomes be documented and fed into deployment plans?
- What contingency plans are in place if the test results are poor?

As part of the Training Plan, super-users will have been identified and recruited from the workforce. Such individuals will have excellent technical skills, understand their business workflows, be good communicators and be responsible individuals who are respected by their team. Super-users will have been involved in testing sessions and helped with the development of training materials.

4.06.02 Solution piloted

A pilot is a test in a real business environment and will provide the best quality data for solution refinement. Pilot tests are carried out in an attempt to avoid a negative impact on workplace productivity and any related costs, should the solution developed by the project prove not to meet the needs of the business. A pilot study is usually carried out with representative of key stakeholder groups who test the design of the project solution as it performs in the workplace.

4.06.03 Solution refined

Testing and piloting of the solution can provide potentially valuable insights that can be added to the refinements of the final solution deployed.

Activity 4.07 **Vet and finalize end-user support materials**

Activity owner and leader	Output or deliverable	CM typology	
		Reference	Theories, models and tools
CM owned and led	4.07.01 Communications and training materials vetted and finalized	18 22	Section 4.3.18 Section 4.3.22

4.07.01 Communications and training materials vetted and finalized

As the solution has been tested and refined, and with the Impacts Disposition Workshops coming to a close, the final solution design and end-user impacts will by now have been fed into communications and training collateral. It is now time to have these end–user support materials finalized and approved. As the Gateway Review Board is likely to include a number of department or division heads, they are a good audience to test materials with before putting them to the Steering Committee for final approval. A coordinated approach will make the best use of everyone's time.

Activity 4.08 **Vet and finalize Go Live Plan**

Activity owner and leader	Output or deliverable	CM typology	
		Reference	Theories, models and tools
PM/CM co–owned and PM led	4.08.01 Go Live Plan finalized	N/A	N/A

4.08.01 Go Live Plan finalized

At this point the deployment plan needs to be validated by stakeholders and project governance teams, before being finalized by the Project Manager. The vetting process is an opportunity to conduct last-minute checks to make sure that the plan is going to work. Where any major obstacles are identified, the project sponsor can work to resolve them. Stakeholders will welcome sight of the plans and the opportunity to influence them before official deployment.

Activity 4.09 **Train Change Advocate Network**

Activity owner and leader	Output or deliverable	CM typology	
		Reference	Theories, models and tools
CM owned and led	4.09.01 Change Advocates Network trained	23	Section 4.3.23

4.09.01 Change Advocates Network trained

It is very important that the Change Advocates Network receive early communications and early training regarding the change. This requirement will have been built into the Communications and Training plans, and now is the time to execute those plans so that the Change Advocates are both informed and proficient with new ways of working. This support will enable them to role-model new ways of working and 'walk the talk'.

Activity 4.10 **Engage Managers and Employees**

Activity owner and leader	Output or deliverable	CM typology	
		Reference	Theories, models and tools
CM owned and led	4.10.01 Managers and employees engaged	16	Section 4.3.16

While individual managers and employees will have involved with the project for activities such as the Think Aloud sessions and Change Readiness Assessments, this will be the first time that all managers and employees are officially informed about the project and its impending rollout.

4.10.01 Managers and employees engaged

The purpose of these pre-launch communications is to give these stakeholders a broader awareness of the initiative and provide any necessary instructions. It is also an opportunity to generate some excitement for the change and share the benefits. It may be that managers are communicated to before employees, using a cascade approach. Communications messages will have been tweaked based on the results of the Change Readiness Assessment to ensure that the right messages get to the right groups and at the right time. Delivery channels may include on-demand videos and traning, job aids, 'Limited Transaction Window' communications (see below), plus invitations to training, eLearning and webinars.

Activity 4.11 **Launch Limited Transaction Window Communications**

Activity owner and leader	Output or deliverable	CM typology	
		Reference	Theories, models and tools
CM owned and led	4.11.01 Limited Transaction Communications launched	18	Section 4.3.18

4.11.01 Limited Transaction Window Communications launched

Where the project involves a window of time whereby existing tools will not be available to the workforce before the new tools are deployed, this needs to be planned for and communicated. 'Limited Transaction Window' (LTW) communications that were developed in Phase 3 can now be launched as part of the early communications to ensure managers and employees are ready for the change.

Activity 4.12 **Develop Phase 5 Plan**

Activity owner and leader	Output or deliverable	CM typology	
		Reference	Theories, models and tools
PM owned and led	4.12.01 Phase 5 Plan	N/A	N/A

For Phase 4, this activity will be similar to previous phases.

Activity 4.13 **Gateway 4 Review Board Meeting**

Activity owner and leader	Output or deliverable	CM typology	
		Reference	Theories, models and tools
Jointly owned/ PM led	4.13.01 Project team gateway readiness determined 4.13.02 Gateway 4 documentation assembled 4.13.03 Gateway 4 meeting logistics 4.13.04 Gateway 4 meeting pack 4.13.05 Board recommendation and secured	N/AN/A	

4.13.01 Project Team Gateway readiness determined

Once again, the team will gather to review their gateway plans and ensure that they have done all that needs to be done to ensure that approval is secured to proceed to the next phase. Below are some points for them to consider:

- *Business Case* – Has it been updated to reflect progress and any revisions to milestones, benefits, etc.?

- *Stakeholders* – Have we engaged with the right stakeholders for reviews, testing of the solution and development of the rollout plans?
- *Risks and issues* – Has the project risk profile been kept up-to-date?
- *Project governance* – Have we the right roles and responsibilities resourced?
- *Objectivity* – Have we kept impartial to individual agendas and pre-ferences?
- *Readiness for next phase* – Have we developed a clear and robust Phase 5 Plan that will provide governance committees with a good sense of Phase 5 objectives, work packages and activities?

4.13.02 Gateway 4 documentation assembled

For Phase 4, this activity will be similar to previous phases.

4.13.03 Gateway 4 meeting logistics

For Phase 4, this activity will be similar to previous phases.

4.13.04 Gateway 4 meeting pack

For Phase 4, this activity will be similar to previous phases.

4.13.05 Gateway Review Board recommendation secured and documented

For Phase 4, this activity will be similar to Phase 3.

Activity 4.14 **Gateway 4 Steering Committee Meeting (SCM)**

Activity owner and leader	Output or deliverable	CM typology	
		Reference	Theories, models and tools
Sponsor owned and led	4.14.01 Gateway 4 SCM logistics 4.14.02 Gateway 4 SCM Meeting Pack 4.14.03 Steering Committee decision secured and documented 4.14.04 Next steps communicated	N/A	N/A

For Phase 4, this activity will be similar to Phase 3. The Steering Committee will need to be convinced that the solution is ready, that business is ready and that robust contingency plans are in place.

Activity 4.15 **Team Performance and cultural assumptions reviewed**

Activity owner and leader	Output or deliverable	CM typology	
		Reference	Theories, models and tools
CM owned and led	4.15.01 Team performance review 4.15.02 Cultural assumptions realigned	21	Section 4.3.21

For Phase 4, this activity will be similar to previous phases.

Activity 4.16 **Wrap-up: Phase 4**

Activity owner and leader	Output or deliverable	CM typology	
		Reference	Theories, models and tools
PM owned and led	4.16.01 Outstanding issues closed out 4.16.02 Lessons learnt documented	N/A	N/A

For Phase 4, this activity will be similar to previous phases.

9.5 Phase 5: Go Live

Success during Phase 5 is dependent on early consideration of how this deployment could be impacted by other projects (e.g. where different technologies are being deployed over the same timeframe and may have unforeseen impacts on the end-user experience), proper execution of previous activities and work packages that involved organizational and end-user requirements, ensuring that these informed the solution chosen and solution built appropriately, and robust deployment plans which include end-user support after going live.

Success in the 'Go Live' phase will be measured by:

- The smooth rollout of the solution to end-users.
- Developments monitored and effective remedial action taken as necessary.

5.01 Kick off Phase 5
5.02 Brief the Implementation Team
5.03 Conduct 'Go/No Go' assessment
5.04 Launch 'Go Live' communications
5.05 Launch 'Go Live' training
5.06 Facilitate local change adoption
5.07 Develop Phase 6 Plan
5.08 Gateway 5 Review Board Meeting
5.09 Gate 5 Steering Committee Meeting
5.10 Team performance and cultural assumptions review
5.11 Conduct Phase 5 wrap up

Figure 9.12 PCP methodology: Phase 5 activities and work packages

Activity 5.01 **Kick off Phase 5**

Activity owner and leader	Output or deliverable	CM typology	
		Reference	Theories, models and tools
PM owned and led	5.01.01 Phase 4 lessons learnt review 5.01.02 Phase 5 Plan finalized 5.01.03 Iterative documents updated 5.01.04 Team kick off	N/A	N/A

For Phase 5, this activity will be similar to previous phases..

Activity 5.02 **Brief the Implementation Team**

Activity owner and leader	Output or deliverable	CM typology	
		Reference	Theories, models and tools
CM owned and led	5.02.01 Implementation team briefed on 'Go Live' plan	25–28	Sections 4.3.25–4.3.28

5.02.01 Implementation Team briefed on 'Go Live' plan

Before implementing change, gather all implementation partners together for a briefing. This group will include the Change Advocates

Network, representatives from the Help Desk, HR and IT, vendor partners and any administrators who have been assigned a support role. Walk them through the vetted and finalized 'Go Live' plan, taking questions and addressing any concerns. Clarify roles and responsibilities for successful implementation, and how they can help individuals and teams adopt change. Generate genuine excitement for the change and trust that it is in their capable hands. Highlight that the project team will be staying on for a while to support the organization with embedding of the change, but the success or failure of change now ultimately rests with the business.

Activity 5.03 **Conduct 'Go/No Go' assessment**

Activity owner and leader	Output or deliverable	CM typology	
		Reference	Theories, models and tools
CM owned and led	5.03.01 'Go' or 'No Go' decision confirmed 5.03.02 Decision communicated to project team	N/A	N/A

5.03.01 'Go' or 'No Go' decision confirmed

Once the implementation team has been briefed, conduct a final check to ensure that everything is in place for a smooth rollout. The criteria used for such an assessment can include the following:

• Implementation partners and key stakeholders have been briefed on the Go Live plan.
• Communications have been successfully developed and executed.
• Any new business policies and processes are well defined and have been communicated.
• Service commitments and related SLAs have been defined and communicated to support staff and end-users.
• Change Advocates have been trained and training plans for end-users are ready to be executed.
• End-user tools have the necessary equipment and applications installed to begin using new applications.
• The Help Desk is properly resourced and on standby to support end-users.
• Go Live risk mitigation plans updated/completed with no critical issues still open.
• End-user Validation Testing (UAT) has been completed (if appropriate).

The project sponsor will need to be involved in this process and project governance will need to agree acceptable thresholds for each criterion. If, upon assessment, any items are raising concern, then they will need to be addressed before the project can 'Go Live'.

5.03.02 Decision to Project Team

Once a decision has been made, it needs to be communicated to the project team so that they can take appropriate action. If the decision at this point is a 'No Go' they need to mitigate any risks identified. The Change Manager will need to have ready a communication to send to the business explaining the reason for the delay and when an update on project status can be expected. Where the decision is 'Go', then the project team can execute deployment plans.

Activity 5.04 **Launch 'Go Live' Communications**

Activity owner and leader	Output or deliverable	CM typology	
		Reference	Theories, models and tools
CM owned and led	5.04.01 'Go Live' communications launched	18	Section 4.3.18

5.04.01 'Go Live' communications launched

In the Change Management Strategy, it will have been determined what level of excitement for change will be generated on Day One of implementation. For a technology deployment, you don't really want everyone logging on to use new tools and overloading the system, so a more subdued 'business as usual' approach might be preferred. But for a product launch, you might want the whole lot – fireworks and all.

On Day One, an article can be posted in the online newsletter or intranet site and an email sent out by the project sponsor or the CEO. Ensure that leaders and members of the Change Advocate Network are armed with Communication Toolkits and a robust set of FAQs in particular to share in local team briefings. Provide information to stakeholders on where to reach out to for support and encourage the use of the Help Desk, online discussion forums, instant messenger (IM) and chat groups. Whether the approach chosen for 'Go Live' is subdued or full-on, going live with change is an achievement and a milestone to celebrate.

Activity 5.05 **Launch Go Live training**

Activity owner and leader	Output or deliverable	CM typology	
		Reference	Theories, models and tools
CM owned and led	5.05.01 'Go Live' Training launched	22	Section 4.3.22

5.05.01 'Go Live' training launched

On Day One of implementation, training will be available to everyone. Many employees will have availed of early pre-launch invitations to training, but there could be a lot of people who have yet to sign up. It sounds so obvious, but from experience I know it needs to be said. Make sure the workforce knows how to access online training resources. In some organizations, a labyrinth of intranet sites can mean that only those who have the web address of a particular site can access it. Also, if too many controls are placed on training sites, end-users may not be able to access the resources. Ideally, training resources should be available on demand in bite-sized chunks that help people solve particular practical problems they have using their new tools and/or understand aspects of the change in more depth at their own pace. Many pressures in the modern workplace can make it difficult for one to find the time to fill in training registration forms and attend formal training sessions. While face-to-face training numbers can make it easier for a training function under threat to validate its existence, the choice of tools used for deployment should be chosen to address the needs of end-users and the organization.

Activity 5.06 **Facilitate local change adoption**

Activity owner and leader	Output or deliverable	CM typology	
		Reference	Theories, models and tools
CM owned and led	5.06.01 Local Change Adoption Plans review 5.06.02 Health Check report conducted	N/A	N/A

5.06.01 Local Change Adoption Plans reviewed

Progress against local 'Change Adoption Plans' will be reviewed with the Change Manager on a regular basis. Local adoption rates will be reported for the Change Manger to review them against local projections and adoption rates achieved elsewhere in the business so as to identify trends. It may be that a high-performing part of the organization has insights that can help other parts of the organization drive up their adoption rates, while low-performing parts of the business will need close attention and remedial action.

5.06.02 Health Check Report conducted

Once change is rolled out to the business, the baton for ownership of the success or failure of the change is passed to the business. Change Management support will continue on *as an enabler*.

Now more than ever, the Change Adoption plans and processes need to be in place. Conduct a Health Check on general housekeeping to identify any risks that need escalation. Criteria to check against can include:

- Appointment of Business Change Adoption Manager for each part of the business, and appointment of a local sponsor;
- Change Adoption Plan in place for each part of the business;
- Quality of plan;
- Regular meetings set up between each Business Change Adoption Manager and the Change Manager;
- Meetings attendance;
- Trends regarding progress against targets;
- Sharing of best practices and lessons learnt across different parts of the business.

Consolidate the result of the Health Check and share with the Steering Committee. Having spent a good deal of energy over the course of my career driving and tracking adoption plan progress, I can say without any hesitation, 'No Change Adoption Plan, No Change Adoption'. If resistance is presenting itself, get the support of leadership and nip it in the bud as soon as possible. A lack of action on their part will signal dysfunction in governance that the Change Triad needs to discuss and address.

Activity 5.07 **Develop Phase 6 Plan**

Activity owner and leader	Output or deliverable	CM typology	
		Reference	Theories, models and tools
PM owned and led	5.07.01 Phase 6 Plan	N/A	N/A

For Phase 5, this activity will be similar to previous phases.

The focus on the Phase 6 plan will be on supporting the workforce in ways that anchor change in the business, ensuring a smooth handover as the project closes out, and positioning the business for optimal business benefits realization.

Activity 5.08 **Gateway 5 Change Review Board Meeting**

Activity owner and leader	Output or deliverable	CM typology	
		Reference	Theories, models and tools
Jointly owned/ PM led	5.08.01 Project team gateway readiness determined 5.08.02 Gateway 5 documentation assembled 5.08.03 Gateway 5 meeting logistics 5.08.04 Gateway 5 session meeting pack 5.08.05 Board recommendation secured and documented	N/A	N/A

For Phase 5, this activity will be similar to previous phases. Below are those key questions that the team needs to answer to move things forward.

- *Business case* – Has it been updated in line with other project documentation to be handed over? Does it outline transitional arrangements and the transfer to BAU?
- *Stakeholders* – Have we engaged the different tiers of stakeholders in a timely and appropriate manner across the project lifecycle?
- *Risks and issues* – Have we been proactive in assessing and managing risks? Have we kept the Risk Management plan updated?
- *Project governance* – Have we ensured that the Steering Committee and Advisory Committee are getting the right information? Have we reviewed membership to ensure governance teams are well constituted?
- *Data and sources* – Have we used credible data and sources to inform decision making?
- *Objectivity* – Have we kept impartial to individual agendas and preferences?
- *Readiness for next phase* – Have we developed a clear and robust Phase 6 Plan that will provide governance committees with a good sense of Phase 6 objectives, work packages and activities? Have we established a business side Change Management function (i.e. local sponsors and the Change Advocates Network) that will be accountable for driving up local adoption of the change?

Activity 5.09 **Gateway 5 Steering Committee Meeting (SCM)**

Activity owner and leader	Output or deliverable	CM typology	
		Reference	Theories, models and tools
Sponsor owned and led	5.09.01 Gateway 5 SCM logistics 5.09.02 Gateway 5 SCM Meeting Pack 5.09.03 Steering Committee decision secured and documented 5.09.04 Decision and next steps communicated	N/A	N/A

For Phase 5, this activity will be similar to previous phases.

Activity 5.10 **Review team performance and underlying cultural assumptions**

Activity owner and leader	Output or deliverable	CM typology	
		Reference	Theories, models and tools
PM owned and led	5.10.01 Team performance review 5.10.02 Team cultural assumptions realigned	N/A	N/A

For Phase 5, this activity will be similar to previous phases.

Activity 5.11 **Wrap-up: Phase 5**

Activity owner and leader	Output or deliverable	CM typology	
		Reference	Theories, models and tools
PM owned and led	5.11.01 Close out outstanding issues 5.11.02 Lessons Learnt documentation	N/A	N/A

For Phase 5, this activity will be similar to previous phases.

9.6 Phase 6: Embed and Close

Most projects close out soon after the deployment of the solution, but to ensure that the organizational change implemented now sticks, and can be built upon, a sixth phase is necessary – 'to embed sustainable change'. Plans need to be executed to ensure the organization realizes the benefits the project was designed to achieve.

The aims of this phase are:

- Strong, visible change advocacy.
- Supported end–users, working in a change-friendly work environment.
- Ensuring the organizational change implemented now sticks.

6.01 Kick off Phase 6
6.02 Facilitate local change adoption
6.03 Solution fine-tuning
6.04 Launch post Go Live communications
6.05 Launch post Go Live training
6.06 Institute new practices to sustain new current state
6.07 Measure results
6.08 Final steering committee meeting
6.09 Assess project team culture
6.10 Develop Lessons Learnt Report
6.11 Transfer ownership
6.12 Wrap up Phase 6

Figure 9.13 PCP methodology: Phase 6 work packages and activities

Activity 6.01 **Kick off Phase 6**

Activity owner and leader	Output or deliverable	CM typology	
		Reference	Theories, models and tools
PM owned and led	6.01.01 Phase 5 Lessons Learnt review 6.01.02 Phase 6 Plan finalized 6.01.03 Iterative documents updated	N/A	N/A

For Phase 6, this activity will be similar to previous phases.

It's now the 'moment of truth'. The amount of thought and effort that has gone into developing a solution that meets the needs of end-users, and into planning for a smooth implementation, is going to be reflected in the business and end-user experience. Post-implementation, it's all hands on deck to ensure that the workforce have the support they need, and that workplace processes are supportive of the change. Project Management practitioners will have started disbanding, but the Change Management team will be working overtime.

Activity 6.02 **Facilitate local change adoption**

Activity owner and leader	Output or deliverable	CM typology	
		Reference	Theories, models and tools
PM owned and led	6.02.01 End-users supported 6.02.02 Feedback gathered	18 20 25–28	Section 4.3.18 Section 4.3.20 Sections 4.3.25–4.3.28

6.02.01 End-users supported

Provide individual support for end-users as they try to adopt the change. Make sure that 'Launch Communications' and 'Launch Training' materials are well advertised, easily accessible, with tips and points easy to grasp and apply. The Help Desk team should be well trained and resourced to support end-users with their queries.

6.02.02 Feedback gathered

To keep a finger on the pulse, the Change Manager and team will be networking and proactively soliciting feedback from different parts of the business. Through ongoing 'Change Adoptions Plan' meetings, a clear line of sight will be created to show how implementation is unfolding in different geographies. Gather that feedback and pass it on to the remaining project team.

Activity 6.03 **Solution fine-tuning**

Activity owner and leader	Output or deliverable	CM typology	
		Reference	Theories, models and tools
PM owned and led	6.03.01 Solution enhanced	N/A	N/A

Based on feedback proactively gathered from the business using a number of different channels, fine-tune the solution where necessary so that it better suits the needs of the business.

Activity 6.04 **Launch post Go Live communications**

Activity owner and leader	Output or deliverable	CM typology	
		Reference	Theories, models and tools
CM owned and led	6.04.01 Launch post Go Live communications	18	Section 4.3.18

After the change is implemented, the job of the Change Communications Lead is far from over. Post Go Live, communications play an important role is helping build and maintain momentum.

6.04.01 Launch post Go Live communications

Suggested themes for post Go Live communications are as follows:

- *Solution refinements related* – Where changes are made to the solution, the business and end-users will need to be informed immediately and preferably in advance.
- *Success stories* – As the organization starts using the solution, individuals and teams will start to benefit from the new ways of working; it is very important that these success stories are shared on a regular basis. Plan in advance so that regular slots are held in communication channels to share and celebrate these wins. This will build the credibility of the solution in the business.
- *Awards* – Reward a job well done and results achieved using new ways of working. If possible, and where applicable, ensure customer feedback informs the selection of award winners.
- *Merchandise* – Print posts and cheat sheets to reinforce change.
- *Two-way communication* – Use surveys and internal social media to establish feedback loops and ensure two-way communication. Keep the drivers for change visible to maintain momentum.

Activity 6.05 **Launch post Go Live training**

Activity owner and leader	Output or deliverable	CM typology	
		Reference	Theories, models and tools
CM owned and led	6.05.01 Launch post Go Live training	22	Section 4.3.22

Post Go Live, the Change Training Lead will also be busy helping to build and maintain momentum in the business.

6.05.01 Launch post Go Live training

Where refinements are made to the solution based on feedback, the business and end-users may need additional training. Make sure they know it is available.

Activity 6.06 Institute new practices to sustain new current state

Activity owner and leader	Output or deliverable	CM typology	
		Reference	Theories, models and tools
CM owned and led	6.06.01 New current state sustained	20	Section 4.3.20

6.06.01 New current state sustained

Since Phase 3, the Change Manager has been working closely with the Business Change Adoption Managers to develop Change Adoption Plans that realign local culture embedding mechanisms with the change. This effort creates a workplace that supports the change, rather than working against it, and makes it much easier for end-users to adopt new ways of working.

On a strategic level, the Change Manager will also work with business operations to adjust and align business policies and procedures to support the change and ensure that ends users have a supportive environment. He or she will also work with Human Resources to ensure that new ways of working are written into job descriptions and induction programmes.

Activity 6.07 Measure results

Activity owner and leader	Output or deliverable	CM typology	
		Reference	Theories, models and tools
Jointly PM owned and led	6.07.01 Measure results	14	Section 4.3.20

Now that the change has been implemented, data can be collated in line with those metrics agreed in the Benefits and Measurement Plan (see Chapter 2, section 2.12.01). This data will serve as a baseline for measurement activity further down the line when end-users have had sufficient time to learn the new ways of working. It will inform leaders on the culture adjustment achieved directly after the change was implemented, and how far there is to go yet.

It is all very well and good to talk about measurement and business benefits, but the maturity and culture of your organization will very much determine its appetite for such work. Small, nimble organizations need to be close to the customer with a keen eye on the competition in order to survive. Being results focused goes hand-in-hand with that world-view and sets the stage for a results-focused organization – number of widgets sold, number of new customers, etc. Very large organizations, on the other hand, are often characterized as slow and inward-looking with more energy spent on politics and navel-gazing. Activity in this context can become an end in itself, rather than a means to an end with success measured by how busy a person looks. Any attempt at an intelligent and results-focused approach to measurement could be rejected in an activity-centred culture that doesn't want to look too closely at actual benefits achieved, so when planning measurement activity it is important to understand your context, what will be acceptable to 'the organization', and what you can get signed off.

Activity 6.08 **Final Steering Committee Meeting**

Activity owner and leader	Output or deliverable	CM typology	
		Reference	Theories, models and tools
PM owned and led	6.08.01 Commitment secured regarding the ongoing support for the change	N/A	N/A

6.08.01 Commitment secured regarding ongoing support for the change

For Phase 6, only the Steering Committee will meet, this time to ensure that all final plans are being executed. The Steering Committee should confirm plans for transfer of ownership of solution and supporting documentation. Steering Committee members should also agree how they will support the change in their BAU roles once the project rolls up. They can reward and recognize key change agents, and develop career paths for them. Or if they are moving on from the organization, they can make sure that their knowledge and experience is captured, and that induction and training programmes are clear on both old and new ways of working. New recruits should have an explicit remit to support change, and stakeholder management should be ongoing so as to dilute any post implementation resistance.

Activity 6.09 **Measure Project Team Culture**

Activity owner and leader	Output or deliverable	CM typology	
		Reference	Theories, models and tools
CM owned and led	6.09.01 Measure project team culture	21	Section 4.3.21

During Phase 1, Activity 1.7, the Change Triad signed up to team cultural assumptions relating to a culture of partnership between Project Management and Change Management. During Phase 2, Activity 2.02, the project team explored these and their culture was assessed in terms of these cultural assumptions. At this point, baseline data was established, and over the course of the project, the team actively worked to embed a culture of partnership. At some point in either late Phase 5 or during Phase 6 (before too many of the team disbands), conduct the project team culture assessment again to see how much progress has been made by the team. Repeating this work across project delivery teams will build Change Management Maturity in the projects environment and lead to greater success.

Activity 6.10 **Develop Lessons Learnt Report**

Activity owner and leader	Output or deliverable	CM typology	
		Reference	Theories, models and tools
Jointly owned/ Sponsor led	6.10.01 Lessons Learnt Report	N/A	N/A

For Phase 6, this activity will be similar to previous phases.

Activity 6.11 **Transfer ownership**

Activity owner and leader	Output or deliverable	CM typology	
		Reference	Theories, models and tools
Jointly owned/ PM led	6.11.01 Ownership for the change transferred to the business	N/A	N/A

For Phase 6, this activity will be similar to previous phases.

6.09.01 Ownership for the change transferred to the business

With PCP methodology, the transfer of ownership from the project to the business is the penultimate step before project wrap-up. All too often, Project Management methodologies recommend an almost immediate transfer of ownership once the change goes live. This encourages Project Managers to mentally let go and physically move on. In Phase 6, there will be plenty of work to do and the project team will need to be suitably resourced to complete Phase 6 activities that will create sustainable change. Once those activities are completed, it is then timely to transfer responsibility, accountability and authority according to a plan and to previously identified owners. They will want supporting project documentation and the opportunity to ask questions before the project team disbands.

Since Phase 1 and throughout the whole engagement process, line ownership for the success or failure of the change has been made clear to stakeholders. The project has now delivered the preferred solution in line with business requirements and Change Management has acted as an enabler. Now, it is time for the business to step up. Momentum should be maintained with ongoing communication, recognition and reward programmes, and resources should not be diverted until change is embedded.

Activity 6.12 **Wrap-up: Phase 6**

Activity owner and leader	Output or deliverable	CM typology	
		Reference	**Theories, models and tools**
Jointly owned/ PM led	6.12.01 Outstanding issues closed out	N/A	N/A

For Phase 6, this activity will be similar to previous phases.

Any outstanding issues will need to be closed out, and lessons learnt and all other project documentation will need to be archived as a resource for further projects.

Once all loose threads are tied up, celebrate with the team and reward and recognize them for their efforts.

9.6 Chapter summary

A successful organizational change project delivers an effectively designed, developed and delivered solution that meets a business need, and that is embraced by stakeholders and adopted by end-users. To achieve successful delivery, project delivery teams need to nurture new ways of work that embed a culture of partnership between the Project Management and Change Management disciplines and professions. This involves establishing a joint-value proposition and the thoughtful integration of Project Management and Change Management activities and deliverables on a number of levels: operating assumptions and key principles; measures; framework; plus activities, work packages and other outputs, and tools.

As mentioned earlier, PCP methodology is more than a bundle of work packages and activities; it is a philosophy that acts as a guide for project team attitudes and behaviours. That philosophy is articulated in cultural assumptions that are interwoven into formal and informal structures, policies and processes during each phase of the project lifecycle and reinforced at the end of each. This lays the foundations for a culture of partnership on project teams. It can only lead to better project and programme results.

Bibliography

Journal

Cooper, R. G. and Edgett, S. J. (2012) Best practices in the idea-to-launch process and its governance. *Research-Technology Management*, 55 (2): 43–54.

Online

www.independent.ie/irish-news/michael-oleary-dubbed-it-the-taj-mahal-now-terminal-2-could-be-the-most-vital-part-of-dublin-airport-30943909.html

Conclusion

It is fair to say that the practice of managing organizational change is in silly season now, and the high failure rates are proof of that. Not enough Organizational Development (OD) is being practised in business-as-usual, and not enough Change Management is being practised on projects. Not enough thought and way too much activity!

The effects of this are being felt in the workplace. DeClerk (2007) writes about how changes leave employees to experience the emotions of aggression, anxiety, apprehension, cynicism and fear. This can lead to performance decreases. Given the scale of the disruptive change we are dealing with, it is surely time to press the 'pause' button and rethink our approach to managing change. When we do press the 'reset' button, our new way of doing things needs to involve:

- More OD in daily operations, building not only individual and team capability to embrace change and align with the external environment, but organizational capability also and with a particular focus on culture.
- A two-legged model for project delivery that employs both Project Management and Change Management throughout the full lifecycle, so as to maximize synergies and business benefit realization.

For projects delivery, a joint value proposition that is built on a culture of partnership between Project Managers and Change Managers will help ensure:

- Alignment of the product of the project with business requirements;
- Business readiness to accept the product of the project;
- The effective transfer of the product of the project to stakeholders and business operations;
- Adoption of the product of the project to levels of proficiency that will achieve business benefits:
- Organizational capability building in making organizational change stick.

Bibliography

Journals

Cooper, R. G. and Edgett, S. J. (2012) Best practices in the idea-to-launch process and its governance. *Research-Technology Management*, 55(2): 43–54.

DeClerk, M. (2007) Healing emotional trauma in organizations: An O.D. framework and case study. *Organizational Development Journal*. 25(2): 49–56.

Online

www.independent.ie/irish-news/michael-oleary-dubbed-it-the-taj-mahal-now-terminal-2-could-be-the-most-vital-part-of-dublin-airport-30943909.html

Appendix: Change Manager

Job description

The role

The Change Manager will play a key role in ensuring that the project solution is accepted, adopted and embedded in the organization, partnering with the Project Manager throughout the end-to-end project lifecycle to ensure a joined-up approach to work packages development and delivery, integrating Change Management interventions into project plans.

Core responsibilities

- *Partner with the Sponsor and Project Manager* to agree project governance, roles and responsibilities.
- *Help establish the project Change Triad*, which positions the Change Manager and Project Manager as peers reporting into Sponsor, *and inform clarification of roles and responsibilities.*
- *Apply a joint-proposition structured approach* such as PCP methodology to integrate Change Management with Project Management through the end-to-end project cycle.
- Lead on the definition of Change Management work packages and activities, and co-own the development of jointly shared work packages and project plans.
- *Act as Subject-Matter-Expert* and Trusted Adviser for leaders, providing coaching and guidance to build change advocacy.
- *Conduct assessments* on organizational readiness, organizational change maturity, etc.
- *Impacts Identification* – ensure that end-user impacts are identified at a granular level to inform Change Management Plans, in particular those relating to stakeholder engagement and overcoming resistance, communications, and training.
- *Maximize support, minimize resistance*, and enable the business to maximize adoption and proficiency levels.
- *Culture alignment* – Develop a plan to ensure culture alignment and support for the change via culture embedding mechanisms..

Requirements

- *Key knowledge and skills* – A strong academic and practical background in Change Management, Organizational Development or a related field, with experience leading a Change Management team on three similar projects.
- *Leadership* – Ability to lead a team made up of a Change Communications Lead, a Change Training Lead, an Organizational Culture Lead and two Change Analysts.
- *Budget* – Ability to manage a Change Management budget of (£000).

Index

Taylor & Francis eBooks

Helping you to choose the right eBooks for your Library

Add Routledge titles to your library's digital collection today. Taylor and Francis ebooks contains over 50,000 titles in the Humanities, Social Sciences, Behavioural Sciences, Built Environment and Law.

Choose from a range of subject packages or create your own!

Benefits for you

» Free MARC records
» COUNTER-compliant usage statistics
» Flexible purchase and pricing options
» All titles DRM-free.

| REQUEST YOUR **FREE** INSTITUTIONAL TRIAL TODAY | **Free Trials Available** We offer free trials to qualifying academic, corporate and government customers. |

Benefits for your user

» Off-site, anytime access via Athens or referring URL
» Print or copy pages or chapters
» Full content search
» Bookmark, highlight and annotate text
» Access to thousands of pages of quality research at the click of a button.

eCollections – Choose from over 30 subject eCollections, including:

Archaeology	Language Learning
Architecture	Law
Asian Studies	Literature
Business & Management	Media & Communication
Classical Studies	Middle East Studies
Construction	Music
Creative & Media Arts	Philosophy
Criminology & Criminal Justice	Planning
Economics	Politics
Education	Psychology & Mental Health
Energy	Religion
Engineering	Security
English Language & Linguistics	Social Work
Environment & Sustainability	Sociology
Geography	Sport
Health Studies	Theatre & Performance
History	Tourism, Hospitality & Events

For more information, pricing enquiries or to order a free trial, please contact your local sales team:
www.tandfebooks.com/page/sales

 Routledge
Taylor & Francis Group

The home of
Routledge books

www.tandfebooks.com